At Home in the Journey:
Theological Reflection for Missioners in Transition

Jo Ann McCaffrey

Chicago
CCGM Publications
2005
ISBN 0-9677245-6-2

Dedication

In gratitude to all who are with me "in the journey."

Together we have given birth to this book.

Cover Design

The front cover features the
Frauen-Gedenk-Labyrinth of Germany.
The labyrinth is one of the world's oldest archetypal
symbols. It represents the soul's journey to the
center and its return to rebirth.

The Chicago Center for Global Ministries (CCGM) is an ecumenical venture of Catholic Theological Union (CTU), Lutheran School of Theology at Chicago (LSTC), and McCormick Theological Seminary (Presbyterian Church USA) (MTS).

Its mission is to provide an ecumenical context for theological education and scholarly research from the perspective of the church's catholicity in an increasingly globalized world. CCGM coordinates and seeks to develop the faculty, student and curricular resources of the three schools in the areas of
* world mission
*cross-cultural studies
*study of and dialogue with the world's religions
*urban ministry
*justice, peace and the integrity of creation

CCGM Publications aims to disseminate the results of scholarly collaboration among faculty and students of the CCGM schools and to make more available the proceedings of lectures and conferences sponsored by the Center.

Also published by CCGM Publications

Stephen Bevans, Robert J. Schrieter and Eleanor Doidge, eds., *The Healing Circle: Essays in Cross-Cultural Mission* (2000)

Stephen Bevans and Roger Schroeder, eds., *Mission for the Twenty-First Century* (2001)

Eliseo Pérez Álvarez, *We Be Jammin: Liberating Discourses from the Land of the Seven Flags* (2002)

José M. De Mesa, *Inculturation as Pilgrimage* (Luzbetak Lecture #1)

Mary Douglas, *Other Beings, Post-Colonially Correct* (Luzbetak Lecture #2)

Darrell L. Whiteman, *Anthropology and Mission: The Incarnational Connection* (Luzbetak Lecture #3)

Aylward Shorter, *Inculturation in Africa: The Way Forward* (Luzbetak Lecture #4).

Table of Contents

Preface

As I say, perhaps this book will only have its full impact if you have lived in another nation or culture. It was taken for granted in the past that the *hard* part of cross-cultural living, or of mission and ministry, was *leaving* and *acculturating*. Coming home was easy–after all it was *home*. Several years ago, one of the general chapters of the Society of the Divine Word (SVD) issued a beautiful and inspiring document about how the essence of being a missionary was "passing over"–really *leaving* the places where we have become comfortable and really *entering into* another land and worldview.

But as many cross cultural workers and foreign missionaries have discovered, coming home is not an easy adjustment at all, and it might even be the hardest part about crossing cultures. In the SVD document I referred to just above, there was no mention at all about the "passing over" involved in returning home– sometimes after years of service, sometimes because our lives were threatened, sometimes even because of failure. And when we return "home," things have changed. People have changed, former friends have grown distant, the culture has changed–even the way people *speak* has changed. And it seems like nobody really cares about where you have been, what you have done, and how living in another world had changed *you*. Sure, people will ask "How *was* the Philippines?" or "How was it living in El Paso?" But when you try to *tell* them you soon see signs that they *really* don't want to know. Coming home, you discover, is just as difficult–if not more so–than *leaving* home in the first place. I have always felt that our SVD general chapter should have spoken not only of *leaving* and *entering*, but also of *returning*.

What Jo Ann McCaffrey has succeeded in doing in this marvelous book is to take this process of returning seriously, to recognize the pain of women and men who struggle and suffer after years of service in other lands and other cultures, and to devise a way of working through such pain and disorientation so that they can come to a new place. A person returning from an extended period of time in another cultural world cannot really come *home*, for he or she no longer has a home. What Asian theologians Jung Young Lee and Peter Phan (Lee 1995 and Phan 2003: 234-231) say about Asian immigrants applies equally to persons or ministers in transition: they are no longer *in* their home context, they are *both* in and outside of their home context, and therefore they are *in-beyond*. If they have a home at all, it is a home on the journey, a sense of wholeness and peacefulness with the fact that they will always be a little foreign, a little different, a little strange. Once a person has determined to cross a culture, my colleague Tony Gittins says, she or he will always be a stranger, a kind of outsider, both to the guest culture and to her or his own culture when she or he returns (Gittins 1989).

As I say, this book will only have its full impact if you have lived happily and successfully in another nation or culture. But it can also speak eloquently to *anyone* who is in a major transition in life–after having left a job you loved, or having been let go from it, or in the wake of the collapse of a relationship, or the death of a loved one. These moves *from* comfort and security *through* grief, anger and loss, and *to* another place are certainly journeys from a "place" that has changed us to a "place" of conversion and faith.

Women and men who are in any transition from "feeling at home" to being "not quite at home" will only find wholeness when they become, as the title of this book indicates, *at home in the journey*. Jo Ann McCaffrey shows us how to do this, as we move *from* the place we have come to love or where we feel safe, recognize our losses and learn to grieve, *through* the desert where we process all of this in meaningful theological reflection, and *to* a "new home" on the journey of constant conversion.

This is a book not so much to be read as to be worked through. It is not a book that holds answers as much as it offers a way to wrestle with gnawing but ultimately life-giving questions. It is a book to be read with faith and hope in the one who "emptied himself" (Phil 2:7) to "pitch his tent among us" (Jn 1:14) and revealed to us as he journeyed along the roads of Galilee that our true home is the "Kindom" of God.

Jo Ann McCaffrey does not make the journey easy; she does not promise a smooth ride. But she will give you hope that such a journey is possible, and she proves to be a wise, compassionate and patient guide.

Stephen Bevans, SVD
Louis J. Luzbetak, SVD Professor of Mission and Culture
Catholic Theological Union, Chicago

Introduction

The geographical pilgrimage is the symbolic acting out of an inner journey. The inner journey is the interpolation of the meanings and signs of the outer pilgrimage. One can have one without the other. It is better to have both (Merton 1967: 92).

This book is about that "inner journey," the experience of "coming home": not only geographically, but psychologically and spiritually. Life is continual change, and human beings are always in some kind of transition. "Life is a continuous process of consolidation and detachment" (Hall 1977: 23). Yet at the same time human beings have the need to be "at home" in the midst of this transition. We need a certain sense of security or homeostasis in the midst of change. We human beings cannot *always* be "in transition," living in a perpetual "limbo," belonging neither here nor there. I believe this is true as well for missioners who may well understand themselves to be pilgrims always "on their way" to the Kingdom. We have a need to "belong" somewhere, to have a sense of "home" in some way. Living in "liminality," a continual non-state of "in-betweenness," implies insecurity, inconsistency, ambiguity. To remain there throughout one's life, it seems to me, would be to regress psychologically and spiritually. Arnold van Gennep, in his classic study on the rites of passage, did not romanticize the pain of transition, even going so far as to say that "in a liminal phase one is a threat to oneself and to the group" (see Gittins 1987: 322).

The onset of transition is usually triggered by some sort of "crisis," which can be both painful and confusing. Yet ironically, while sometimes dangerously risky, authentic crisis also provides an opportunity. For those who have entrusted their lives to God, spending themselves for the coming of God's kingdom in this world, this can be a time of incredible growth. In the following pages I suggest that a time of transition, this moving from the familiar and secure to the new and unknown is an essential part of the spiritual journey. Passing through painful experiences of separation and grieving, confronting again limitations and loneliness, feelings of alienation or anxiety: all of this can be both an exciting and excruciating process of "coming home"...to one's authentic self, to others, to God. This implies, above all, discovering (or rediscovering) one's deepest self, this privileged place where one also meets the invisible God. And this meeting takes place–not apart from or even because of–but precisely *in the midst of* the journey.

At Home in the Journey grows out of my own experience of transition. I spent almost thirteen years in the Democratic Republic of the Congo, then Zaire. I had come to love its great green forests and winding rivers, its red clay that turned to mud in the rainy season, the sights and sounds of its cities. Above all, I had come to love its people: their strength and sheer determination to survive against all odds, their joy and laughter in the midst of incredible hardship. They lived–and still live–in my heart. It is no exaggeration to say that letting go of Zaire was possibly the hardest thing I had ever done in my life.

Thus when I returned to the United States I embarked upon a difficult "re-entry" experience which was to go through different phases over a period of several years. That transition, which also involved the discernment and ultimate decision to leave my religious community of almost twenty-five years, is what gave birth to this book.

Before continuing, a word about Zaire. In 1997, the government reclaimed one of the country's former names, "The Democratic Republic of Congo" (or DRC). During the years when I lived there, however, under the dictatorship of Mobutu, the country was called "Zaïre," as was its currency, and its citizens, Zaïrois (or Zairians, in English.) Because of the narrative nature of this work, the emotional content which the name "Zaire" carries for me, and in order not to be anachronistic, I will refer to the DRC as "Zaire" throughout this book.

Once I was back "home" in the U.S.A., there were several significant people to support me during my transition. One of them was Larry Lewis, a Maryknoll priest who had spent some years in China. His doctoral dissertation was entitled "Waiting," and it was with his help, through spiritual accompaniment and many tears, that I learned how to wait (See Lewis 1983, 1997). To wait patiently–but *actively*–is like being on "night watch" waiting for the dawn. This initial "watching" period in my life was like a long night, at times confusing, startling, anxious, awesome. But after almost a year in darkness, a glimmer of dawn appeared on the horizon. I cannot remember the exact moment, but I know that gradually the light grew brighter and stronger, until a sense of clarity came. It was as though a "cloud lifted," and I could finally continue on my journey.

This "cloud" was not so much a "cloud of unknowing." Rather, it was a cloud of intuitive "knowing". I was conscious of the divine presence enfolding me, like a cloud. Exodus tells us that when the cloud settled on the meeting tent, "*the glory of the Lord filled the Dwelling. Whenever the cloud rose from the Dwelling, the Israelites would set out on their journey. But if the cloud did not lift, they would not go forward; only when it lifted did they go forward*" (see Ex 40: 34-38). If the "cloud" in which I seemed to dwell during those months of discernment was, in any way, one of "unknowing," it was not knowing which way God would lead me, or which door God would open. But I knew that God was "in that cloud," and that, sooner or later, God would in some way indicate to me "the way in which I should walk" (Ps 31: 8). When clarity finally came, after over a year of intense discernment, I experienced that moment as one of "the cloud lifting." After that I felt that I could move, and God began to lead the way. "In the daytime, the cloud of the Lord was seen over the Dwelling; whereas at night, fire was seen in the cloud by the whole house of Israel *in all the stages of their journey.*"

Climbing the Mountain

A few years ago while vacationing with my sister on the coast of Maine, we spent some time in Acadia National Park. One early morning, as we sat on one of Acadia's rugged cliffs watching the rising sun glisten across our little piece of the Atlantic's waters, a group of mountain climbers approached a neighboring cliff, not far from where we were seated. We watched them as they set up their ropes along some difficult cliffs that jut out over the ocean. It was the first time I had seen any mountain climbing at close hand and I was fascinated. I asked myself, what is it that motivates people to undertake this kind of sport? The sense of adventure? The risk involved? The thrill of arriving at a mountain top after a challenging climb, or the breathtaking views that one would never know without being able to scale the slick sides of that mountain? Or was it simply the challenge of being able to say, "I did it!"

As I examined the composition of the group more closely, I realized that they were a *family* of climbers. I approached an older member of the group and asked if he were the father. Yes, he and his wife had been climbers, and had initiated their children into the sport, who, in turn, were initiating their children! We spoke a little, then I let them get back to leaning over the cliff and watching one of their sons scale the granite wall below us.

My sister Angela, having done a little amateur climbing, knew a little more about the sport than I did. She explained some of the techniques involved in what they were doing: the skillful handling of the rope, (the climber's wife was learning how to hold the rope for him, tightening up on it or giving him slack, as he needed it), the handholds and footholds, the importance of the "lead climber" knowing just the right crevices in which to pound the spikes they call pitons. She told me how exciting it is to hear them call to one another with special codes and signals, their voices echoing up and down the mountain. She said, "Climbing has its own special language—it's like another culture."

Angela talked me into attempting a little climb ourselves. We would go up to a spot called "Bubble Rock." She had done it a few years earlier and assured me that it was an "easy climb." Having embarked on our little adventure, however, and the further we got along the trail, she realized that this was *not* the same one that she had taken before. Actually this approach to Bubble Rock was much more difficult and risky than she had expected, demanding skills that neither of us had—certainly not me! The further along on the path we climbed, the more steep and treacherous it became. We both realized that even though the climb was becoming more and more strenuous and challenging, to turn back and try to return the way we had come would have been even more treacherous. My sister knew there was an easier way down—*if* we could just make it to Bubble Rock. As we got closer to the top, we came to what seemed to be an impasse. We tried to find a way to continue.

Angela went first and finally managed to hoist herself up to a plateau near the top. After looking at the rest of the path ahead she called down to me, "If you can just make that one climb, we're 'home free'." She reminded me to be sure to have a good firm handhold on the rock I was moving to, before letting go of my foothold on the rock where I was presently standing, and where I felt secure. I made several attempts, but I felt like my legs weren't strong enough to pull me up to the next landing. I realized I was really afraid. I didn't dare look behind me, which was straight down. Angela was afraid too, but she kept encouraging me, knowing that there really was no turning back. We just had to keep going and get through this scary moment. She kept coaching me with the little knowledge she had, "Lean into the rock . . . Get a secure handhold on the same rock I used . . . Take your time . . . Just keep leaning in . . . You can do it . . . ."

And finally, I *did* do it! Somehow I found the strength to pull myself up to the next rock. At the moment, it seemed I was just so glad to have made it. I kept going the short distance which remained. Upon reaching the top, though, I immediately became aware of some signs of the stress my body had been under: my heart was beating hard and fast; my hands–in fact, my whole body–was trembling; even my liver (a weak point since my bout with hepatitis while in Africa) was "in a quiver," as a friend puts it. Yet as we sat there on top of "Bubble Rock," taking in the spectacular view surrounding us, it felt good to know that I had summoned up (from somewhere!) the strength–both physical and moral–to make that climb, the courage to overcome my fear. I had *literally* been "between a rock and a hard place," and I had gotten through it.

"It has its own special language . . . it's like another culture . . ." My sister's words began to echo in me and I began to think about these "worlds" of mountain climbing and the "world" of mission. A missioner in the midst of a significant transition probably experiences what most mountain climbers feel each time they attempt a new climb. Missioners, like climbers, are people with a sense of adventure, not afraid of risk, willing to accept the challenge of "a tough climb," in fact one that sometimes seems impossible. Missioners have been "climbing" for centuries, and they keep on climbing, working their way to the heights–and sometimes falling into the depths. They live a life which, for most outsiders to this missionary "culture," seems incomprehensible.

Each time missioners make a cultural transition, whatever it be, they face a new and different challenge than the one before. Granted, they have learned some of the skills of crossing culture. It's certainly not like that very first "climb" when *everything* was new. Nevertheless, climbers say that no climb is ever the same. Even if you've taken that mountain before, each climb in itself is a new experience. Likewise, each move, each moment of *every* transition is both challenge and adventure for the missioner, however "experienced" he or she may be. And perhaps the hardest "climb" of all is the one inward, the journey home.

Re-entry, Culture Shock, Transition

"Implicit in the conflict and tension posed by the transitional experience lies the potential for authentic growth and development, the transcendence from environmental to self support" (Adler 1975: 14). For Christians, this sense of being "on the move" toward the Kingdom is an essential part of the Christian life, and even more so for those who, within the mission of the Church, are called to ministry in a culture other than their native one. Yet how are *missioners* called to live in this time and space called "transition" when returning to or while living in their "home" culture? It is my observation that more attention has been given to *preparation* for cross-cultural mission than to what is typically called "re-entry." While indebted to *FROM (From Mission to Mission)* for their singular contribution in this area of re-entry, very little systematic, well-researched written material is available which addresses this particular topic. In addition, I often find that "re-entry" is equated with culture shock and is approached as something negative to be "gotten through" and overcome. My aim is to place this experience of cross-cultural transition, admittedly at times confusing, alienating, anxiety-producing, ambiguous, in the overall context of something *positive*: a process which can be psychologically and spiritually transformative, leading to greater personal development and integration, necessary for growth in wholeness and holiness. As the body goes into a temporary state of shock for its own protection and healing, so does our psyche. My theological perspective, then, is that the *crisis of transition* carries within it the *potential for transformation*.

Being "missionary" is an affair of the heart. Part of the pain and the gift of such a life is knowing that on some deep level one has become a "stranger in a strange land"–whether in the host culture to which one has been sent, or in one's place of origin. "Once a missioner, *always be missioner.*" However, being a stranger is not to be understood as "bad." In fact it is one of the most important gifts the missioner has to offer: to the church at large, to the host church and culture, and to the local church and culture "back home." (See Gittins 1989).

At Home in the Journey is designed for Christian sojourners who have themselves been through the process of transition, i.e., returning from mission in other countries, or from cross-cultural contexts within their own country, and who are now attempting to accompany other such missioners during a similar transition. It might also be helpful for those who are on sabbatical or home leave, for those who are, studying or in a period of discernment about ministry, or for those who have definitively completed their mission assignments in other cultural contexts. It might be relevant for those who are experiencing *any* kind of transition in their lives, e.g., marital separation or divorce, mid-life crisis, job or career change, etc. These reflections are intended to respond to the very real need of those who are "betwixt and between" changing situations in their lives.

This work is particularly addressed, however, to those ministering in cross-cultural situations, whether in their own countries or in other parts of the world. And while cross-cultural transition is an integral part of every phase of a missionary life, this book is especially helpful for those in a stage of "re-entry," i.e., those experiencing *separation from* a place of ministry or mission, (for whatever reasons and for whatever period of time); *grieving through* an "in-between" period; *movement toward* a new perspective, a new vision, a new beginning. At times the new beginning may occur geographically, but hopefully, always psychologically and spiritually.

In the Method is the Meaning

This reflection comes not only from my own personal experience, but from the shared experiences of other cross-cultural missioners as well. The contributing participants were members of different "focus groups," made up of women and men, parents and children, members of religious congregations and ordained. The groups have been racially, culturally and ecumenically diverse, all missioners who recognized themselves to be in a time of cross-cultural transition. They were all experiencing the effects of transition--albeit in different phases and forms. Together they reflected upon their past and present experience of transition, seeking to find meaning in it and support from others going through it. I believe that what is *most particular* in human experience is also the most *universal*. It is my belief, then, that the experiences and insights of a few, shared in these pages, will find resonance and response in the lives of many.

I hope to engage the reader of this book in a holistic process of reflection which unfolds in five movements, represented by each chapter. The process is based on a method developed by Patricia O'Connell Killen and John de Beer (Killen and de Beer 1994). They maintain that a truly *theological* process of reflection *cannot happen* without being intimately connected to the *human drive toward meaning*. When these two processes merge, new meaning and insight occurs, leading one toward better *integration of one's past experience into the present*. This integration happens in the context of a larger circular movement which I will often refer to as simply *"from → through → to → from →* paradigm used by Larry Lewis in an integration seminar he taught at Catholic Theological Union in 1992). A missioner might understand this in terms of one's own "rites of passage." These movements intertwine throughout the process of transition, as various melodies flow in the background of a movie or the scenes of an opera. While each chapter treats each of these movements as though it were a separate happening, keep in mind that they are not so easily identifiable when one is in the midst of transition. Rather, like the stages of grieving, they flow in and out of each other, all mixed together within the person who–while sometimes *feeling* very fragmented--is still a "whole" person, seeking to reestablish his or her sense of self and equilibrium.

Entering Experience

In Chapter One the reader is invited to enter into his or her own experience of mission, leave-taking, and transition. We reflect upon identity, i.e., who and how he or she has been in mission. I both explain this process and illustrate it through autobiographical stories as well as those of other missioners (see also Sullivan 1991 and Stroup1981). Entering into one's experience is done primarily through focusing on some particular aspects of it. For example, I describe in detail an event from my life in Zaire, the particular place, the persons involved etc., concentrating on the "who, what, when, where, and how?" The "why" of an experience is better deferred to a later moment, to avoid the tendency to make a premature judgment on what happened, or doing what I call "spiritualizing," which often means repressing or ignoring one's feelings.

Attending Feelings

In the second chapter readers will be invited to pay attention to the *feelings* that they are *currently* experiencing, as well as to "re-member" feelings from the past, possibly discovering unexpressed joys or uncovering unhealed hurts. Feelings are "clues" to the meaning of our experience. Naming and claiming feelings is not only a healthy psychological movement, but as Killen and de Beer suggest, a necessary "spiritual discipline." (See Killen and de Beer 1994: 27-30). Some ways recommended for attending to these feelings are through journaling, creative imagining, prayer and dialogue with others in similar circumstances.

Exploring Images

Attending to feelings will naturally give rise to *images,* because images are capable of expressing our feelings in ways that words often cannot. This is an area which is often neglected. "Images symbolize our experience. They capture the totality of our felt response to reality in a given situation . . . they encourage multiple aspects of meaning in an experience to come forth" (Ibid.: 37). In fact, our ordinary everyday language is full of metaphorical images: "I feel flat as a pancake . . . dead as a doornail . . . higher than a kite." Or "chill out . . . cool down . . . get fired up!" Or simply, "He's down today . . . She seems up tonight." "As a metaphor or symbol, the image is both concrete, referring to a particular event, and universal, connecting that event to human experience at a deep level. The more it captures a very particular experience, the more it invites resonance with the experiences of others" (Ibid.: 39-40). The third chapter explores the power of images for capturing and embodying experiences and feelings, as missioners explore key images of their own. After exploring some personal images, we turn to Scripture, as a fertile source for images related to the life of a missioner. *The Pilgrim God* (John of Taizé 1985) will be our main "guidebook" for exploring the missioner's "sojourn" in the desert.

Examining "The Heart of the Matter"

Articulating feelings through images helps us to notice the energy we have around a *key issue or cluster of issues* which we may be unresolved or perhaps only recently surfaced. This significant issue is called the "*heart of the matter*" (Killen and de Beer 1994: 61). In Chapter Four readers are encouraged to identify and articulate their own "heart of the matter." We help one another by the sharing of our images, or other expressions of an identifiable pattern, a key issue or concern which we may have at this time in our transition. A turning point occurs when we engage this "heart of the matter" in conversation with the resources of our spiritual tradition.

Genuine conversations are a reciprocal movement full of surprise, sometimes delightful, sometimes sobering. This is what we aim for when we put the heart of the matter, or the most energy-filled point of an event, into conversation with the wisdom of the Christian heritage (Ibid.: 64-65). This kind of dialogue actually calls one to a kind of "conversion." Mark Searle describes conversion as the successful negotiation of crisis or change . . . as a form of "passage" or "transition" whereby a person may pass through to a new lease on life and enter into a new set of relationships with self, the world, and with life itself (Searle 1980). Using the example of my own unexpected "conversion," as well as the insights gleaned by others during theirs, I offer this attitude–being called to "conversion"–as the challenging space in which to examine one's transition or "re-entry."

Integrating Insight

In this final chapter, we explore some of the spiritual challenges involved in this journey with self, others and God. The sometimes imperceptible movement through experiences, feelings, images, and issues, if faithfully carried out in dialogue with one's true self and one's sacred tradition, will usually enkindle "insight." Insight occurs when "reasons of the heart are made known to the mind" (Dunne 1981: 3). And each insight is an invitation to transformation. Thus, as missioners arrive at these moments of insight, I encourage ritualizing them in some way, personally or communally, which helps to integrate them into our current situation. This, in turn, enables us to move into new experiences and new life. A missioner's integrative process, as I develop it in this book, consists in *being faithful to the unfolding movements of their own life.*

So now I invite my readers to put on their "hiking boots" and their "backpack" and dare to do a bit of "mountain climbing" with me. It is my sincere hope that in the following chapters you will recognize your own "sojourn" and that of other "mountain climbing" missioners you may have met along the way.

Chapter One
"Welcome Home!": Entering Experience

*It's not easy coming back to this country. It's not like any
other country in the world. Most North Americans don't
know that, because they live here, and have never been
anywhere else, except maybe the Caribbean, which is like
a big beach . . . or Europe, which is like going to an old
museum. Europeans sit at tables with knives and forks.
They have beds and sheets, toilets and garbage cans.
Africa is different. The expatriates there will tell you that
the reverse culture shock of coming back to North America
can be worse than the shock of going to the Third World in
the first place (Dooling 1994: 1).*

The Context of a Missioner in Transition

"Welcome Home!"

"Welcome home! How was Zaire?" "Oh fine," I would numbly
reply, not knowing quite what to say or where to begin, not yet ready or
able to describe the life I had been living for half of my adulthood.
Strangely, my simple answer seemed enough to satisfy most of those who
asked!

How well I remember my initial days back in the United States after
being almost thirteen years outside of it. I arrived in the States in August,
1992, right at the time of the Barcelona Summer Olympics, and I remember
that everyone was talking about the "Dream Team." When I asked, "What's
the Dream Team?" the group stared at me incredulously and said, "You
haven't heard of the *Dream Team?!?*" "Well, I've been in Africa for the
last 13 years," I would explain rather apologetically. (I don't think I really
understood what the "Dream Team" was until four years later, when the
next Olympic games rolled around.) "How does it feel to be back home?
. . . I'll bet you're in culture shock, huh?" How often well-intentioned

friends and members of my family would ask me that question. I remember saying that I guessed I was in culture shock, but I wasn't exactly sure what that meant at the time. Was it feeling totally disoriented, and equally stupid, about almost everything around me? Was it not knowing how–or sometimes simply not wanting or not having the energy to answer all those questions? Was it being overwhelmed by a "new language." "If I'm not home, just leave me a message on *the machine.* Do you have voice mail yet?" *Voice mail?* (I knew that I probably had intestinal parasites, but someone had arranged a doctor's appointment for next month.) "Are you on-line yet?" *Am I what?* Whatever culture shock was, I think that I must have been in it!

Family and friends are important at this time because they love us. But this is not enough. Although they try to be supportive and understanding, sometimes their attempts are more obstacle than aid to the challenge of re-new-ing oneself that is being called for at this critical time. Well-intentioned family, community and friends want to be helpful and to help us adjust. But they want to "make it all right." They want us to feel and act "normal." They want us to be at ease, to be glad to be "back home." It is hard for them to listen to our stories–they don't understand that strange world from whence we've come–and to which they usually hope we'll never return. They just "can't relate" to where we've been and what we've experienced–and most importantly, to what we're currently experiencing. For many of us "returning missionaries," we just kind of fold up like a flower at night, keeping inside that other world, that other life, that other "self" which has become a part of who we are. And if we ever open up enough to dare to say that we hope to go back next year–others are usually dismayed. They just don't get it! Why would anyone want to go back to that!? "All that we're hearing about that place in the news lately . . . What about all the violence . . . ? There's lots of mission work for you to do right here at home . . . ." Sometimes what they say is objectively true. But that's just not what we need to hear at this moment.

When I returned from Zaire in August, 1992, I was fortunate to have been advised to take a class at Catholic Theological Union (CTU) in the Fall entitled "Mission/Ministry Integration Seminar." This class, facilitated at that time by Larry Lewis, M.M., had a powerful methodology which sparked the beginning of my own long journey "home." The method can be described in three key movements: "from → through → to → . . .": geographically, but also psychologically and spiritually.

Thus, I began my explicit theological reflection on my own departure *from* Zaire, *through* transition, *to* integration. This integration of one's past mission life into one's current experience of "mission" does not usually happen in a ten week seminar! It might take months or even years before one begins to see some "light" as to what one is about–or more accurately, what God is about–in our seemingly disrupted lives. The ongoing personal and group reflection that I still do regularly continues to provide me with new insights as I move into my future.

A fundamental principle of that Integration Seminar was that *every* experience, no matter how small or insignificant it may seem to be, has the potential of becoming a *formative* experience. In order for this potential to be realized, the experience must be the subject of reflection. This reflection enables us to discover, as much as possible, that which can be revealed in this experience. Some experiences in our lives are like flowers. It is as though one gently observes petal after petal of the rose gently unfolding, revealing its splendor in color and fragrance. Other experiences, however, are more like onions. One must peel off layer after layer of an onion in order to fully know the whole of it. As many of us know, in "onion peeling" the process is not without its "sting." I have found that the movement and growth involved in holistic theological reflection on an incident in my life can often bring tears. But through those very tears comes new awareness and insight, new life and growth. Finally, it is in moving through the transition, acting on our new or rediscovered insights, that integration can happen. We begin to know ourselves strangely "at home" in this missionary journey in which we are continually moving *"from → through → to → ...."*

This movement *"from,"* as we mentioned, is not only from in a geographical sense, but it is also the psychological, emotional and spiritual places where we have come to feel settled, comfortable, "at home." The movement *"through"* can mean, in the same way, many types of "liminality," which we will discuss more fully in the next chapter. Finally, *"to"* represents the movement *toward* new psychological, emotional, spiritual and sometimes geographical spaces, in which we begin again to feel "at home." Theological reflection on our experiences makes us more insightful. This final movement will be explored in Chapter Five. We become more aware that our life as Christians, and in an even more explicit way as missioners, is a continual journey in which we are already "at home" in the Reign of God, in whatever space we find ourselves. Yet at the same time we know ourselves to be pilgrims, and our sometimes dark and difficult journey *"from → through → to → ..."* reminds us that neither we nor God's Reign have fully arrived.

How long did those "initial days" last? It's hard to remember. I know that the days turned into months, and the months to years. And somehow, gradually, I began to be able to let go of all that had become familiar, the places and people in Zaire whom I had grown to understand and love, the country which I had learned to call "home" for over twelve years. And, after over ten years "back home," I am now able to call this place where I am living "home." How did this movement from disorientation through transition to a new sort of "homecoming" happen? Well, that's what this book all about. I know that it happened with the support of certain people who were providentially in my path. They were willing and patient enough to *listen* to me as I struggled to tell my story, over and over again in many different ways, scene by scene narrating the drama of my own journey. Leaving "home" for a "strange land," crossing cultural boundaries, slowly breaking down barriers–exterior and interior, my own and those of others. A missioner, seemingly without "a mission," I needed others who could in some way understand my journey–who could "watch and wait" with me until I was ready to move on again, because for a time it seemed as though I did not know how to move nor which way to go. As I write this I am conscious of having spent many years "in transition" (and all that it implies), and in some ways, I still am. The difference is that I am beginning to be "at home" on the journey. Perhaps it is valid to say that a Christian missioner will in some ways always be "in transition," a special sign of God's Reign, which is "already" but at the same time "not yet."

Liminality: Some Characteristics

The heart of any transition is living through a "spaceless space" and a "timeless time" often referred to as "liminality." Missioners must attend to what they are feeling in the present, *through* this "liminal" time. This is a very important and often neglected part of integrated theological reflection based in human experience. The term itself was made a commonplace among anthropologists through the work of Victor Turner, whose classic essay, "Betwixt and Between" is generally considered to be the seminal classic on the subject of ritual liminality, although it is itself built on the classic work of Arnold van Gennep (Turner 1967; van Gennep 1960). William Bridges has referred extensively to Van Gennep's stages (separation, liminality, reincorporation) and their accompanying rites of passage in his popular work, *Transitions* (Bridges 1980). He speaks of them as "Endings," "Neutral Zone," and "Beginnings." James and Evelyn Whitehead also make use of van Genne['s structure for their description of an adult crisis as a religious passage in *Christian Life Patterns* (Whitehead and Whitehead 1979: 51-53).

I prefer the translation "liminality," however, because it seems to better express that "betwixt and between" reality that informs this part of the transition. Turner also refers to this time as "mid-transition" (Turner 1967: 105). For a missioner we can see this liminality expressed clearly, even in simple terms of place and time. Separated from his or her mission, yet not yet reassigned to another, a missioner literally is a man or woman "without a country" . . . without a place to call "home." In his essay Turner points out certain characteristics of this liminal phase of the transitional process as contrasted with the "status quo" (see Figure 1.1 below). Although Turner's research is in an entirely different context (Turner's research in ritual, myth and symbol took place primarily among the Ndembu people of Zambia in central Africa.), some of his insights and conclusions might help us to deepen our own understanding of the situation of the "passenger," in order to better facilitate the missioner's "passage" through transition.

During this liminal period "the state of the ritual subject (the "passenger") is *ambiguous*; he or she passes through a realm that has few or none of the attributes of the past or coming state"(Ibid.: 94). The pain of this liminal state is that one is neither what one was before, nor what one will eventually be. Ambiguity is something that none of us is comfortable with. Most of us like some clarity in our lives–we like to be able to define things for ourselves. Most of us are happy when things are relatively black and white: living with the gray is at best, challenging. Many missioners have, perhaps unconsciously, defined themselves by their role precisely as missioners, or by their identity with a certain country or population. The need to do so is even stronger when we are in this time of transition.

I remember when I began studies at CTU in Chicago after a few months back from Zaire. Each quarter at the beginning of each class the participants would each briefly introduce themselves. I would never identity myself as being from Georgia (although that was indeed where I was born), but from Zaire. I recall sometimes struggling with what to say when people would ask, "Where are you from?" or "Where's your home?" I would sometimes say, "Zaire." Often they might laugh and say, "Were you born there?" It took me several years to let go of identifying myself as having "worked in Zaire for over twelve years."

On the other hand, there is, as Turner puts it, "the peculiar unity of the liminal: that which is neither this nor that, and yet is both"(Ibid.: 99). He reminds us that the Latin root for liminal means "threshold" (Turner 1969: 94-95). In liminality, missioners are indeed "standing on the threshold." We are not what we were nor what we will be. At the same time we are what we have become, and what we are becoming. I always wince when someone introduces me as "a former missionary." I've

LIMINALITY CONTRASTED WITH STATUS SYSTEM
Transition/state
Totality/partiality
Homogeneity/heterogeneity
Communitas/structure
Equality/inequality
Anonymity/systems of nomenclature
Absence of property/property
Absence of status/status
Nakedness or uniform clothing/distinctions of clothing
Sexual continence/sexuality
Minimization of sex distinctions/maximization of sex distinctions
Absence of rank/distinctions of rank
Humility/just pride of position
Disregard for personal appearance/care for personal appearance
No distinctions of wealth/distinctions
Unselfishness/selfishness
Total obedience/obedience only to superior rank
Sacredness/secularity
Sacred instruction/technical knowledge
Silence/speech
Suspension of kinship rights and obligations/kinship rights and obligations
Continuous reference to mystical powers/intermittent reference to mystical powers
Foolishness/sagacity
Simplicity/complexity
Acceptance of pain and suffering/avoidance of pain and suffering
Heteronomy/degrees of autonomy

Figure 1.1 Liminality contrasted with status system (see Turner 1969: 106-107)

never been comfortable with that term It tends to identify "missioner" with a role at a given place and in a given time. I rather think that it has more to do with a quality of being. If one has a missionary heart, no matter where she is, no matter what he is doing, that person will always be a missioner. All those qualities that we have acquired and fostered as missioners in another cultural context, we bring to whatever we do in the future.

Another aspect of this liminal process is its *invisibility*. "The subject of passage ritual is, in the liminal period, structurally, if not physically, "invisible" (Turner 1967: 95). Turner points out that "the structural "invisibility" of liminal *personae* ('threshold people") has a twofold character. They are at once no longer classified and not yet classified. The former is frequently represented by symbols involving death and dying. The latter, by symbols of gestation and birth (Ibid.: 96-97—we will discuss symbolism more in depth in the next chapter.) For missioners in transition, as well as for friends and family who surround them, this "invisibility" or not being "classified" is at best, awkward, at worst, devastating. When I would come to the States on a home visit every few years for a few months I was always "the missioner." *"This is my daughter, JoAnn." "Oh, is this the one who works in Africa?"* Now sometimes my father, in his own struggle to sort out my transition, will say to his friends when they ask about his daughter, "Which one? I have four daughters." It takes time and patience for all of us to get used to one's no longer being "the one who works in Brazil . . . Taiwan . . . Bolivia . . . ."

Turner also tells us that liminality may be described as *a stage of reflection:*

> [Those undergoing this passage]are withdrawn from their structural positions and consequently from the values, norms sentiments, and techniques associated with those positions. They are also divested of their previous habits of thought, feeling, and action. During the liminal period, neophytes are alternately forced and encouraged to think about their society, their cosmos, and the powers that generate and sustain them (Ibid.: 105).

Transitional people, says Turner, *have* nothing. "They have no status, property, insignia, secular clothing, rank, kinship position, nothing to demarcate them structurally from their fellows. Their condition is indeed the very prototype of sacred poverty" (Ibid.: 98-99). Similarly, missioners in transition, particular in "reentry," often *have nothing."* They have been stripped, as it were, of all that was familiar, of all that gave meaning to their ministry, their vocation—and sometimes to their life. Indeed, at times this time of transition is an invitation to the missioners to live poverty as they have never lived it, even though they may have slept in the simplest of huts or walked the most of rugged roads. Oftentimes living in liminality, with all of its ambiguity, is the most radical and rugged "faith walk" missioners have yet had to make in their missionary life. How can the missioner be helped to name and claim these elements of liminality: ambiguity, invisibility and being in a stage of reflection, in order that they work toward his or her transformation? This question leads us to consider the meaning of *"communitas."*

"Communitas"

> *I spent the first year of my "sabbatical" feeling angry, closed, bitter, almost antisocial. It was only after a year or more that I began to realize how angry I was, and that somehow I had to deal with it. . . . I began to journey with a group of missioners who were also on sabbatical, studying, regrouping, returning, moving on. . . . Gradually I began to gain trust in this group, having my experiences accepted, my feelings understood. I began to gain the confidence I needed to look within myself, to begin this inner journey...the most difficult I had ever made . . . (Eileen, Winter, 1997).*

Transition, and particular the liminality which is the heart of it, can become "transformation" if missioners are given the time, space and accompaniment which will enable them to reflect seriously and theologically about *"their* society, their cosmos, and the powers that generate and sustain them." Many missioners today, upon returning from their place of mission or during a period of sabbatical, are indeed given this opportunity. But what is important to emphasize here is the need for community and accompaniment during this time of confusion and crisis.

However, as Anthony Gittins puts it, "Van Gennep did not romanticize the pain of transitional states, and noted that in a liminal phase one is a threat to oneself and to the group (Gittins 1987: 322). Turner also recognizes what Mary Douglas called "the potency of disorder" in this transitional state. At the same time Van Gennep, Douglas, Turner, and others building on their insights, all acknowledge that this disorder can also be potential for creativity and growth. Two important factors will influence the way in which this potentially dangerous phase will enable transition to become, in fact, transformation: these are ritual and community, in particular a spontaneous form of community which Turner calls *communitas*. He prefers this Latin term to "community" to distinguish this "modality of social relationship," i.e., *communitas* from an "area of common living" i.e., community (see Turner 1969: 96).

Turner thus defines communitas as a specific context, differentiating it from the more common form of society which is "structured, differentiated, and often hierarchical." By contrast, a model which "emerges recognizably in the liminal period, is of society as an unstructured or rudimentarily structured and relatively undifferentiated *comitatus,* community or even communion of equal individuals who submit together to the general authority of the ritual elders"(Ibid.: 96). Thus we understand that communitas often arises spontaneously among those in similar situations of transition, ambiguity and stress, and in particular the liminal or in-between phase of this transition process.

What I want to emphasize here is the need for a community of support during this time, the kind that missioners experience especially when they are with "their own kind." How many times have we sat in a circle while someone recounts their experience, feelings, confusion, etc., and all of the heads in the circle are nodding with affirmation. "Yes," we're saying to one another. "Yes! That's exactly how it feels." "Yes, I know what you mean!" "Yes! I understand." Anthony Gittins suggests that "if the liminal person is encountered and embraced in suffering, not primarily by functionaries or persons of a particular status or authority, but by the right kind of significant others–peers, fellow campers . . . or community–there may well be a deep and salvific experience, a real conversion which will redirect the individual and set a new course for the future. It will also modify the community and exemplify real co-ministry, 'ministering with,' rather than professionalism or 'ministering to' (Gittins 1987: 326).

Missioners need to laugh together at the crazy moments. I recall one of our group relating her experience of wading through a Bolivian swamp. At one point they saw what seemed to be the head of a snake poking up through the water. Before she knew it she had literally jumped into the unsuspecting arms, and was clinging for "dear life" to one of her Bolivian companions–who was at least a foot shorter than she! We can also cry together at the pains, the losses, the hurts, the injustices, the oppression that we have sometimes witnessed, sometimes been a part of–in one way or another. Again, as we have seen, traumatic events have often shattered the sense of connection, the trust, that a missioner would normally have with others, with any community. Gradually restoring or rebuilding that sense of trust can be an important part of this process of missioners traveling together through transition, trying to make their way to that safe place again within themselves we can call "home."

The Identity of a Missioner

A person's identity is never static because personal history is always unfolding and there is no self-understanding apart from an understanding of the historical horizon or tradition which serves as the context to the interpretation of identity (Stroup 108-109).

So who is this strange breed of a human being we call a "missioner" anyway? What makes him or her tick? The onlooker might undoubtedly look at missioners in much the same way as I looked at those mountain climbers, wondering, "What makes them do what they do? Why take such risks? Does he really enjoy scaling that bluff? Looks like nothing but hard work to me." I remember one time while I was on home leave from Zaire for a few months and visiting my aunt and godmother in Georgia. As we were driving across town she said to me that sometimes her friends asked her why I, her niece, did what I did. She told me how she had explained to them one day, "Well, it's kind of like garbage collecting–somebody has to do it!" I have no idea how I responded at the moment. My aunt doesn't remember ever saying that, but obviously it made an impression on me. I have since thought about what she said. We all attempt to make sense out of things we just don't understand. Her explanation satisfied her–even if it seemed a bit incongruous to me!

Mission, and missioners or missionaries, have been variously defined and understood over the years by outsiders and insiders alike. Webster's pocket dictionary puts it this way: "Missionary: a person commissioned by a church to propagate its faith or carry on humanitarian work. Missioner: a person undertaking a mission and especially a religious mission." This simple two-lined "secular" definition seems to include some essentials: a person *commissioned,* i.e., a person called and sent, given, as it were, a mission, which the missioner *undertakes.* Most missioners are impelled to do what they do because they believe that they have been *called* by God, and *sent,* usually by a church or community. And what is the nature of that mission? It is *religious:* i.e., *propagating faith* or *humanitarian work.* Perhaps these would be put differently today, but Webster is not far off the mark.

Michael Collins, in his *Spirituality for Mission,* summarizes a list of the most common motives that seemed to characterize the spirituality and life style of missionaries over the last three centuries. They include the glory of God and service of Christ, being called by God and commanded by Christ; pity and/or compassion for "lost souls," as well as humanitarianism for their temporal well-being; establishing and nurturing the church, along with–consciously or unconsciously–one's cultural "civilization" (Collins 1978: 129-31). David Bosch has a listing of similar motifs that had shaped missionary thinking since the middle of the eighteenth century: "the glory of God, a sense of urgency because of the imminent millennium, the love of Christ, compassion for those considered eternally lost, a sense of duty, the awareness of cultural superiority, and competition with . . . missionary efforts–had blended together to form a mosaic" (Bosch 1991: 342).

"Missionary Myth"

But this mosaic is beginning to break into pieces. The last half of the twentieth century and the post Vatican II era has brought about a significant change in the world of mission and the missioner. There is growing feeling in the church worldwide of what Bosch refers to as a "missionary malaise" (Ibid.: 345). This malaise is due, at least in part, to a church that has been permeated by what Anthony Gittins calls the "missionary myth (Gittins 1994)." Gittins analyzes the growing "missionary malaise" in terms of the breaking down of this myth. The unraveling of the "missionary myth" has touched all involved in the missionary endeavor of the church. Protestants and Catholics, religious and lay alike, have been living through a powerful and transforming "identity crisis" in mission in the last half of this twentieth century.

Himself a missionary anthropologist, Gittins uses the term "myth" not in its technical anthropological sense, but more because it was a reality in the lives of both missioners and non-missioners alike. They *believed* in the myth, and believing in it, they continued to create and sustain it. Exactly what is this "missionary myth"? Gittins defines it as:

> A portmanteau term embracing the explanations, projections, and rationalizations shared by missionaries explicitly or implicitly, and serving to bind them together as a unitary group with common work, aims and understanding . . . the web of relevancies which largely unconsciously, missionaries wove around themselves and each other, and within which they survived and grew, despite and sometimes because of, other worlds of meaning or patterns of relevance which abutted or threatened theirs (Ibid.: 145).

Missioners, not unlike the rest of humankind, need myths to live by.

It seems inevitable, however, that the old missionary myth had to give way to a new one, more in keeping with a radically changing world. The economic, political and technological revolutions that characterize our globe at the turn of the century demand an equally revolutionary understanding of mission both from within and without the church. Such concepts as conversion, competitiveness, "baptisms," and planting churches, have been called into question. Although mission would nevertheless remain highly theocentric, christocentric and ecclesial, Vatican II and later Paul VI's extraordinary *Evangelii Nuntiandi* ushered in a new era in missiology, marked by such concepts as inculturation, contextualization, development, ecumenism and dialogue.

The traditional forms of mission embodied a response to a world that no longer existed, and even if we do not have to negate the traditional mission as such, we are challenged to respond in a very different way today (Bosch 1991: 345).

In A World of Violence

In addition to this kind of "missionary malaise," missioners today must contend with many other factors which may make their time of transition more difficult or even traumatic. One of these factors is the reality that today we all live and work in a world strongly marked with violence. We need only glance at the newspaper or listen to the daily news. As I write these reflections, thousands of Iraquis still remain without infrastructure because of the recent U.S. led invasion of their country; refugees flee Bunia in the Democratic Republic of the Congo (formerly Zaire) in fear of being caught in the cross-fire of recent outbreaks of violence threatening genocide; thousands are taking to the streets of Lima protesting political and economic instability; gun-fire and suicide bombings still erupt in the Middle East as world leaders try once again to broker a fragile peace between Palestine and Israel; and the list could go on and on.

There are also many more subtle forms of terrorism and violence that mark our lives. Living in fear from day to day, just *not knowing* what might happen next in your neighborhood or town; being "on a list," suspected of collaborating with "the enemy;" knowing that others are "disappearing" around you, living in fear–or guilt that you have been spared; or sometimes the confusing anger and shame of having been raped, tortured, or imprisoned.

Many missioners are being increasingly affected by this violence in varying degrees. In journeying with groups of "transitioning" missioners over the last few years, we have increasingly found the impact of terrorism and violence on their lives to be powerful and sometimes very painful. One friend had worked in Peru for over twenty-five years, and was there during the height of the reign of terror of *Sendero Luminoso* ("Shining Path") during the late 1980's and early '90s. He had been almost a year in the States for study when he began to have recurring post traumatic symptoms, not unlike he had experienced before in the midst of the terror, when close friends and parishioners were "being disappeared" or killed, and he was privilege to a lot of information and consequently, a lot of fear and pain.

Another friend, in a workshop of returning missioners sponsored by FROM, shared with us an excruciating experience that he had not been able to talk about with anyone until that moment, although he had been back in the U.S. for almost a year. Although a "foreigner" in a Muslim state, as a teacher and priest he had been invited by some of his student friends to be part of a rally and an evening of dialogue for peace. An informer had leaked their gathering place. This missioner had been witness to an overt and intentional massacre of hundreds of young men and women who had been gathered. He had helped gather the wounded and carry them to the hospital. He had to walk through hundreds of dead bodies strewn across the plaza where they had been meeting. The next morning, the massacre headlined the morning news. And yet because of the tense political situation, and his own paralyzing fear, he had never been able to share with anyone–not even members of his local religious community–that he had been present at the event.

Self-Images of a Missioner

As the "missionary myth" has begun to crumble in our midst, and the global situation becomes increasingly more violent, many missioners find that maintaining self understanding and a sense of purpose has become more complex. What is the missioner's self-image today? In an article entitled "Seeing Mission Through Images," Stephen Bevans maintains that theologies of mission are concentrated in various images of the missionary. He acknowledges that missionaries have always seen themselves through various images, some of which remain valid today "if properly understood." But he notes that today "times and attitudes have changed." He points to the U.S. Catholic Bishops' 1986 pastoral statement, "To the Ends of the Earth," noting that, since Vatican II "we have been living in a world that provides a new context for missionary activity."

Bevans maintains that "missionaries need to go about mission work differently, and they have to understand themselves and be understood by others through different images" (Bevans 1994: 159). He then goes on to reflect upon eight different images through which a modern church might understand its missionaries: "(1) treasure hunter, (2) teacher, (3) prophet, (4) guest, (5) stranger, (6) partner, (7) migrant worker, and (8) ghost" (Ibid.: 158-169). These titles in themselves reveal a bit of the complexity of what it means to be a missioner in today's today's world church.

In view of our reflections here, we would like to look at one of these images more closely, namely that of *stranger*. Part of the complexity and pain of the missioner's life is knowing, on some deep level, that one has become a permanent "stranger in a strange land," whether in the host culture to which one has been sent, where one is a "guest," or in the "home" culture from which one has come. This latter reality can be a very disorienting discovery for missioners who are returning to their countries or cultures of origin, either definitively or for a temporary time of discernment, rest, study, etc. Furthermore, women and men who once have been "missioners" will *always be missioners.* In this sense we find ourselves in some way "misfits" (see Lewis 1997), and it is painfully disconcerting not to "fit," to always feel like a stranger. As Gittins puts it, "So many of us wriggle or fidget as we resist the discomfort" (Gittins 1989: 112).

One of my favorite descriptions of a missioner says a lot about this image of "stranger." It was written over sixty years ago and comes from Bishop James Walsh:

> The task of a missioner is to go to a place where [she] he is not wanted to sell a pearl whose value, although of great price, is not recognized, to people who are determined not to accept it, even as a gift. To do this he [she] must so conform to the place as to make him[her]self, first tolerated, then respected, finally esteemed; and yet his [her] conformity must not be total, for all the time he [she] must conserve that precious foreign clan that will unceasingly nerve his [her] campaign of active propaganda until his [her] people begin to see some value in his [her] offering. He [she] must become Chinese while remaining American, thus conforming and resisting at the same time. It is easy to become wholly oriental, and it is easier still to remain wholly occidental; but the adaptation needed by the good missioner is a judicious combination of the two, and that is a feat. He [she] must absorb a new and fascinating

civilization, while eschewing its philosophy; he [she] must adopt new view points, while retaining old ones; he [she] must learn and wield a new language, while clothing in it, not its own shopworn tags, but his [her] own vigorous foreign thoughts. He [she] must absorb not only the language itself, but what lies behind the language: the mentality that made it and is at once expressed and revealed, and even at times disguised, by it. He [she] must know and adopt many customs that are quite strange to him [her]; some others he[she] must know without adopting. She [he] must doff all sorts of habits and prepossessions, and must don many others, so that he [she] finds himself obliged to maintain through life a flexibility of both mind and body that makes of him [her] a perpetual gymnast" (Walsh 1976: 3-4).

It is difficult and challenging, but it is not to be understood in a negative way. It is in fact one of the most important gifts that a missioner has to offer to the church, both to the local church in which he or she has been serving as a "guest," as well as to a new local church in a new culture, or to the church "back home." Bevans points out a growing phenomenon in the worldwide church today:

Returned missionaries, by sharing their experiences abroad and their continuing strangeness in their home culture, can perhaps help their brothers and sisters contribute more actively to the church's mission to the ends of the earth (Bevans 1994: 165).

But this kind of "reverse mission" is easier said than done. First the missioner must negotiate the sometimes long and arduous process of "transition." In this next section we will explore this time of transition from the point of view of missioners themselves in conversation with sources from psychology, anthropology and the humanities.

The Nature of Cross-Cultural Transition

From birth to death, life is punctuated by separations, many of them painful. Paradoxically, each separation forms a foundation for new stages of integration, identity and psychic growth (Hall 1977: 223).

The General Nature of Transition

Transition has become quite the popular term in some circles, especially in the western world. It is not uncommon to hear that someone or other we know is "passing through a transition." We know that we all go through many natural developmental transitions in our lives: from childhood through puberty to adolescence; from adolescence to adulthood, and so on. James and Evelyn Whitehead call these "scheduled " changes. "The change may not be desired or preferred, but it is known to be inevitable or at least highly likely" (Whitehead and Whitehead 1979: 35). There's the now infamous "mid-life" transition, more often called the "mid-life crisis." We must move through later adulthood into our senior years–and, even if we are blessed with a long and healthy life, we eventually go through that final transition called death.

As the Whiteheads point out, when these transitions happen "on schedule," as it were, they are much easier to negotiate. Although they may be critical and significant, the upheaval of the "crisis" associated with every transition will be less severe. They make reference, however, to other kinds of transitions that are worth mentioning here, namely the "unscheduled," the "misscheduled" and the "overscheduled."

The *unscheduled* or unexpected life transitions would include those induced by the loss of a spouse or other loved one, or the change or loss of a job. As one might expect, these kinds of crises usually make the transition a much more turbulent and dark time. A *misscheduled* transition might be a premature marriage or a couple dealing with their own intimacy issues after their children leave home. *Overscheduling* refers to those kinds of transitions that one is expected to make at a given age, or in a certain lifestyle, in a given culture. The Whiteheads give the example of young adults in the USA being *expected* to get married in their early twenties, whether or not they feel ready for this personally (Ibid.: 36).

There are several other terms that it would be well to clarify concerning this subject. William Bridges, in his simple yet profound book *Transitions*, makes a helpful distinction between *change* and *transition*. While every change implies a transition, he notes that they are not the same thing. A change in jobs or missions will inevitably provoke a transition, because every change means an *ending . . .* and a *beginning*. Change may happen abruptly, or slowly, but it happens and it's over. But what the change ends implies a *loss* of some sort or other: this is where the transition begins. As Bridges puts it, "Every transition begins with an ending" (Bridges 1980: 11). This seems rather obvious, but sometimes it's very difficult to pinpoint when something ended, and something new began. That's because of the space—or non space—in between the beginning and the end. And this is, as we will see, the heart of the transition.

Another term that is sometimes used in connection with transition is "crisis." For many of us this term "crisis," probably sounds more formidable and foreboding than "transition." We often hear the term crisis in a negative context, e.g., the sudden illness of a family member becomes a crisis; a country stricken by famine or civil war is in crisis; domestic abuse sends out an alarm for "crisis intervention." However, Indian missiologist Michael Amaladoss offers another view. He points out that crisis can be a time for growth.

> Crisis can be a time for growth. I think that the theory and practice of mission is in a crisis today. Some speak of paradigm shifts: the focus of mission has changed from the church to the Reign of God. Others are concerned that mission is losing its very center: Christ. Some are asking whether "foreign missions" are still relevant? Missionary Institutes are questioning their identity and revising their methods. This crisis is the result of two related developments: the field of mission, namely the world, has changed; the theology of mission has had a rather rapid development in recent years. (Amaladoss 1991: 359).

The Missioner in Transition

The connotation of "crisis," therefore, like its character in written Chinese, can mean both danger *and* opportunity. I like to think of crisis as a crossroads, where we have an opportunity to make a new turn, take a new path, follow a new route—but we have to choose. We have to "cross the road," and this moment of crossing can be risky. Being in crisis is also risky—and sometimes one has reached an "impasse" and cannot decide which way to turn. Once the route is chosen, it can be a long, long way before we arrive at a new destination—or sometimes at another crossroads! A "crisis" is often the moment or event which often triggers a transition. Sometimes a crisis is precipitated by a series of decisions or intuitions of some sort which lead up to it. For the missioner in transition, this triggering event is often changing mission assignments or what is even harder, leaving "the missions" altogether.

How do missioners experience times of change and transition, especially when they are "in-between cultures," i.e., moving from one mission assignment to another, discerning the next phase of their life? A missioner, you might say, is used to change. A veteran missionary friend of mine would say, "Hey pal, it's what we signed up for!" Missioners leave home; they leave their base of identity. Often they spend a few months or a year in one place learning the language. Then they move on to their first "real assignment." The children of lay missioners grow up with change: new schools, new neighborhoods, new friends. A missioner is no stranger to changes, and to the crises and transitions that they often evoke. But most of us need a certain sense of security or stability in the midst of change, and often missioners must deny or repress that need.

Leaving an assignment is not easy–no matter how pleasant or unpleasant, "successful" or "unsuccessful" that assignment was. This is especially true because of the special kind of motivation that prompts missioners to cross cultural boundaries in the first place, and to stay–for however long they do–in the second. I believe that today, however, missioners who are in "transition," i.e., in between assignments, permanently leaving one parish, region, country or continent for another, or returning "home" definitively (implying another kind of assignment altogether)–may experience a uniquely difficult or confusing transition.

In addition, some changes are less expected, and sometimes less welcome, than others. I'm finding that this sense of the "expected" or "unexpected" plays an important role in the transition of a missioner. One who has in some way anticipated the change from one mission to another, or who has known that ultimately, he or she will return "home," will none the less have to move through the experience of transition. But it may be somewhat less disruptive or devastating than for one who has ignored or denied an inevitable change. I once saw a poster whose saying was attributed to Shakespeare: "The readiness is all." But sometimes we're "just not ready." Sometimes the move is abrupt or forced upon us. What about the missioner who had planned to stay "for life," but senses that he or she is no longer needed, or no longer able to support the climate or the lifestyle? What about the one who contracted for ten years, but is asked to leave after three? What about that missioner who senses that she or he has "overstayed their welcome." Or what about those who must be evacuated from their mission in one hour's time, because of a sudden eruption of violence in the country? And what about the transition of one who discovers his or her companion left behind, disappeared or killed? My own personal experience, as well as that of others, teaches us that this can be a very traumatic time in a missioner's life, precisely because it is so unexpected. In my own case, I left my mission in Zaire for a time of study or sabbatical. I was tired, maybe "burned-out," confused with a vague sense of uneasiness about my lifestyle and ministry. Fully expecting to return after a year or two of study and rest, I found myself plunged into a time of questioning and discernment, needing–without ever intending it–to re-evaluate everything: my ministry, my vocation as missioner, even at times the meaning of my life. (This "re-evaluating" is especially common when the missioner's change or sabbatical coincides with the period of midlife.)

Reverse "Culture Shock"

Culture shock has traditionally been thought of as a form of anxiety which results from the misunderstanding of commonly perceived and understood signs and symbols of social interaction . . . . [It] is primarily a set of emotional reactions to the loss of perceptual reinforcements from one's own culture, to new cultural stimuli which have little or no meaning, and to the misunderstanding of new and diverse experiences. It may encompass feelings of helplessness; irritability; and fears of being cheated, contaminated, injured, or disregarded (Adler 1975: 13).

The "identity crisis" of the missioner is even more difficult due to the simultaneous experience of "culture shock." A missioner who is supposed to be "home," instead finds her/himself in a *new* environment, feeling that he or she just can't understand or can't adjust to this new way of doing things. As missioners we expected to find ourselves in "culture shock" when we left home, even if we didn't know what it would look like or how it would feel. But few of us really expect such a shock when we return. This lack of readiness is what makes it that much more disorienting.

What some of us don't fully realize, even though we may know it intellectually, is that when we return from mission, we are *not the same person who left for mission* however many years before. Inevitably, we have been *fundamentally changed* by our mission culture, often depending upon the degree to which we inserted themselves into that culture. We humans are social beings, and as such we are continually in the process of changing, adapting, growing. It is a presupposition of cultural psychology that the person and the culture are continuously *mutually* influencing each other, a "making each other up," as it were (see Shweder 1991).

Let us consider the missioner who has been serving in a highly context-dependent or, as some would say, "holistic" society, one in which relationships and the group are the strongest factors influencing one's understanding of oneself and one's purpose in life (see Shweder and Bourne

1991). In an African context, a person's perspective is perhaps, as philosopher and theologian John Mbiti has put it, "I am because we are; and since we are, therefore I am" (Mbiti 1969: 141). I remember once while in Zaire a boy in his early teens telling me about the technical school that his parents were sending him to. I asked him, "Is that what you want to do?" I recall him looking at me with an almost bewildered expression saying, "I've never really thought about what I *want*. It's just what I'm going to do."

The point is that a missioner may have been living in a culture with a fundamentally different worldview, a different conception of life, a different anthropology, psychology, spirituality. She or he may have been influenced by a different system of values, of individual-social relationships, of understanding one's "self" in relation to the other, to environment, to God. When that missioner returns to a low-context, highly individualistic, capitalistic society is it any wonder that he/she feels lost, confused, disoriented, hesitant and vulnerable. An American missioner friend recently said to me, having spent over thirty years in Taiwan, "My family members don't really know me anymore." I'm sure that many of you reading this have felt that way, or at least known someone who has. Sometimes this creates a deep loneliness on the part of the missioner, as well as much frustration and a sense of powerlessness on the part of family and friends.

We need to be convinced that, as "returning" missioners, we are, in fact, experiencing a "new" culture! We are indeed experiencing again that sense of alienation that comes from "culture shock" and all–or at least many–of the accompanying feelings that come with it (see Figure 1.2.). We will explore these kinds of feelings more fully in Chapter Two.

The computer revolution is one good example of this "new" culture. In Zaire, I had grown accustomed to using an old portable manual typewriter, sometimes with a few well-worn sheets of carbon paper for copies. When I returned to the States to study, I was elated to find an *electric* typewriter at my disposal! Friends kept telling me to learn to use a computer! "Jo, it's so easy to get used to a computer, you'll *never* go back to that typewriter again--especially for writing papers!" Of course, they were right, but it took me about 6 months and lots of persuading before I finally attempted it. Then it took a few more months and many frustrating moments before the computer and I began to call a truce. And I have missioner friends who take much longer to convince! One was paying a typist to do his papers, until he realized that he was going to go broke over a year or two of papers! He learned to use a word processor.

Symptoms of Culture Shock

Homesickness
Boredom
Withdrawal
Need for excessive amounts of sleep
Compulsive behavior (eating, drinking, cleanliness, etc.)
Irritability
Marital stress
Family (community) tension and conflict
Chauvinistic excesses
Stereotyping others (nationals of former host country or of country of "reentry")
Hostility toward others (especially toward current host nationals)
Loss of ability to concentrate or work effectively
Unexplainable fits of weeping
Physical (psychosomatic) illnesses (headaches, colds, muscle pain, etc.)

Figure 1.2. A list of some typical symptoms that may occur in relatively severe cases of culture shock (Adapted from Kohls 1984: 65)

Unpacking the Baggage

Missioners, however, do not have to remain "in transition" forever, as though in a sort of perpetual culture shock. On the contrary, it is the presupposition of this project that transition can become, in fact, *transformative*. Peter Adler proposes that the alienating experience of culture shock can be transformed into what he calls a "transitional experience," whereby the time spent "betwixt and between" can become a privileged time of growth:

> Although culture shock is most often associated with negative consequences, it can be an important aspect of cultural learning, self-development, and personal growth . . . The problems and frustrations encountered in the culture shock process to an understanding of change and

movement experiences . . . transitional experiences [which] can be the source of higher levels of personality development . . . Implicit in the conflict and tension posed by the transitional experience lies the potential for authentic growth . . . . (Adler 1975: 14).

This kind of growth, however, does not usually happen automatically. It can be a long, slow and sometimes painful process before we find ourselves capable of feeling at home and useful again. It means rediscovering the skills and gifts that first enabled us to adapt to a new culture, and reinvesting ourselves "back here," as we once did "over there." We need to be patient with ourselves in this process, as we begin to "unpack the baggage" we've brought with us.

There may be different kinds of heavy burdens that missioners carry around with them, often well packed away within them somewhere, as they return for study, sabbatical, discernment or maybe just a vacation. The significant emotional and cultural upheaval in their lives is even more profound and life-changing, because of the way in which missioners usually try to enter into their adopted mission culture, in spite of the many ambiguities within and hardships without that this adaptation often causes. At the same time, within the church–both local and universal–there is a widespread growing ambivalence toward the very concept of mission and "missionary" from critics and supporters alike. This ambivalence only weakens an already unsteady "missionary myth," both "at home" and in their countries of mission. The depth and challenge of a missioner's tumultuous transition might in some way seem to threaten the commitment which has marked their lives, the way in which they have tried to be faithful to their missionary call.

Need for Support

There is a legitimate need for missioners "in transit," be it geographical, psychological, spiritual, or all of the above, to be able to share their story with someone who "gets it"–usually because, in some way or other, that someone has "been there" too. Sometimes others such as family, friends or a religious community are unsuspecting and unaware of what a missioner among them might be experiencing. A clearer understanding of the impact of these changes in the life of the missioner may also help others grasp the nature of their transition better. It is because of these and many more factors that we ropose that missioners–despite their frequent reluctance–be strongly encouraged to enter into some program or structure which will help them process their transition or reentry. Whatever the framework, it exists only in order to help the missioners get in touch with their own stories, and their feelings–often repressed–about their mission, their "successes" and "failures," their pain and their anger, their fear or disillusionment. Many missioners testify that it is in sharing these stories and feelings among those who can understand and empathize with one another, that they are both strengthened and at the same time, challenged. They say that it is through this kind of peer support, more than through an academic program in missiology, that they come to arrive at new insights, accompanied by new and renewed feelings about themselves as missioners, and about mission in general, even in the midst of profoundly shifting paradigms.

The Narration of One's Experience

The memory is a living thing; it too is in transit. But during its moment, all that is remembered joins, and lives–the old and the young, the past and the present, the living and the dead (Eudora Welty, quoted in Sullivan 1991: 103).

Killen and de Beer remind us that any reflection on one's life (theological or not) begins with entering one's experience, and that we enter that experience by recalling it and describing or narrating it with as much descriptive detail as possible. A narrative description of a concrete human experience intensifies that experience in a way that makes it begin to resonate with and relate to the stories of others. This resonance does not occur on the level of the particular topic of the story. It sounds on a deeper, symbolic level where the quality of the particular event, conveyed in the dominant feelings that were experienced in it, relate us to the humanness of all events characterized by such feelings. A narrative description of an event, then, can reveal the profoundly symbolic and interrelated quality of our lives (Killen and de Beer 1994: 24).

The rule for narrating an incident for reflection is to "tell enough for ourselves and others to see what we saw, feel what we felt, smell what we smelled, experience the fear, joy, peace, that we knew" (Ibid.: 25). This, I believe, is the first step for missioners moving through transition: telling one's story.

A conch shell blew to signal that things were about to start. We all gathered around the "banis"(an enclosure

*built of dried palm fronds). The commentator said a few
words of introduction, and the drums began inside the
banis. The singing began at something like a low hum and
increased gradually in volume and speed. As the singing
increased in intensity, first one side of the enclosure began
to shake, then another, then another. One side fell, then the
other three. It was as if the sides of a gigantic cardboard
box collapsed outwards. And there in the middle sat Peter
Kamposi, looking cool and relaxed.*

*The drums stopped one rhythm and began another, one to
walk and dance to. The drummers and singers began a
stylized movement toward the cathedral, followed by the
concelebrants and the consecrating bishops and Peter (the
first Papua New Guinean bishop). Then came the throng
of people in the typical local style of procession. Formless
as it may have appeared to some overseas visitors' eyes,
the clear awe and wonder on the children's faces showed
that something special was going on. I could feel a sense
of anticipation all around (Rick, Fall, 1992).*

The above excerpt was the beginning of a long process of transition
and healing for the missioner who wrote it. It seemed unassuming enough
at the time of its first writing, but in his own words:

*The experience I relate above did not seem to me to have
any formative implication at first glance. We had been
asked to pick an experience that we would not mind
sharing with the group, to avoid any experience that was
too personal or soul-searching. Fine. But through guided
reflection upon this "innocuous" experience . . . a lot of
thinking and praying over it . . . I have, much to my own
surprise, come to recognize that God is working in my life
even when I am not aware of it . . . Gradually in the
reflection process, it became clear to me that I had been
measuring my self-worth according to how much I
accomplished and according to how much affirmation I
was receiving from people whose good opinion I valued.
The more items I could check off on myth "to do" list, the
better I used to feel . . . I began to discern a pattern in my*

life that I had not been consciously aware of. Instances
where I was not in control were becoming more numerous
in my life, and I was becoming more and more resentful
toward others, and with my own inability to live up to my
own expectations . . . . (Rick, Spring, 1993).

Thus the process is not an individual one, although it will be
intensely personal and unique. In my experience with missioners returned
for study or sabbatical, one of their greatest needs is to know that they were
not alone in their journey. Together with a much needed time of solitude,
they also need "guided reflection," to be able to *tell someone* what they are
thinking and, more importantly, feeling. And most importantly, we need to
see that someone or those someone's nodding their heads in understanding,
which says, "Yes, I've been there too." A group that I was associated with
for a few years, calling ourselves "Missioners in Transition," grew precisely
out of that need to be with others who had experienced in some way what
we had. There were commonalities, even though we might have been in
entirely different cultures or even different continents! What we had in
common produced a sense of solidarity: we were travelers together on this
journey, looking for the way "home." Not unlike those mountain climbers,
we have a sort of "culture" that we live and move in. As we saw earlier,
perhaps this is partly because we share a common myth, whatever shape it
may be taking at the present moment. This is all the more true with
missioners who find themselves in some sort of "limbo," when they are
"between assignments." For this reason I invite missioners who find
themselves in this sort of "limbo" while transitioning, to intentionally get
in touch with their experience.

Exactly when this process is best begun is different for everyone.
FROM recommends that people be back from their assignment at least six
months before making a re-entry workshop. This is probably to assure that
they have recovered from the initial reverse "culture shock," sometimes a
time of "euphoria" or just "spaced out," not unlike our first months in our
new mission culture. It can take some time before we come to *recognize*
that we are disoriented, still living in the place we left behind, or simply not
quite "right." For some, this recognition may never come. For others, for
one reason or another, a sense of disorientation may never be felt. Perhaps
this is related to the degree or nature in which a missioner was integrated
into the society in which he/she had been serving. In most cases, however,
whether they know it or not, some process of reflection will be necessary
for an integration of their past mission experience with their present and

future. Addressing the nature of human experience, as I do in the following section, can help us in this process.

The Nature of Experience

"Life history," like personal identity, is an interpretive concept used to bring order out of a person's unstructured past and in so doing to imbue it with a particular significance or worth. The identity of any person is an interpretation culled from that individual's personal history (Stroup 1981: 106).

Killen and de Beer describe experience in a broad sense as "the flow of interaction between an individual and the people, places, events, material conditions, and cultural factors that make up that person's identity, context and world" (Killen and de Beer 1994: 58). They speak about all of this "flow" of interaction as "Experience" with a large "E." "Experience" can in turn be separated into many "experiences" with a small "e." There are four categories which make up our experiences, each an integral part of all of human Experience. They are *Action*: one's lived narrative, which we normally think of as experience); *Tradition*: the religious wisdom that one accepts as authoritative; *Culture*: ideas, social structures, ecological environment; and *Positions*: standpoints, attitudes, opinions, beliefs, convictions (Ibid.: 54-60).

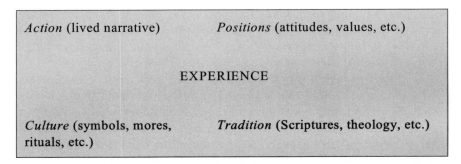

Action (lived narrative)   *Positions* (attitudes, values, etc.)

EXPERIENCE

Culture (symbols, mores,   *Tradition* (Scriptures, theology, etc.)
rituals, etc.)

Figure 1.3 The elements of Experience

I deal implicitly, and sometimes explicitly, with all of these experience sources throughout this book, because they are, in reality, inextricably interconnected. The smallest, seemingly insignificant moment in our experience is inevitably influenced by all of these "sources." They are, like the air we breathe, always a part of us, and we exist by inhaling and exhaling that air, though most of the time without any particular awareness that we are doing so. That "air," fresh or polluted, stormy or still, is a part of every movement we make, every thought that we think. So too are our lives informed by our culture, religious tradition (or the absence of one), and our beliefs, convictions, attitudes, values and standpoints. We might say that the "action" of our Experience *embodies* the culture, tradition and positions by which we have been formed and informed. It is primarily on the actions, the *lived and living narrative*, that we want missioners to focus as they begin their own process of reflection.

But these "actions," events or incidents do not happen in a vacuum. They take place in a context, a context which is also part of the missioner's broader "Experience." I have found it helpful for missioners to begin the process of narration by situating themselves in the context of their vocation, their mission, their ministry. There are many ways to do this, formally and informally. One that we have used in the Mission/Ministry Integration Seminar in recent years is to invite the missioners to think of their cross cultural or mission experience as a sort of "novel," or at least to think of their ministerial life in story form.

We cannot reflect, however, on our vast experience "in general." As Killen and de Beer have put it, "we need to reflect on humanly manageable pieces of our experience":

> In order to reflect, the flow of experience must be stopped. We cannot reflect on experience in its entirety. We need manageable pieces of experience in order to reflect, so we take a single event or issue and focus on that for reflection. We freeze Experience in a moment of time and separate into aspects or sources (Ibid.: 58-59).

It is in focusing on specific experiences that we can begin to discover the issues that may be hidden within. We have come to believe, from our own experience and from working with others, that if we *recall any experience*, however small and seemingly unimportant it might be, it is a like a microcosm of all of our Experience. That is, within that one experience are contained the same key issues or concerns, which Killen and de Beer call "the heart of the matter"(Ibid.: 61), that we would find if we recounted ten experiences, or better, one "major" event or incident that *we judge* to be of great importance. In other words, we might say that "in every acorn there is an oak."

The Importance of Narrating Our Experience

In the field of religion, a paradigm shift always means both continuity and change, both faithfulness to the past and boldness to engage the future, both constancy and contingency, both tradition and transformation (Bosch 1991: 366).

Missioners who have left their previous place of mission, either temporarily or permanently, might ask, "What's the point of recalling the past? Rehashing old events? Digging up buried hurts? Remembering good times that are no more?" I'd like to argue that there is much to be said for missioners in transit, taking the time and the space they need to tell their story, first of all for themselves, and then for others who are there, wanting to receive it.

What about the missioner who is being asked to leave or change assignments, after years of learning a language or a culture? Or, what does one say about the one who doesn't know how to deal with the tension and stress of a new approach to mission, or his or her own physical limitations due to age, sickness, or the general "wear and tear" of another climate and culture? What about the missioner who has been living amidst overt or subtle violence and is beginning to experience the physical and emotional signs of its impact? What of the missioner who is experiencing what is called "burn-out," who is simply physically, emotionally and spiritually exhausted, and needs a change of environment? And there are those missioners who come "home" for a year of sabbatical or study, and unexpectedly begin to discover some neglected inner needs or motions that are demanding attention, who somehow realize that they are being called to "move" in the mysterious journey of their mission vocation, and yet don't see at all clearly what that "new movement" is all about? Whatever the circumstances, telling one's story is essential to a positive integration of the past with the present in order to move into the future with courage, confidence and hope.

Narrative and Identity

Perhaps the stories of those who are "in transit" in their missionary life, express a searching for personal and/or vocational *identity*. They find themselves asking questions like: What should I do now? Is there anything I *can* do? Has what I've been doing made any sense? Is there any purpose to my life? Have I been wasting my time and energy? What am I doing here? Should I continue? Should I go back? Where am I going? These are identity questions, which may coincide with the issues arising at mid-life. They are questions which *demand* to be answered, issues which–once raised–will be buried no more, challenges to be addressed for the articulation of personal identity. In this regard, George Stroup asks a relevant question:

> Is narrative simply an imaginative way of entering into theological reflection, or is there something about the nature of human being and the structure of human experience that makes narrative the appropriate and even necessary form for the articulation of personal identity? (Stroup 1981: 100).

Using the work of Hans-Georg Gadamer, Stanley Hauerwas and Stephen Crites, Stroup leads us to understand that if one's identity is bound up with one's past, it is also bound up with one's memory.

> By means of the memory *an individual selects certain events from his or her personal history and uses them to interpret the significance of the whole.* The claim that human beings are inextricably tied to history simply means that *they search for meaning and unity of self in some pattern of coherence in their personal history . . .* Personal identity, therefore, is always a pattern or a shape which memory retrieves from the history of each individual and projects into the future...The identity of any person is an interpretation culled from that individual's personal history (Ibid.: 105-106, *italics* mine).

Stroup further points out that Crites takes an even stronger position, believing that the very quality of experience through time is *inherently narrative*. Crites holds that the "past, present, and the future are the 'tensed modalities' which are *inseparably joined in every moment of experience* (Ibid.: 112, *italics* mine). It is the fusion of these modalities which is expressed in our "stories," whether they be "mundane" or "sacred," whether expressing the "ordinary" day to day unfolding of our history, or the deeper meaning found in patterns of "internal coherence." Thus the missioner moving "from → through → to → . . ." is experiencing the "fusion" or coming together of his or her past present and future in this present liminal moment which I'm calling "transition."

TRANSITION

→ From → Through → To → From → Through → To → From → Through →

How does all of this relate to the missioner's integrative process? One who is in the midst of transitional upheavals as described above, will find her or himself struggling to renew–or in some cases retrieve–personal identity, and even vocational or ministerial identity. The very act of telling one's story, of putting together a narrative of one's life, in particular one's mission history, is a way for missioners to articulate and affirm their identity–especially at a time when they are feeling particularly disoriented and estranged. In the simple act of selecting (even unconsciously) the events and moments that will go into our narrative, we begin to find a pattern. Finding meaning in the past, helps make sense of the present, and this has the power and momentum to carry us into the future. "To tell a story," says Hauerwas, "often involves our attempt to make intelligible the muddle of things we have done in order to become a self" (quoted in Ibid.: 112). In being able to tell his or her story, the missioner is beginning to find a new way to live out the original call. This may involve a confirmed, renewed or in some cases transformed identity which is in the process of new growth. Let us take a look at some particular elements of story-telling which facilitate this process.

Non-Judgmental Narration

In narrating our experiences it is important to be non-judgmental, i.e., avoiding evaluation, judgment, or premature interpretation of it. When describing an event, we often tend to interpret it as we go along, even for ourselves. This robs it of its original impact. The time for interpretation and evaluation will come, but later. It is important to first simply try to relate the stories as they come to mind, as we remember them. Killen and de Beer give us an important rule for non-judgmental narration. First, they remind us of what most of us learned in grammar school in language or writing class, i.e., the classic questions of "Who? What? When? Where? and How?" At this point we *don't* yet ask the question "Why?" This will be asked later on as we seek understanding and insight.

Answering why yields an interpretation of the event. Whatever our interpretation is at the beginning, it is most likely inadequate and unsatisfying, or we would not be reflecting on the situation. Answering why too soon smothers the actual experience. It prematurely distances us from the event and rationalizes what happened. This short-circuits the revelatory power of the experience (Killen and de Beer 1994: 25).

But sometimes this description of our lives is not as easy as it might seem. Irving Polster in *Every Person's Life Is Worth a Novel*, stresses paying attention to the "ordinary" details of one's life. Not many of us do this very well, nor very often. And yet these very "ordinary" things, described in vivid color and in the context of the dramas of day to day living, are the very stuff that good novels and movies are made of. Yes– "every life *is* worth a novel!"

The Power of the Written Word

Another point I want to stress here is the value of *writing* one's story before orally sharing it with others. The emphasis here is the need for the missioner to recollect her or his memories first by letting them flow from the head, to the fingers, through the pen, onto the paper. Paula Farrell Sullivan tells us in her work on autobiographical writing, "Whatever comes through our fingers, trust that it is truth as each reader of this book has experienced it"(Sullivan 1991: 9).

This has been my experience over and over again when working with missioners in transition. They need time and quiet space, first to get in touch with their experience, events of the past which come to mind, and then to allow them to flow onto paper, as in a written "stream of consciousness." They are sometimes amazed how the act of writing seems to jar memories that they had not originally thought of or intended to record. The act of writing stirs the creative imagination to "fill in the blanks" that may be left by memory. This is helpful in a narrative description of past events. It might be well to note here, in this age of computerization, that the creative and therapeutic response is not the same when typing at the computer as when writing by hand. Some of you may also be aware that handwriting analysts tell us that there is much more expressed in and through our handwriting than merely the content of our thoughts and words. The *way* we write, the force, the slant, the size, the way we dot our i's and cross our t's. All of this is an expression of who we are and what we have to say.

Something very direct happens as we pick up a pen to write; mind connects to body through fingers grasping both pen and the truth of our experiences. Writing stimulates memory and thought, memories and thoughts stimulate writing (Ibid.: 8).

The importance here is not in the "objective accuracy" of the narration, but in its meaning and significance for the rememberer. Besides, there is no totally "objective" memory. Experiences are "subjective" as they happen, and as they are recorded in the memory or suppressed in the unconscious. They will also be subjective when they are recalled and narrated. When missioners come together in a group (or with a counselor, director or friend) they can usually recount only a small part of what they have written, often simply due to time and logistics. At the same time, as we tell our story or event, it is difficult not to begin to alter it, often interpreting it, making explanations or judging our actions or those of others. The narration might be influenced by the self-consciousness of the narrator, or one's degree introversion or extroversion. It might also depend on the amount of confidence that the members of the group have built up in one another.

Creativity in Expressing One's Own Experience

Writing may not be the best method for everyone, although it is the most common. It has long been a pedagogical principle that the more senses one employs in the learning process, the more one learns. A student learns from listening in class, but even more when also interacting through questions or discussions. One learns from taking notes; still more from reading the material ahead of time and going over it afterwards. And finally we optimize learning when we creatively put the material into practice through actions, e.g., art, skits, or role-playing. Some of us may want to re-enact our finger painting days, or prefer to do modeling with clay. These can often be meaningful and powerful ways of expressing ourselves, instead of or in addition to the written word (See Appendix III for suggestions of materials, symbols and rituals which may be helpful).

Another tool that may be helpful in giving our memories or creativity a jog is that of using films or fiction. Through these media, stories are told that missioners can relate to and can often be both a reminder and a validation of what we have lived through. Because these fictitious or autobiographical accounts are in narrative or story form, not only the content, but the form itself can help us give shape and voice to our own stories. You can undoubtedly call to mind many examples of autobiographical writing or film (A list of films and other forms of fiction that missioners may find helpful can be found in Appendix II). One missioner commented after viewing the film, *At Play In the Fields of the Lord*:

> *I found the whole film frightening as well as thought provoking. The total defeat in the end is very telling, "It would have been better for this people not to have known us . . . We are getting out of here!" Meanwhile, the village of the native people is ravaged by an epidemic . . . The film, however, is powerful. It emphasizes for me the need to approach mission and ministry with a sense of humility and reverence. At the same time it urges me to examine my style of doing mission. Do I confuse the message of the faith with material things, for example, the students passing their exams at the end of the year? While this cannot be neglected, I have to be careful to ensure that I am establishing the bonds of human relations, and building bridges across cultures (Kate, Fall, 1995).*

Moving On: Some Concluding Comments

Let us review briefly a breakdown of how we "enter into" this experience. Missioners are invited to think of their cross-cultural mission as a sort of short story or novel, keeping in mind of course that our lives are far more than a novel or a film. They are, in fact, a living "salvation history," the story of God's saving action is in our own lives and the lives of those around us. The shaping of that story is the first and perhaps best place to look for God. Probably, for most of us, the thought of seeing God acting in the life of those we work with is not a difficult one. Nor is it perhaps hard to recognize God working through us in our ministry. But how often do we think our life as an actual living example of God's "salvation history"?

We begin, then, by reflecting on one particular event or incident in our past mission experience. This does not have to be a "spectacular" event. It can be quite "ordinary," long or short, humorous or serious, etc. Keep in mind that it doesn't matter whether it's "positive" or "negative" (in the missioner's mind). What is important is that it is an event that spontaneously comes to mind when you're invited to think back and choose a particular moment. This experience, together with the feelings and images which accompany it, will be the source of further reflection throughout the process, and often reveals the entire "plot" of one's story. The narrated event is the key for naming feelings, identifying images, and discovering the primary issues, (the "heart of the matter") which are often the source of the transitional "drama" in the missioner's life. It is in attending to these feelings, images and issues, that we will begin to integrate the insights gained throughout the process, and–hopefully-begin to feel "at home" again on our life journey. Now let's see how the process unfolds in the next chapters.

Chapter Two
"Betwixt and Between": Attending to Feelings

The world is falling apart.
I want things . . . the way they were.
How do I mend this broken world?
How do I hold on to the Past . . . yet move into the Future?
How do I change, without changing,
Die without dying?
How do I get New Life . . . without giving away the Old?
How do I accept New Wine Skins . . . when I like the old ones
better?
I rebel . . .
Against others . . . against God . . . most of all, against myself.
I am confused, disorientated, frustrated, lost and helpless.
Help! My world is falling apart (Jim, Fall, 1992)

In this chapter we will examine more closely the *feelings* involved in the experience of transition or liminality, as described in Chapter One. We've been invited to recall and "re-enter" experiences *from* our past when we were in our mission home, as well as what we are experiencing in the present, as we pass *through* transition. Now we notice that when we enter our experience, if we observe it non-judgmentally and attentively–we are filled with feelings. In addition, these feelings may sometimes be associated with experiences of violence, trauma, or other forms of psychological and physical abuse in varying degrees. We need to be prepared for such possibilities.

Getting In Touch with Feelings

One day last year a friend and fellow missioner studying at CTU asked me to trim his hair. (Having spent many years in India where his wife was his "hairdresser," he didn't worry about my lack of expertise in the area!). We proceeded to lay sheets of newspaper on the floor and got on with the haircut. As I was clipping his straight graying wisps of strawberry-blonde hair I was–without realizing it at the time–careful to put the cut pieces into the wastepaper basket as I cut, trying to keep it from getting on the floor, or even on our carefully spread out newspaper. When finished, we carefully folded up the sheets of newspaper and put them into the trash basket. After we had cleaned up and he had gone, my eyes fell on the wastepaper basket with the freshly cut hair lying in little mounds amidst the crunched newspaper. As I looked at those strands of hair I recalled another haircutting session one day in Iboko, Zaire, about twelve years ago.

I had only been a few months in this village of equatorial Africa when I and an American friend visiting for a few days took the opportunity to give each other a haircut. We installed ourselves outdoors, so that there wouldn't be any hair to sweep up later. In the midst of our cutting, two of our Zairian sisters came out to join us. As they watched, they were shocked. "No, no! You mustn't just cut each others' hair out in the open like that, letting the hair be picked up by the wind or carelessly thrown away. You must be careful to bury or burn it!

I can't recall if they explained their reasoning to us. If they did, it didn't make an impression on me at the time. It would be several years before I would come to understand the significance of "hair" in their culture, and the implications of allowing hair to be carelessly carried off by the wind. I learned that hair is an important symbol in many African cultures, believed to possess the life-spirit of the person. One indication of the power of hair is that it is commonly used in witchcraft. Often the sorcerer demands a lock of hair of the person to whom harm is intended by a client. Or in an altogether different context, friends might exchange locks of hair much as they exchange blood, in ritually confirming kinship.

As I looked at the wisps of hair in that wastepaper basket, I realized that I was feeling as though I had committed a sacrilege, treating something sacred without proper respect. There I was looking at "the embodiment of my friend's spirit" lying crumpled in that waste can. How could I just walk away and leave it there, in full view of a passerby!? I began saying to myself, "Jo Ann, you're in Chicago now. No one here worries about cut hair!" But as I looked at that hair, I knew that I just couldn't leave it like that. For some reason within myself, I had to attend to it in some more "sacred" way.

I then proceeded to carefully gather the little wisps and mounds of

"Peter's spirit." I carefully wrapped them in paper toweling, folding it into a package so that nothing could be seen or fall out. Then I gently laid the wrapped package back into the wastepaper basket, somehow feeling that "it was enough." I felt that I had ritually disposed of the hair in an appropriately respectful way. I had thus appeased my own spirit.

There have been many similar moments in my life since I've returned to the United States from Zaire, when I realize, reflecting on my own behavior, that somehow in some fundamental ways, *I have changed.* Oftentimes many of us are not at all in touch with what we are feeling, and find it very difficult to articulate. We can usually say what we *think*, but what we *feel* is another question altogether. Killen and de Beer suggest that naming feelings, accurately and non-judgmentally, is a necessary "spiritual discipline . . . an essential practice of Christian asceticism for our time" (Killen and de Beer 1994: 30). One way for missioners to face and explore these feelings evoked by their transition is through dialogue with others who may be experiencing–or possibly repressing–similar feelings. Exploring those feelings and what might be their origin is the work of this chapter.

Defining "Feelings" and "Emotions"

Feelings can generally be defined as "embodied affective and intelligent responses to reality as we encounter it . . . . They are clues to the meaning of our experience" (Ibid.: 27). I like thinking of feelings as "clues." I'm a mystery fan, and any good mystery writer gives subtle hints, clues to help the reader figure out "who dunnit." We must be very attentive to the clues, often hidden, or found in unsuspecting places. So too as missioners narrating our stories from the past or present, we–and those who walk with us–must be attentive listeners to the clues our body and emotions give us. What are we *feeling* within ourselves, when we are speaking or listening to one another?

While Killen and de Beer refer to "feelings" in a general sense, some authors prefer to make a distinction between "feelings" and "emotions." Some aspects of this distinction might be helpful as we look at different phases of the transition process. Psychologist Magda Arnold describes feelings as the physical or somatic signs which accompany an appraisal of something as good or bad, but refer to the *person* doing the feeling rather than to the object of appraisal (see Arnold 1960, 1970). Feelings, in this more restricted sense, are like reactions, either pleasant or unpleasant, painful or delightful. Thus for example, one can say, "I feel

good" or "I feel sad." These feelings are like the perceivable "envelopes'"
for the "emotions" which usually accompany them, e.g., love, anger, ot fear.
Emotions, on the other hand, are the "action tendencies" produced by the
appraisal, rather than the "felt" physiological signs. For example, a
"positive" emotion is a felt tendency *toward* something which we
intuitively appraise as good for us. A "negative" emotion moves us *away*
from anything which we intuitively appraise as bad or harmful. According
to Arnold's theory, this attraction or aversion is accompanied by different
patterns of physiological changes organized toward approach or withdrawal.

Sometimes the *same feelings* can accompany very *different
emotions*. For example, "I feel good because you love me," and "I feel
good because I finished my work." Obviously, there are different appraisals
of desirable objectives in these two cases. Another example might be a
"flushed" feeling: red face, fast heartbeat. What emotion is the person
experiencing in this case? It could be anger, embarrassment or maybe love.
Whatever the case, emotions and the decisions we make because of them
are always connected to our self esteem. In most situations of conflict
between two or more parties, if we look carefully, we will find that an issue
of self-esteem is at stake. Our emotions are geared toward *enhancing or
protecting our self esteem* as we perceive it in relation to some intuitively
appraised "object" (see Solomon 1976: 140-141).

Although this may seem to have little to do with our subject, I think
that it might have some bearing on understanding the *felt* reactions and
responses of missioners in transition, especially as they try to identify what
it is they are "feeling." I recall many times my counselor asking me, "How
do you feel about that?" or "What are you feeling as you tell me this?" I
would respond and often enough she would say, "That's what you *think*, but
you still haven't told me what you *feel*." Gradually I began to distinguish
between the two, and to articulate better what I was *feeling*, i.e., the
sensations and emotions involved, which would indeed gradually give me
a clue as to the *meaning* of an experience, situation or dream.

Once in a small group, a woman was recounting an experience from
her time on mission. As she was speaking, I found myself feeling chilled.
Later when I was responding to her, my gut was actually trembling, as was
my voice. I recognized that energy had gone out of me in listening and
responding to her story. This apparently simple sharing on her part had
generated strong feelings in me. This was more than an empathic response.
Something in her story was connecting to something in mine, evoking a
feeling response within me. At this point the *reason* for such an emotional

response may not yet be apparent. It will eventually reveal itself if we are faithful to the process: *attending our feelings, exploring the images they evoke, moving through the "conversion"* that is demanded, and eventually embracing and *integrating the insights* revealed along the way.

Encountering Feelings from the Past

One evening, one of the "missioners in transition," "Kathy," recalled the night when one of the women from the base communities had come to talk with her and shared her burden with "Kathy." This was after about one and a half years since her arrival in Brazil–and about thirteen years before. "Kathy" had only recently gotten in touch with what happened to her on that night, after over two years back in the States for study. She describes how, for the first time since she had arrived, she really *felt deeply* with that woman. For the first time she identified with the poor in this woman's concrete situation. In her words:

> *I don't know how to describe it except I "felt her pain." Poverty and oppression were no longer a nameless face, just another "poor person." The poverty, the injustice, the oppression took on a face, a name, a reality that I could never forget. I felt overwhelmed by it all. I was angry. I felt powerless. I can't exactly say what happened, but I knew from that moment on everything had changed . . . . I had changed and would never be the same. After the woman left, I found my two companions in the sitting room still up that night. I began to tell them what had happened and how I felt. I began to cry–for the first time since I had been in Brazil. They listened, but they must not have been comfortable with my tears. They began to give me advice about how I must learn to distance myself from these things . . . not to get too emotionally involved (Winter, 1997).*

Again Kathy couldn't exactly explain what happened to her at that moment. This memory of that night with her companions is less vivid than the time spent with the woman from the fávella. She only knows now that they couldn't receive her tears, her pain, her vulnerability, and that something within her "turned off." She makes a wrenching gesture toward her gut as she says with a trembling voice,

That night, something within me shut down. I knew that
from that moment on I had to become hard, tough,
invulnerable. From then on I became "the crusader." In
my fury I began a stream of ceaseless activities aimed at
changing the situation. "Even if no one else will help them,
even if they don't seem to want to help themselves, I will
help them."

And for the next nine years "Kathy" spent all of her energy
organizing, strategizing, developing, doing . . . .

Toward the end of my time in Brazil it dawned on me very
forcefully–so forcefully that I was once again brought to
tears–that all of my work, plans, strategizing was not one
bit helpful. It was changing nothing, and keeping me at a
distance from those whom I was trying to help. All my
effort was not alleviating the pain of what I saw and, at
times, experienced with those who suffered. I could not
help the situation either. The tears were tears of useless
time spent on too much activity, and tears of compassion
as I identified with the futility of their lives and my own.
All I could do was "get out." I was "a mess" and so angry
(Kathy, Winter, 1997).

Kathy acknowledges now that when she left Brazil to come to the
United States for a sabbatical, she was indeed "a mess." But at the time she
wasn't fully ready to recognize it, much less the reasons why. She spent the
first year of this "sabbatical " feeling angry, closed, bitter, almost antisocial.
It was only after over a year that she began to realize how angry she was,
and that somehow she had to deal with this anger. Angry at whom? About
what? At the Brazilians? At her religious congregation? her companions?
The injustice of "the system"? Herself? At God? She needed to get to "the
heart of the matter," the key issue or issues which were causing her so much
anger, so much pain.

She began to journey with a group of missioners who were also on
sabbatical, studying, returning, moving on. Gradually as her experiences
were accepted, her feelings understood, Kathy gained trust in this group.
She also gained the confidence to look within herself, to begin this inner
journey–possibly the most difficult she had ever made. She realized her

need for spiritual direction and counseling. She began to pursue both. This movement *from* past events and lived narrative, *through* feelings and the images and other feelings they evoked, led *to* a certain liberation from all those feelings that had been "shut down" for over ten years. Only after two more years, however, did she begin to see some glimpses of light in her darkness, to begin to get some clues as to what was happening to her and within her. Gradually these clues became insights which would begin to further free her to move on, into some new light, new clarity and insight, enabling her to take some initiative, to make decisions and to take action about her future.

Kathy's journey, although unique, is, at the same time, not unlike the journeys of countless other missioners who come home with "unfinished business" or "unpacked baggage." Rather than deal with that baggage however, missioners often just push it under the bed, as so many of us do, or put it down in a basement somewhere, hidden from everyone's view, even their own. But something within us knows it's there, that unpacked bag, and keeps reminding us—sometimes in subtle or disguised ways—that we have to eventually deal with it. A friend told me that he *literally* shoved a full trunk under his bed when he first returned from a mission assignment. He didn't unpack it until six years later! Some say, "Let it go," or "Forget it," but we will never be fully "at home" nor readjusted to a new situation until we "unpack that bag."

This chapter is all about "that baggage." We may have been carrying it around with us for a long time, or maybe only since we left our mission. For some this "baggage" may represent a very complex reality, while for others their bags may be relatively light. Certainly, for most if not all missioners, the liminal stage of transition "betwixt and between" may carry with it a vast array of feelings which might be attributed to any number of factors. In addition to the cross-cultural "missionary" transition, for example, a person might also be facing other challenging life crises: health problems, family difficulties, the death of a significant person, radical changes in what once were familiar surroundings. Again, while some of what missioners are feeling during transition may be closely connected to the past, for others it's what they anticipate or fear regarding the future. Often we have mixed feelings about what we are moving toward.

The emotions driving us, and the feelings expressing them, are obviously all interconnected. They are not neatly divided into categories: "past," "present" and "future," or "grief" and "trauma." For our purposes in this chapter, for the sake of better understanding this aspect of a missioner's transition, we will treat each of these emotionally charged time frames and categories as though they were experienced separately. But the transition affects *all* of the missioner's self, including his or her spirituality. Since we cannot possibly address all of the many feelings which may be experienced during any given transition, I have tried to focus on what I consider to be three major pieces of "baggage " often carried during that liminal time, namely, *loss*, *grief* and *trauma*. I have found that the many faceted process associated with the act of *grieving* provides an especially appropriate prism for understanding the dynamics of the liminal feelings experienced by a missioner in transition. Let us take a look at that prism in the light of our current reflection.

The Nature of Loss

> *[The] adjustment that caused me the most trouble and grief was the great amount of loss and change I was forced to experience suddenly. The only thing that did not change in my life was a few pieces of clothing and a few articles I brought with me to America. Everything else . . . was either altered or completely lost. Everything: people, relatives, friends, cars, climate . . . nature–Everything! It was almost as if I was (and I believe I was) dealing with thousands of deaths at once, including my own. (A young returnee, in Storti 1989: 176).*

In *All Our Losses, All Our Griefs*, Mitchell and Anderson discuss six major types of losses, as well as several possible variables (1983: 36-51). I believe these losses are worth mentioning in some detail here, because the missioner in transition is usually affected by not merely one or two, but often all of these different kinds of loss. In my own experience I can now identify that when I returned from Zaire, I was dealing with each of them in a significant way. I will name and briefly define each, using Mitchell and Anderson's schema and complementing it with Sullender's perspective. At the same time I'll give a few examples of these kinds of losses using my own and other missioner's experiences.

Material Loss

"Material loss is the loss of a physical object or of familiar surroundings to which one has an important attachment" (Ibid.: 36-37). Sullender refers to this as "loss of external objects [which] can be losses of such things as money, pets, special mementos, home or even homeland" (1985: 15-17). He goes on to say:

> The loss of one's homeland, even if by choice, is a complex phenomenon that also involves the loss of roots, identity, support and familiarity . . . The loss of one's home can also be by disaster, by changing homes or by leaving homes. 'Home' often involves more than just a building. It also includes one's family, security, childhood, familiarity, etc. (Ibid.: 16).

Material loss is perhaps the easiest to identify for missioners in transition. I remember when I first came back from Zaire, I surrounded myself with all kinds of material objects which seemed to "bring Zaire close": I liked to wear my "limputa," the wraparound piece of bright African cloth which is not only the basic clothing for women there, but also serves at least a dozen other purposes. On my dresser was the carved African Madonna that spoke to me of the elegant simplicity of the people. I listened endlessly to homemade cassettes of popular Zairian music or to a copy of the vibrant liturgies that I had become my way of worshipping.

I longed for the sights and sounds of Zaire: women calling to one another across the road or marketplace, "Mbote! Okei wapi?"; the drumbeats of a distant celebration; the children–always and everywhere, the children–laughing, singing, hopping and jumping with the games I could never master. I missed the sun burning through the morning haze of the dry season, the distant sound of the rain approaching, moving across the lush forest like the hooves of an angry herd coming closer and closer. I longed to place my feet again on Zairian soil, and look up at night into the vast diamond studded African sky. Instead, I had to be satisfied with listening to vague news reports about the refugee crisis in eastern Zaire, the "rebels taking over one fourth of the country," the endless reports and television's gaunt faces of hunger, starvation and death in the land I had come to love.

A missioner may actually be engaged in uprooting him or herself from that which has actually become "home." Such a process will depend upon many variables: the time spent by the missioner in the host culture, the emotional investment in relationships and work, the effort at acculturation, whether or not the decision to leave is voluntary or involuntary, the age and experience of the missioner. This kind of transition will necessarily mean dealing with questions of identity and the loss of a part of one's sense of rootedness.

Relationship Loss

Relationship loss is the ending of opportunities to relate oneself to, talk with, share experiences with, make love to, touch, settle issues with, fight with, and otherwise be in the emotional and/or physical presence of a particular other human being (Mitchell and Anderson 1983: 37-39).

I believe relational loss is the most significant and often the most difficult to accept of all losses. Sullender puts this category first in his discussion, since when we mention loss and grief, we most readily think of separation from persons. He simply calls this the "loss of a person," whether by death, divorce or separation of any significance (Sullender 1985: 7-12). In recent years, I have had reason to do much more traveling than I might wish. I have relieved the boredom of waiting in airports by engaging in the wonderful pastime of "people watching." I've become quite a keen observer of humankind. Through this pastime, I've become convinced that one can learn a great deal about grief in airports. At every departing gate one can find embracing couples, crying children, and weeping parents. The pain of separation, however brief, is the pain of grief. Every good-bye, however temporary, is a prelude to the final good-bye. We fight off that pain with "promises to write," gestures of affection, gift exchanges, taking pictures "to remember her by" and so on. Yet all of these assorted rituals only point to the reality of the loss and the inevitability of grief feelings (Ibid.: 12).

The loss of relationships is inevitable for missioners transitioning to new forms of mission. We indeed try to console ourselves with promises to keep in touch, but we know that the relationships that we have formed in our adopted culture, the familiarity and intimacy with which we have lived them, will never be the same. One missioner, after several months back from Brazil, shares a part of a letter he received from a friend:

> *"Listen to me . . . every friend who has entered into our lives always takes with him/herself a little bit of us and lets a piece . . . stay with us. A piece of you, which is here with me, makes me remember that which has gone away . . . . For three months I have been waiting for some words from you . . . I am very sad and also, maybe more, worried about you . . . ."*

The missioner reflects:

All of the letters I receive express clearly their grief and also my grief. I have also written many letters to some of them in the same tone. Many times the grief comes strongly whenever we think that this separation is a permanent one . . . no more opportunity to get together, no more working as a team . . . . (Frankie, Fall, 1995).

My closest Zairian friend was my first tutor. She eventually became my "kinship sister." It was she who unlocked for me the door to many aspects of the culture. Other Zairians became my "sisters and brothers," many of them affectionately called me "Mama leki," which is "maternal aunt" in Lingala. I can see the brave, long-suffering women, wives and mothers, workers of the fields and the marketplaces. I also can recall some proud and hardworking fathers, who did their best to provide for their families under impossible circumstances. I remember the "forest people" of Iboko, who taught me much more than the literacy and life skills I tried to teach them.

One of the strongest people I knew was Anna, who bravely raised her three grandchildren in conditions of extreme poverty and in the face of unbelievable obstacles. It was on a routine visit to one of the base communities in Mbandaka that she asked me to take a look at her youngest grandson, Gaylor. He was almost two years old but he looked like a shriveled up little old man. He was suffering from "kwashiorkor" (extreme lack of protein) and general malnutrition. Mama Anna was doing her best to fill him up with "kwanga and mpondu," i.e., cassava bread and greens–the only diet that most Zairians could afford. She didn't understand what was wrong with him. She only lived about three blocks from "Mama Mobutu," the general hospital, but she had no money and was afraid of taking her child there, afraid of what would happen. With a little support, more moral than financial, I was able to convince her to take him for the consultation that would be the beginning of Gaylor's long road to recovery. When I left Zaire about six years later, he was a robust, husky, rough and tumble eight year old who could hold his own in any argument, and was also doing well in school! I remember the day he and his grandma came to say good-bye. She fell to her knees on the red clay floor of the little pagoda outside our house, tears in her eyes and a basket of papaya and pineapple in her hands. She thanked God for me, and I was overwhelmed with a sense of unworthiness compared to this courageous woman. From time to time I

still get a letter from her, handwritten in her broken Lingala. I don't think
I could ever forget Anna and little Gaylor.

Intrapsychic Loss

Intrapsychic loss is the experience of losing an emotionally
important image of oneself, losing the possibilities of "what might have
been," abandonment of plans or a particular future, the dying of a dream.
Although often related to external experiences, it is itself an entirely inward
experience. An external event may be paralleled by a significant sense of
inner loss. What makes such a loss intrapsychic is that what we lose exists
entirely within the self (Mitchell and Anderson 1983: 40-41).

As we saw earlier, missioners today must deal with intrapsychic
loss constantly, as the image of what it means to be on mission is being
continually re-visioned, e.g., a "foreign" missionary, a "home" missioner,
a cross-cultural minister, a global minister. How much more complex is
what it means to be "missionary" for one who is also in the midst of a
personal transition. Intrapsychic loss involves our self image, which for
many missioners is intimately connected with their role as missioner or
minister in a particular context. Sullender refers to this as loss of "some
aspect of self":

> "Self" is defined as an overall sense of identity or self
> image. We all tend to define ourselves by those ideas,
> roles, things and relationships to which we are emotionally
> attached. In a sense then all losses involve a loss of some
> aspect of the self. Yet, in this category, I want to focus in
> particular on those non-physical losses, such as the loss of
> status, an opportunity, an anticipated outcome or an ideal.
> These losses can be very powerful and subtle (Sullender
> 1985: 12-13).

Becoming a "self" involves the unique patterning of perceptions
and values centered around our lifelong task of creating, sustaining, and
actualizing ourselves (see Switzer 1970: 78). Given this understanding of
self, we can see how a missioner "without a home" or confused about sense
of purpose, about his[her] "lifelong task," is at risk of a serious crisis of
identity and of threat to one's self. As we saw when we looked at the
dynamics of grief and of reverse culture shock, this perceived threat to self

creates anxiety. One missioner writes, reflecting on this part of her process:

> *Probably the biggest intrapsychic loss that I had to deal*
> *with when I got back was the loss of the image I had had*
> *of myself as the wife of the guy I was engaged to before I*
> *left for Africa. I had grieved the loss to some extent after*
> *we broke up, but I had to come back to the issue on the*
> *spiral. . . . I had to deal with the dying of the dream I had*
> *had about being married . . . ."* (Susan, Fall, 1995).

My own case involved several layers of loss which could be called intrapsychic. An "inside" robbery of our fledging cooperative/credit union had triggered within me a significant loss of meaning, purpose and motivation. I was depleted of energy for several weeks, if not months. At this same time, no doubt connected with my psychological and emotional state, I found myself struggling with issues of intimacy. Confusing and challenging at any time in one's life and in one's own familiar culture, how much more so when compounded by cultural and language differences, loneliness or spiritual desolation. Because of my emotional fatigue and the upheaval in my life at that time, I asked to leave Zaire for what I thought would be one year. Once back in the United States I realized that I had some "inner work" to do.

Functional Loss

Powerful grief can be evoked when we lose some of the muscular or neurological functions of the body, what is called functional loss. Functional loss often carries with it a loss of autonomy. Gone is the sense that "I can manage"(Mitchell and Anderson 1983: 41-42). Sullender includes this under the category of loss of an aspect of self. It may be that a missioner has experienced an incapacitating illness or accident, literally lost a limb or the function of an organ. One missioner shares:

> *"I had to learn that I am not as physically, spiritually or*
> *mentally strong as I thought I was. I'm not even as good at*
> *language learning as I thought I was" (March, 1996).*

In my own case, in spite of continued preventive quinine derivatives (which have their own lasting side effects), I still had many bouts with malaria. I also contracted a severe case of hepatitis. In addition to the months it took for me to regain my normal strength and energy after the hepatitis, my liver was damaged, and I still experience it as a vulnerable point in my body. I have to be conscious of what I eat, getting enough rest, etc. If not, I feel–as a friend says–"a quiver in my liver" and have overall reactions: headache, nausea, fatigue. It's nothing "serious," I can readily say–which is objectively true. Nonetheless, I have to live with a certain "functional loss."

Sullender also discusses the inevitable losses one encounters as one advances in age. Much has been written about the sense of loss and transition which accompany mid-life changes for both women and men. There is also beginning to be some significant study and literature being written concerning the later adult years (see Faucett and Faucett 1991, Whitehead and Whitehead 1979 and 1995, Levinson 1978 and Sheehy 1976). To quote just one of many authors in this area: "At mid-life a part of us is dying and changing. We are no longer who we used to be. A part of us feels dead, and, in fact, a part of us is dead. . . . The task is to *discover* and to *grieve over our losses"* (Faucett and Faucett 1991: 50).

I mention this here in terms of functional loss for missioners in transition because I believe that for many, though certainly not all, the change in missions or the return to one's country of origin often coincides with the transition of mid-life or sometimes entering the "third age." That is to say that while the missioner is having to negotiate losses and changes associated with aging, she or he may also be dealing with the significant separation from all that has been familiar for ten, twenty or thirty years. This not only involves psychological changes and losses, but these are usually related, as we know, to actual physiological changes and "functional losses." A woman missioner in her fifties may not only be grieving the separation from her adopted home of many years, but she may also be experiencing the physical and psychological turbulence of menopause. She may be asking herself those mid-life questions such as, "Is that all there is?"

Likewise a male missioner in his mid-forties will typically pass through a difficult transition of reevaluating his entire life course, as he begins to note the ache in his back or legs and the decline of his youthful energy. This can be very threatening to a one's ego and acquired sense of identity. Quite so for someone who has prided himself on the miles he could trek, through the forest or over the mountain, as he visited the Christians of a vast church or parish territory. One missioner reflects:

Many, many times what I expected or predicted turned out

*very different. Even things I had been taking for granted
begin to change and in the process upset many of my
plans. One of these was my health. I had always enjoyed
walking and exercising and was proud of my physical
fitness. Then in March of 1991 I got a sore ankle. I thought
nothing of it at first, but the pain lingered on. The more I
tried to exercise it out by walking, the worse it became. I
tried pain-killers; I went to see a doctor; I tried gout
medicine. Nothing worked. With the loss of my ability to
walk for exercise, I also began to notice myself taking out
my anger and frustration on others more and more. Then
I began to apologize for my behavior more and more. I
didn't like what I was seeing in myself. . . .   I was
becoming discouraged with myself, with what I was not
accomplishing, with others who were not meeting my
expectations, with life in general. What was happening to
me? . . .   The physical problem I was having with my
ankles kept on getting worse in the middle of all this,
compounding what was going on. Sometimes I would try
to hide it, trying to "brave it" through situations that
required a lot of standing (such as teaching catechists).
And a few times I even used the pain to get sympathy by
exaggerating my limp, so that I could just withdraw and be
alone . . . . (Rick, Spring, 1993.)*

For missioners who feel bodily and sometimes mental capacities
literally breaking down, compounded with the fact that they had to
leave–for whatever reason–the mission they have literally *spent their life*
for, these mid-life or later aging processes can easily throw the transitioning
missioner into confusion and grief. As we have seen, the symptoms or
emotions involved in grieving are often identical with those experienced by
missioners in "reverse culture shock."

Role Loss

The loss of a specific social role or of one's accustomed place in a
social network is experienced a role loss. The significance of role loss to the
individual is directly related to the extent to which one's sense of identity
is linked to the lost role (Mitchell and Anderson 1983: 42-44). This kind of
loss is one of the most applicable and relevant for a missioner in transition.

Sullender reminds us that we are continuously changing (intellectually, physically, socially [role, status], spiritually and psychologically), but that it is at certain transition points that we become *aware* of *how* we have changed and of the issues involved (see Sullender 1985: 18). Such "transition points" for a missioner can be home visits and furloughs, (although these are still temporary "visits" and usually the missioner doesn't have to adjust to anything but being, as it were, "on vacation"). Even when we must "work" and do mission appeals, we are still fundamentally relating to others and our environment in our role of missioner. It is clear. We have a sense of security in who we are and what we do. To others here "back home" we are something of a "celebrity." We are used to being introduced as "my daughter . . . brother . . . friend . . . the missionary . . . the one who works in—"

But in a time of changing missions, discernment, or definitive "reentry," when we are actually facing the future, or trying to envision one, *without* being "on the mission," we find ourselves suddenly like a musician without an instrument, no longer clear about "who we are and what we do." For awhile one might be a student. I myself was, and many transitioning missioners, especially members of catholic religious congregations, have the opportunity to do a sabbatical and study. Being a student (especially after ten or twenty years in the bush or the mountains!) is already a significant change in role–quite a feat in itself, as many a "back to school" missioner knows! We have seen in the previous chapter how missioners often tend to strongly identify themselves with the work that they do, their ministry, their *role* in the community, the organization, the church. Oftentimes it is this role which defines *who they are.* One young missioner, upon returning from a year of pastoral internship, put it this way:

> *Probably the loss that most hit me on coming back from Senegal was the loss of a role. I was no longer an American as before I left, and I wasn't a Senegalese. Yet I had characteristics of both. At first I was left without a sense of how to behave in my society. Now I am struggling to decide who I am–what values do I hold, and how do I maintain those values in a society that doesn't easily accept some of those values? How can I be myself when I don't even know who I am anymore? Or maybe I never knew, and I'm just beginning to finally understand. But I find it very hard to be myself, because it doesn't always*

seem to fit what I'm used to. It's like I'm trying on new clothes. I like what they look like on me, but they feel different from the clothes I'm used to wearing. So I go back to my old style, but that style no longer fits, and I feel more uncomfortable and out of place than I do in the new style. How long does it take to get used to this new style? What do I have to do to make it fit? (Mary, Fall, 1995).

Systemic Loss

To understand systemic loss, we must first recall that human beings usually belong to some interactional system in which patterns of behavior develop over time. Even without a strongly personal relationship to others in the system, one may come to count on certain functions being performed in the system. When those functions disappear or are not performed, the system as a whole, as well as its individual members may experience systemic loss (Mitchell and Anderson 1983: 44-46).

In some ways this kind of loss could embrace the loss of homeland and culture. Culture, it has been said, is a term with a thousand definitions and no definition. One image that we have found helpful is that of a "net" or "web" of common understandings, meanings or values which reside within a group or society on some conscious or unconscious level, and are expressed in that group or society's structures, symbols, and world view. Lonergan defines it simply as "a set of values and meanings that informs a way of life" (Lonergan 1972: 7).

Missioners, especially if we've intentionally invested ourselves in new cultures, have learned to live in at least two or sometimes more of them, which we often call our "home" culture and our "host" culture. If culture is a way of designating the web of value and meaning "systems" within which we all live, missioners, then, must learn to function in these different systems of meaning. This is a skill that we must have if we are to survive–and thrive–in our mission countries. Thus, when the time comes to leave or change an assignment, we will inevitably find ourselves experiencing "systemic loss."

How often in our countries of origin we find ourselves feeling "helpless," "useless," "stupid" or just plain "clumsy?" We are overwhelmed by the aisles and aisles of choices in the supermarkets. We don't know how to order in a "fast food line." We don't know how to use a credit card for gas at the "outdoor" pay stations–that is, if we're brave enough to take a car out on the busy freeways! We may have learned how to maneuver around potholes or animals and line up the front tires onto a two-log "bridge," but cars and traffic, well that's another thing all together! We've been in and out of airports and customs; we can manage without running water or electricity. But "the web" or "the net" can be intimidating, or even paralyzing for some. We find ourselves lost in a complexity of new systems, and begin to long for the security and ease of the ones in which we had learned to operate with relative ease.

One missioner's return from Latin American illustrates painfully well her sense of systemic loss. She had come to the hard decision that it would be best to leave her beloved Bolivia after fifty-two years of service there. She felt that she was getting older, less able to cope with the changes and new ways of doing ministry, as well as with the difficulties of travel and climate. After a few months in the United States, she was encouraged to make a re-entry workshop, which she did. It was evident to us that she was struggling with a re-adaptation to the country she used to call "home." She wanted to be of service, to be of use to her religious congregation. But the "systems" involved, however simple or complicated, whether in parish ministry, chaplaincy, even simply "visiting the sick" seemed to be so different than those she had become accustomed to. Just "getting around" (shopping, transportation, leisure activities) in the United States implies "knowing the system." She didn't "know" the members of her congregation in the United States anymore; her friends were in the communities of Bolivia.

In a stage of denial at first, later one of "bargaining," she thought more and more about going back rather than trying to work in *this* country. What could she possibly do here? She was intimidated by this fast paced American culture. She hated working with a computer technology that she didn't understand, just knowing enough to get by–because *that* was a strategy of survival in *this* system. What she knew had to do with village based communities and a Bolivian mentality. The teaching and methods she knew were for a different context and language. Besides, she had no desire to readjust to life in the USA.

> The art of losing isn't hard to master;
> so many things seem filled with the intent
> to be lost that their loss is no disaster.
> Lose something every day. Accept the fluster
> of lost door keys, the hour badly spent.
> The art of losing isn't hard to master.

Then practice losing farther, losing faster:
placesand names, and where it was you meant
to travel. None of these will bring disaster.

I lost my mother's watch. And look! My last or
next-to-last, of three houses went.
The art of losing isn't hard to master.

I lost two cities, lovely ones. And vaster,
some realms I owned, two rivers, a continent.
I miss them, but it wasn't a disaster.

Even losing you
(The joking voice, a gesture
I love) I shan't have lied. Its evident

The art of losing's not too hard to master,
though it may look like (Write it!)
like disaster.
                    (Bishop 1994: 62-63).

When one is in the process of grieving what one has lost, one cannot invest oneself emotionally in what there might be to gain. This is precisely why the returned or transitioning missioner *needs time and patience with self* before it's even possible to begin thinking creatively about what one might do or how one's gifts might contribute to society and church in another context.

Grief and the Missioner in Transition

I had spent almost twenty years as a missionary . . . . Just returning to the States was enough of a shock. I had no choice . . . everything had suddenly collapsed. Like some strange quirk of fate, everything had turned upside down. I felt disowned, a failure. The only choice I could make was to leave. Yet, leaving mission life was like cutting away half my heart, half my life. Death in any form is difficult to accept. Dying often comes slowly . . . sometimes, breath by breath (Tim, Fall, 1993).

One of the main components or essential elements of what is often referred to as "reentry" or "reverse culture shock" is *grief*. As we have noted in Chapter One, transitions involve endings before they lead us into new beginnings. And endings involve leaving, losing, letting go, dying. As the missioner above reminds us, "death in any form is difficult to accept." Even when a couple decides together to divorce, the letting go of the other, and of "how things used to be" is still a slow process. This is equally true of missioners, even when they have voluntarily decided that it is time to move on. This "moving on" is easier said than done. It means a kind of dying. The missioner has experienced a significant loss–oftentimes multiple and complex losses. This is all the more evident if the missioners are a family, and children are involved in the transition. Everyone doesn't grieve nor move *"from → through → to → . . ."* at the same pace nor in the same way. When a spouse or children are involved, This can be even more painful and confusing, since we feel we are "not on the same page" as we were in our mission country (at least in our idealized selective memory of it, so common during transition). On the other hand, being a couple or a family can have its advantages during the time of transition and grieving, since the missioners share common experiences and are an immediate "support group." For more on the re-entry process of missionary families, especially "missionary kids," I recommend the work of Clyde Austin and Craig Storti (Austin 1983, 1988, 1986 and Storti 1989, 1997).

Letting go of "the mission" as one has known and lived it is one of the most challenging tasks for missioners in transition. It is, in effect, a sort of "dying." But most of us aren't too eager or too well prepared to "die." Elizabeth Kübler-Ross's seminal study, *On Death and Dying*, found that people go through stages in the dying process (denial, anger, bargaining, depression, acceptance) (Kübler-Ross 1969). These might be considered as stages of both the grieving process after a loss, as well as what is called "anticipatory grief," when one knows a loss is imminent, and begins to grieve in anticipation of it. Much has been written in recent years about grief as a necessary response to any significant loss in one's life. Grief is a normal emotional response to significant loss...Grief is universal and inescapable, even when its impact and its existence are denied. It is a composite of powerful emotions assailing us whenever we lose someone or something we value (Mitchell and Anderson 1983: 18).

When one has lost a loved one, a spouse, good friend, parent or child–even a beloved pet–one is *expected* to grieve. Family, friends, neighbors, society in general are sympathetic (if not always empathic) to one's sometimes erratic behavior. n his book Good Grief, Granger Westberg insists, as the title suggests, that grief is not only normal and necessary, but that it is *good* for the bereaved (Westberg 1979). With a missioner who is in transition from one mission to another, or from "the missions" to "home," no one really thinks of him or her as *grieving* the loss of the mission, least of all the missioner oneself. Yet one has lost, in a very real sense, everyone and everything that had come to have meaning during the years of his or her missionary service. Of course, as with any loss, its nature and the length and kind of relationships involved will have much bearing on the degree of grief experienced and the time necessary for grieving. In fact there are many variables affecting transition and reentry. The kind of missionary engagement, the time spent, the degree of acculturation to the host culture, all of these will influence the missioner's need to grieve.

Defining Grief

The most significant affective element [in grief] is anxiety, identical in its dynamics with any acute anxiety attack . . . . The anxiety of grief is an experience of separation from or loss of a significant other, perceived as a threat to the life and integrity of the self" (Switzer 1970: 179-180).

According to many psychologists, grief is primarily a form of separation anxiety (See Sullender 1985: 25-41 and Switzer 1970: 93-117). It is not difficult to understand grief in these terms for missioners in transition, especially given what has been said earlier about the changing identity of mission and missioners today. We can assume that missioners may experience this kind of separation anxiety at least twice, and possibly several times during their lifetime. First separated from family, friends, country and culture, missioners have probably done some grief work during their initial adaptation and efforts at acculturation to their mission country. Many attest, however, that this second adaptation, this reverse culture shock, is worse and more difficult than the first.

This could be true for varying reasons: the difference in age and experience, a mellowing of the usual idealism and early fervor of the initial missionary call, or simply the fact that for the first mission assignment one is usually somewhat *prepared* for an initial culture shock and difficulties in adapting to a new environment. (In my own experience, however, the difficulties one *expects* are rarely the most difficult!) One is also highly motivated for the first mission assignments, while one is rarely motivated for the return or even for a change in mission. At best one's feelings are usually ambivalent under these latter circumstances. And no matter how much one is intellectually prepared for the reverse culture shock or for a life-changing transition, the impact of what is happening often doesn't become real until well after one has left the local mission and has been through some months of initial shock, numbness and/or return "euphoria."

Scott Sullender speaks of grief as "a process of . . . 'making real' the fact of the loss." When the griever has been able to do that, to make that loss real, in some way reaching a certain acceptance, then "the new reality no longer hurts" (Sullender 1985: 38). This involves a new kind of "letting go," a living through a time of "liminality," and finally a "moving on" with a new hope and an ability to invest oneself again in new relationships, work, and life in general (see Bevans 1999).

The grieving process, according to Mitchell and Anderson is "the *intentional work* grief stricken persons engage in, enabling them to return eventually to full satisfying lives." Then they add a sentence which we find relevant for us here. "It [the grieving process] can be avoided, though at a very high cost to the one who refuses it" (Mitchell and Anderson 1983: 19). Thus negotiating a transition is essentially "grief work." Grief work actually spans the entire transition from → through → to, but is most evident–and most essential–in the beginning because it is necessary to *name the loss* (and in the case of missioners this can be complex and multiple losses) in order to begin to let go.

I have lived through and seen others live through this process of grief work. I remember the day in which I finally accepted the "reality" of all my losses. My spiritual counselor had said to me on several occasions, "It's over, Jo Ann, it's over." But I hadn't been able to hear or accept that reality until *I was ready.* Once I could say to myself, and to others, with a heavy sigh of relief, "It's over," then–and only then–was I able to begin to remember with joy and celebrate all the years I had spent in Zaire, all the relationships, the ministry, the life, the love. I remember the words of one companion in a FROM workshop when she had finally moved "to" a new phase in her process. Not with exhilaration, nor with sadness, but with a certain serenity she said to me as we hugged each other during a ritual celebration, "Yes, there is life after Tanzania."

I believe that often missioners returning "home" or changing missions do not allow themselves to grieve for many reasons. First of all, many of them do not recognize that they have suffered significant loss and are experiencing grief. For those missioners who belong to missionary organizations in which "sending" and "being sent" are an ordinary part of the "routine," the return or change of a missioner is viewed as something more or less "routine." To recognize and acknowledge such feelings as those symptomatic of reverse culture shock (and of grief) only adds to the missioner's sense of helplessness or uselessness, moments of panic or depression, or a general sense of confusion or even shame at feeling this way. These symptoms typically include homesickness (nostalgia for the host country that has become "home"), excessive tiredness and the need to sleep, irritability, unexplainable sadness and episodes of crying, withdrawal, lack of interest or caring about life around him/her or oneself. In journeying with missioners in transition, first of all, what we need to be aware of is that at the heart of every transition is loss (Whitehead and Whitehead 1979: 37). There has been much material written on grief and grieving, so our purpose here is not to re-explore that territory. It is rather, as mentioned earlier, to help us relate it (more explicitly than we have seen it done elsewhere), to the reentry or transition process of a missioner.

Stages of Grief and Transition

Usually the most characteristic initial reaction to loss is some form of disbelief. Different authors call this stage by different names, but they all express a similar phenomenon. Kübler-Ross referred to it as "denial" (Kübler Ross 1969: 38); others call it "shock" (Westburg 1979; Oates 1981); Anderson and Mitchell (1983) refer to it as "numbness," which Oates considers a second phase after the initial shock (See Figure 2.1). Sullender reminds us that in psychological terms, denial and/or repression is a defense mechanism, and it is one of the most common employed in the grieving process, as it is in the transitional or reentry process of a missioner.

If we consider the reverse culture shock characteristic of missioners in transition this initial phase is typically one of "euphoria," just as we experienced an initial euphoria when we first arrived in our mission country. Storti calls this stage in the transition the "honeymoon" (Storti 1997: 57). As Larry Lewis puts it, "After the glow of 'everything's new and everything Chinese is wonderful,' which faded after about two months of language study, I knew enough to have an idea of what I didn't know" (Lewis 1997: 86). Most missioners experience a similar "honeymoon" when they first come "home," (or when they arrive at a new mission assignment). It's good to be able to stand under a hot shower or soak in a warm tub! Inevitably family and friends invite you over and ask you what you would like eat. I remember just savoring a glass of cold milk! Being asked to speak here and there, people interested in what you have to share–at least for the first few minutes when you first enter the room. Storti has captured this "honeymoon" stage well:

> This is also the time when you do all the things you've missed doing while you were gone: You go that favorite restaurant and have your favorite dish; you have a picnic in the park you love; you go to a decent bookstore, fabric shop, garden center or computer store and stay for hours just looking; you drink all you want of a favorite drink and eat all the strawberry ice-cream or rainbow trout you can stand; you can't get enough of golfing at your favorite course or working in your garden (Storti 1997: 57).

This is often the experience of missioners when they first return on furlough or for a two to three month home visit. One veteran missioner in our group was assigned to the States for formation work. He was just exuberant the first few months. He'd say "Wow, I feel great! Good food, plenty of rest, time to study, a community to pray with. Just a few guys to worry about. This isn't so bad—in fact it's really a good assignment!" But after a few more weeks went by, we noticed that he gradually began to speak more and more about his former mission. He began to reveal his anger and frustration at being brought back here for a few guys who really didn't need much attention, when he had just begun some important work back where he was. At that point he began to throw himself into a serious program of study. Then we heard him beginning to "bargain" with his superiors for time. "I told them I'm just here for two more years, then my time's up. They'd better start looking for someone else 'cause I'm going back."

When I used to return to the States from Zaire every three or so years for about three months, I remember feeling like I was on a train all of the time, just sort of gazing out of the window as everything rolled by me. There were many things that bothered me about this society, but I didn't have to engage myself in it—I didn't have time to. I knew I'd be heading back "home" soon, where I felt I belonged. I let my family and friends pamper me a little, take care of me. I enjoyed many of the delightful simple things this life had to offer, including some privacy and time to just be quiet and really relax. I had left the constant demands and responsibilities of my ministry behind me for awhile. But when, after a few weeks or sometimes months, the missioner begins to remember and realize that *this time it's for good,* life begins to take on a different color. As Storti puts it:

> The vacation-like unreality of the first part of readjustment will start to fade . . . . By now your novelty value has started to wear off; people are used to your being back, though you are far from used to it. Moreover, people expect you to have settled in now and assume that your are happy being among family and friends again. They don't ask you how you're doing during this stage–they think they know–and more or less leave you to your own devices. At a time when you may be suffering the most, everyone assumes you're fine (Ibid.: 59).

With regard to the entire grieving process, most researchers agree that the "stages" involved are in no way neat and orderly, and that the emotions described in the five (Kübler-Ross), six (Oates), ten (Granger), and other stage theories are all "mixed up" (Sullender 1985: 55). (See Figure 2.1 below).

Nevertheless there seems to be common agreement that *there is a process*, and these "stages" sometimes help the griever give a name to an experience that might otherwise be difficult to articulate. We all know how much it helps when we read described in a book, or when someone else puts into words, "exactly what I've been feeling!"

These stages are very similar to the descriptive phases that we find in most "reentry" literature. In most cases we notice the pattern "from → through → to → . . ." If we consider the process of a missioner in transition we see phases very similar to those first named by Van Gennep's in his classic *The Rites of Passages*. A study by Asuncion-Landé suggests four "distinctive patterns of response" to reentry shock: excitement, re - establishment/frustration, sense of control, and re-adaptation (Asuncion-Landé 1978, quoted in Austin 1988: 519). Storti also describes four stages: leave-taking, honeymoon, reverse culture shock, readjustment (Storti 1997: 60-65). Maryknoll missioner Jack Sullivan prefers to refer to reentry as "rediscovery." He speaks simply of a three-stage process: "letting

Stages Experienced in the Normal Process of Grief

Elizabeth Kübler-Ross	*Wayne Oates*
Denial	Shock
Shock	Numbness
Anger	Mixed belief and disbelief
Bargaining	Depression
Depression	Selective memory
Acceptance	Commitment to living again

K. Mitchell and H. Anderson	*Granger Westberg*
Numbness	Shock
Emptiness, lonliness	Expression of Emotion
Anger	Depression, lonliness
Fear and anxiety	Somatization
Sadness and despair	Panic
Guilt and shame	Guilt
Somatization (headaches, fatigue, etc.)	Anger and resentment
	Resistance

Figure 2.1: Stages of Grief

go...letting be...letting begin" (Sullivan 1985: 30-38). Some of this terminology, while quite true, may be a bit deceptive. As we have already begun to see, this "letting go" is often quite complex and painful for a missioner. Even more, the "letting be" or "liminal" phase of transition is anything but "neutral" in the emotional context of the term. It can be the most difficult and confusing part of the process. All of these phases, including "letting begin," involve dynamics of grief and grieving.

The Dynamics of Grief

All my effort was not alleviating the pain of what I saw

and, at times, experienced with those who suffered. I could not help the situation either. The tears were tears for the useless time spent on too much activity, and tears of compassion as I identified with the futility of their lives and my own. All I could do was "get out." I was "a mess" and so angry . . . . (Kathy, Spring, 1997).

As we saw earlier, "Kathy" had spent nine years of her life dedicated to working for the people of Brazil. These few words, expressed spontaneously at a sharing session, contain the most common elements or dynamics found in the experience of grief. They are the expression of one missioner's grief, associated with both the experiences in the *past* as well as with her feelings in the *present*. There are perhaps as many expressions of grief as there are people living with losses. Innumerable variables make descriptions of its dynamics very generalized. The case of missioners in situations of transition adds even more variables of possibility to the kinds and circumstances of losses and subsequent grieving one might experience. Nevertheless much research has revealed that the following major dynamics seem to characterize most expressions of grief. There is no order or chronology to these, although some may be more obvious signs of grief than others.

Tears and Sorrow

Tears are perhaps the most easily recognizable sign that a person is grieving, although they could be a sign of several different emotions. They may be tears of regret or anger, of loss and separation; they may be empathetic tears for the suffering of the people we have left behind. When they are linked with sadness or sorrow, they serve a profoundly necessary and healing function of grief. In some societies tears are an unacceptable form of behavior, especially for males in western society (although this is beginning to change as we enter the twenty-first century). Nevertheless, tears, weeping, wailing are all healthy releases of grief. Tears literally and psychologically "cleanse the soul," sometimes releasing a storehouse of pain. It is important to encourage missioners in transition to get in touch with their pain and allow themselves to just "cry it out." At the same time we need to recognize when someone may be stuck in her or his pain, and tears become a sign of chronic depression, and a warning that perhaps more professional help is needed.

Oftentimes missioners, especially men, have been schooled not to cry–and certainly not for such "silly" reasons as the leaving of a mission. After all, isn't this just part of our life? But for everyone–those who leave and those who stay behind–leaving hurts, especially if a missioner has invested a significant amount of energy and/or years into the ministry, having formed significant relationships. But I've known missioners, as I'm sure you have, who prefer not to say good-bye, sometimes sort of "sneaking away" in order to avoid emotional scenes. Sooner or later they will find themselves grieving, and let us hope that they are accompanied in their grief by others who understand and care. One of my own experiences may serve as an example.

I had left Zaire in the summer of 1992, without bringing closure to my twelve plus years there. Much had transpired in my life during the following two years. My many changes–country, state of life, job, residence–had not allowed me to adequately grieve the separation from the country and the many losses it entailed. I think I began to realize this one day in the Spring of 1994. Civil war had erupted in Rwanda after the plane crash of the president. It was the beginning of what would become one of the world's worst known genocides: several million Tutsis, as well as hundreds of thousands of Hutus, would be massacred at one anothers' hands during the next few months. The refugees began to pour into neighboring Congo, Tanzania and Uganda. The crisis would shock the sensibilities of the world and would last for years. The impact of this genocide on Rwandans, Africans and possibly all nations, would be felt for many generations to come.

Since Zaire was "in the news" for the first time since I had been back two years earlier, quite a few people were asking me about the situation. Some would say things like, "You must be feeling awful about all this" or "Do you know any of those people?" I would answer that this was taking place on the eastern border of Zaire, while I had worked in the western side. I found myself numbed by it all. I didn't seem to feel anything. Then one evening I was sitting alone in my apartment in front of the television, watching the evening news hour, which had a "special" on the crisis. As I was watching scenes of the people fleeing their homes, of slaughtered bodies and mass graves I suddenly couldn't support it anymore. I broke into sobs and found myself weeping and wailing, as do the women at an African wake, until I didn't seem to have any tears or energy left. Finally, I just sat there for a long time, alone with my pain.

I reflected later that, although I was weeping for the victims, and was experiencing deeply the pain and the horror of this devastation, I was also weeping for myself. This was perhaps the first time that I had been able to release the pain that was within me. Perhaps it was "survivor guilt" that I was expressing: being so far away, so removed from them and unable to do anything about their situation. I remember that this was the first time I felt like quitting what I was currently doing. What *was* I doing here anyway?" On the one hand I was tempted to volunteer to go to eastern Africa with some relief organization–but on the other hand I wanted to run away from my own pain and theirs. But I didn't do either. I lived through it, and this experience eventually led me into a deeper compassion, a deeper sense of suffering with others–and with myself.

Stress

Some time ago I heard a commentary about stress on National Public Radio. "Stress" one of those words that has been incorporated into most languages on the globe. The editor was finding the word "stress" popping up in the midst of a string of Japanese, Italian or Swahili! His point was that stress means so many things, embraces so many different ideas, that it can fill a gap in any language for "that certain something" Sullender defines it as "a physiological response to a perceived danger or threat" (Sullender 1985: 44). When a person perceives that he or she is in some way "threatened" the body prepares itself for what is called "fight or flight"–for action!

Adrenaline is pumped into the blood system; muscular tension increases as blood is transferred from other organs to the muscles and the limbs; blood pressure goes up; the heart rate increases; breathing becomes shallow and more rapid; there is an increase of sweating and an improvement in vision; and excess energy is mobilized as glycogen and is converted to sugar (Ibid.).

Sometimes, however, the organism senses the "danger," prepares itself for action when there is nothing concrete to do about the perceived threat! Or maybe the fact that one *doesn't know what to do* increases the reaction of stress. Thus can an individual find him/herself in a chronic state of stress. This state produces "wear and tear" on the entire organism, which eventually begins to "break down" in different forms of sickness. Mitchell and Anderson describe this psychosomatic aspect of grief as somatization. "Headaches, insomnia, loss of appetite, weight loss, fatigue, dizziness, and indigestion, are all common to the experience of grief" (Mitchell and Anderson 1983: 81).

Missioners have much reason to be "under stress" during the

process of transition. We have already described the kinds of disorienting and undermining kinds of situations they find themselves in–from overwhelming shopping malls to computer technology–when they return from or are discerning change in their life mission. It is not unusual that a missioner's psyche feels threatened by this new and unexpected environment. Oftentimes the future is unclear and this is stressful: Where do I go from here? What can I do now? How can I be a contributor to my community, society, church? How do I (and my family) survive financially? What if I can't adjust? What if I can't find a good job? What if I feel this way for the rest of my life? What if . . .? When missioners first come back, or are manifesting any kinds of stress symptoms, probably the last thing they need to deal with is a "stress management workshop" from the point of view of this "foreign" cultural perspective. That would probably only increase their stress by making them feel more inadequate and "out of sync"! But they do need others who accompany them to understand their stressful symptoms--especially when they try to hide them! Those of us who have "been there" and maybe have picked up some stress management along the way, can support and help them as they navigate these uncharted waters "from → through → to → . . ."

Anger

Anything written about grief includes anger as one of its most significant and almost universal dynamics. Anger is a normal and often spontaneous response to loss and separation. It is also an appropriate response to a perceived lack of justice, to feeling misjudged, mistreated, misunderstood, used, abused, neglected, taken for granted . . . . The list could go on and on. Most of us probably think of anger as one of those "negative" emotions. Unresolved anger can be a dangerous volcano seething within a person for the rest of their years. But healthy recognized anger can become a wellspring for healing and growth.

A missioner friend of mine on sabbatical has been struggling with various issues regarding her mission and her presence there: the apparent incompatibility of her missionary vocation with that of her religious congregation, the lack of unity within the pastoral team where she works, the anticipated lack of continuity when her small local community leaves the mission. Since she has been in the United States, she has suffered in greater and lesser degrees from severe stiff neck and back pain, colds and headaches, and most recently a chronic stomach disorder that doctors have called "ripe for an ulcer." She has been through acupuncture and massage therapy; she has spent money on x-rays of her esophagus and stomach; she has sought counseling and spiritual direction. This missioner has been dealing with lots of ambivalence and confusing emotions. She was depressed and beginning to lose all sense of self-confidence. She found herself not only unable but unwilling to pray for many months. Only recently she has begun to "climb out of the pit," as she describes it. She is finally beginning to recognize that she has been dealing with suppressed anger for a long time and only within the past year has been able to get in touch with it.

Anger can be friend or foe, depending on how we approach it and what we do with it. I have heard it said that anger is not a nice nor a gentle friend, but it is a very loyal one. Anger, when it is recognized and expressed in a constructive way can enable us to move "from → through → to → . . . ." It can help us to be assertive and say what we must to whomever we must. It knows when injustice has been committed and raises awareness about it. Anger can help us overcome our fear and take initiative. It can help us seek creative options for the present and future. But we must acknowledge it, own it and befriend it. It will not let us down. But we mustn't be afraid to share our anger with those we can trust. Otherwise, it may turn inward and express itself in another common form or grief: depression.

Depression

I've been looking into myself, and I am not too happy with what I see. And that can still get me very depressed, if I seek the answer in myself, because I know now that there is no satisfying answer with myself. But there is hope, even for me . . . . (Rick, Spring, 1993).

Many of us have probably gone through (and know other missioners who have or are presently going through) periods of what might be called depression. According to the standard clinical definition of depression, it is still best understood as "internalized anger" (Sullender 1985: 49). There is depression which is generated from within and that which is triggered from without. In relation to missioners in transition I am referring to the kind of sadness, lack of energy or enthusiasm, sometimes even lack of hope, which is a consequence of significant loss or separation, violence or trauma. Normally this kind of depression comes "from without." Especially during the "liminal" time of transition, when one is "betwixt and between," it is not uncommon for missioners to feel isolated, lonely, alienated from others and even themselves in this new "foreign" context.

According to a hypothesis by clinical psychologist Leroy Aden, alienation is one of the major problems that all humans wrestle with in life, along with finitude and guilt and all three play significant a role in the struggle of missioners to integrate change and repatriation into their understanding of their missionary vocation (See Aden 1968). Alienation is a feeling of being "cut off from the world above, below, and around . . . . Loneliness and isolation are not the only manifestations of alienation. The problem appears in other forms, chiefly in a sense of rejection, a sense of hate and disgust, a sense of dependency and self-alienation, and a sense of emptiness and despair" (Ibid.: 179). Mitchell and Anderson speak of depression in terms of sadness and despair (Mitchel and Anderson 1983: 80-81). This kind of sadness can range from momentary feelings to long periods of prolonged sorrow. Often it seems to a grieving person that sadness comes in "waves", as does grief itself.

Most grieving people will liken their pain to the rise and fall of waves hitting against the shore. The waves of pain are alternated by lulls of momentary rest. Initially, of course, in acute grief situations the waves are intense and frequent. Gradually, as one is healed the waves are less intense, less prolonged and less frequent (Sullender 1985: 56).

These attempts to articulate aspects of the grieving process only confirm what all the literature emphasizes, namely that the signs and stages are all intermingled and not clearly defined one from the other, neither in content nor in chronology.

Guilt

According to most research the feeling of guilt also seems to be almost universally present in the grief process. You might be asking why a missioner in transition would have to deal with guilt. Guilt has to do with responsibility–and missioners are some of the most responsible people you'd ever want to know! Missioners, however, are often persons of high ideals and expectations. Often during our mission life we let ourselves down, feeling that we have let others down: the local people, our religious community, friends, pastor, superior, co-worker. We feel guilty when we have neglected to do something we should have or done something we shouldn't have. These "shoulds" and "should nots" can come from laws or norms exterior to ourselves, or from internalized expectations we have of ourselves. This latter kind of internal guilt, according to Aden, is the deepest and most important kind. It refers to the inner "gestalt" of the individual, to the norms and demands of one's "essential being" to the individual's failure in the moral sphere of self-affirmation (Aden 1968: 180). One missioner shares about a disagreement with his local assistant:

> *There must be many ways of "losing face" in life . . . . In reprimanding [her] I took away a "good face" . . . perhaps the only "face" she truly liked. I robbed her of the little treasure she had, and did not even notice that I had done it. I was that blind! All she had left was the marred life she knew too well. Thus when her friends came, several days later . . . I still did not realize what I had done. It was only when they said, "Unless you go ask her [to come back to work] she will never come back," that I realized: [She] had "lost face" before her friends because of what I had said.*
>
> *All of my reading about the Asian value of "saving face," and when I ran into it, head on, I did not even see it! I missed it completely. In holding so strongly to my own views of right and wrong, I missed seeing an even stronger value of these new people. But rather than admit my wrong, I still held on to my own convictions. Inside I began to justify my actions and condemn theirs. A proud, ugly "face" was beginning to rise inside me. I hid it as best I could from their eyes, but I needed to get away! I got on my motorcycle and raced off (Tim, Spring, 1993).*

Sometimes the very fact of leaving the mission or even *considering it*, for whatever reasons–including when one is asked to leave–can, in itself, produce guilt feelings in the missioner. For myself, one of the most difficult aspects of my own transition was feeling as though I had abandoned the Zairian people, in particular my Zairian sister companions in the religious congregation to which I belonged there. I knew how much they loved and respected me. It was hard for me to think of them feeling that I had let them down. I imagined them getting the news, first, that I wasn't coming back to Zaire, then, that I was leaving the religious community. They would feel shocked, dismayed, deceived and abandoned. In fact I *had* let them down. And now I couldn't sit down and talk to them about it. Due to the postal situation in the country, I couldn't even be sure that my letters and attempts to explain had reached them. Not only was I dealing with my own loss of our relationship and their friendship, but also with a lack of closure. There seemed to be no way to somehow alleviate my own feelings of guilt, my pain at their pain. "Guilt assumes responsibility"(Sullender 1985: 51). It is my hope that through prayerful reflection on their experience missioners will find the grace to forgive themselves the failings–real or imagined–that they're carrying around in as excess baggage.

Trauma and the Missioner in Transition

In Chapter One I mentioned that we live in a world of increasing violence. One loss which is becoming more and more common among returning and transitioning missioners today is the loss of a sense of safety or of basic trust: trust in other human beings, the environment, oneself, even in God. Often one of the most common experiences of missioners today is that of having been traumatized by violence on some level while in the field. This third type of "baggage," that of trauma, is becoming increasingly prevalent in today's society.

> *I went to sleep that Friday night thinking about the catechism classes that we were going to have on Saturday. I fell into a deep sleep around 10 o'clock. At midnight precisely, (as I looked at the clock on my night-stand to see the green glow of the numbers), I was awakened by a sharp noise, an explosion actually, which I thought was a sky rocket fireworks. I thought to myself that it was strange to shoot off fireworks at this time of the night, although it was not all that unusual. There were those who stayed out all night at the cantinas who launched some on occasion. But then in rapid succession came more explosions. PA-PA-PA-PA-PA...BOOM! Now I knew it was not a celebration for the fund-raiser of the new home for the aged. That was **next** Saturday! As the explosions continued, I couldn't believe my ears! These were the sounds of machine gun fire, grenades handhold rockets, who knows what. I got up to look out the window and saw in the darkness over the cafeteros above the police station, some flickers of light spitting out of some machine guns.*

My realization of what was happening was now confirmed. We were being attacked by the guerrillas! But why? What did they want? How many were they? How safe was anybody?

I felt so helpless and all alone. I was in fact alone in the rectory, as my cook left the house to go to her quarters around 9:30. She lived back behind the courtyard of the parish compound. I did not stay too close to the window for fear of being detected and to avoid any stray bullets. Thoughts ran through my mind. What do I do? What <u>can</u> I do? Where can I hide? Are they going to come for me? I am a foreigner. What about the people in the pueblo? What about the police? Where are the police? Are they responding--fighting back or in any way resisting?

As the outbursts continued I kept asking myself the same questions. What can I do? Nothing--but pray. So I went back to my bed and began to say the rosary. I don't know how I said it or how many times. But I thought about my cook. I thought about some friends who lived next to the station and others across the street. How were they doing? Every once in a while after an explosion, I hear the scattering of glass and shrapnel on the pavement and rooftops. It made a zinging sound that came floating out of the sky. I didn't see anyone I knew. Not a soul from the pueblo was about. I imagined them hiding in their houses, cowering under their beds. Were the guerrillas entering the houses? What were they doing to the people? Does anyone know we're being attacked? Has anyone called for help? Why are they taking so long to come? Where was the army? How are Blanca, Hernando, Martha, Anna and the others?

Every five, ten minutes—who could tell—I peeped out the window to see if anything had changed. The gunfire in the cafeteros had ceased. There was an occasional outburst here and there. Then a few bombs. I felt a chill and put on my clothes and a sweatshirt. "What's taking them so long?" It was now past one AM. No relief yet I continued to pray the rosary or whatever came to my mind. "I wonder if they are now taking hostages?" I knew from conversations with others that they usually leave the

*church and priests alone. I took some comfort in that. But
I thought about the people. How were they doing? At one
point I was going downstairs to check again, for what I
don't know, and I noticed that the patio lights were out."
That's strange," I thought. They were on in the rest of the
town. I didn't continue down the stairs. Back in my room.
More prayers. As the night continued, that became the
pattern: Pray . . . look . . . pray . . . look . . . .*

*It was around one-thirty when the most powerful
explosion that I've ever experienced hit and rocked the
ground. The whole earth shuddered. "What was that?
They're attacking the church," I thought. Again the sound
of glass, metal and wood came zinging down and collided
with the ground. "How many died with that?" I asked.
When will this nightmare end? I put on another sweatshirt.
The minutes slowly ticked by . . . Finally–was it five
minutes or fifty?–I heard some commotion and crept to the
window to see distance light beams approaching the town.
One truck, then I saw two. Were they campesinos returning
from market? Or were they police reinforcements? I felt
some sense of relief. But I still didn't feel safe.*

*Looking out again I saw more people on the street. It
had been quiet now for about half an hour. I noticed some
familiar figures standing around in the midst of soldiers all
over the place. "The guerrillas are gone." The army had
finally arrived. "What do I do now? Do I stay here? Do I
go out to see what happened? What would the people want
me to do?" As these thoughts continued, interspersed with
prayer, drowsiness took hold of me after awhile . . . .*

*At daybreak I arose and saw people still milling
about, as though I had not left them at all. I readied myself
for the day with morning prayer. Blanca, my cook, entered
the house before I was finished. She was racing up the
stairs and I met her halfway to let her know that I was all
right. Questions were flying. Fears were relieved.
Anxieties remained. She had knocked on the back door
during the night to see how I was. I never heard her
knocking. She was the one who had turned off the patio
lights. The police station was gone. The lieutenant in*

charge, Fabio, was dead. He had been killed in cold blood. One shot to the head. Another in the heart. He had been alone on duty in the station and apparently had tried to hide in the bathroom. He was only nineteen, two years out of high school and just starting his career. Fabio used to go with us on our visits to say Mass in the villages. He was a generous young man . . . .

How can one describe the scene? People were everywhere. Soldiers with their various types of hardware roamed the streets. Men, women and children were looking, talking, asking, wondering. The police station was no more. Only the two side walls and back wall remained. TELECOM was a shell of its former self. Bricks, wood and steel lay about as if a tornado had ripped them from their place. I saw the spot where Fabio was killed. It looked so ordinary. I saw the bullet holes in the back wall of the station, and the burn marks of a bomb that never exploded to give death. Men pointed out to me where the guerrillas had been hiding in the cafeteros, behind the banana trees and cisterns . . . .

As we stood around talking, looking and wondering, a blue Chevy approached in the distance. Driving over the glass, wood and metal, our superior and several seminarians parked and got out. They had heard the news on the radio that morning and had set out immediately to see how we were. Again, more questions and answers. They were relieved to see me okay. They were saddened by Fabio's death. We all knew that there could have been more dead, and we thanked God that there were not. With rumors and fears in the air, they were concerned about my safety and thought it best that I not stay in the pueblo over night. We arranged that I go to the neighboring parish that evening. I returned the next morning for the Sunday masses in our parish . . . .

What this experience brought home to me is the reality that many live with every day. There are always reports in the news about this or that town that was attacked by guerrilla groups. But the violence had never touched me until now. Now I knew the terror that the people live with. One feels very vulnerable living through

an experience like that. You have no control. You are at
the mercy of the aggressor. You feel helpless (Joe, Fall,
1996).

Today when missioners return "home," whether definitively, on furlough, for a time of sabbatical, or a visit between assignments, they are often carrying "trauma" as a part of their internal baggage. While I don't want to over-exaggerate this point, neither do I believe that we should underestimate the impact that traumatic events may have had on missioners in transition today. Oftentimes this only complicates what is already a difficult passage in their lives. Many of the kinds of symptoms associated with reverse culture shock are also those connected with what is generally known as Post-Traumatic Stress Disorder or PTSD. This disorder may be discovered by a set of symptoms, often referred to as "Post Traumatic Stress Syndrome," e.g., trouble sleeping, recurring nightmares, withdrawal, feeling helpless (Figure 2.2). While I'm not suggesting that all returning or transitioning missioners have been victims of trauma-producing events, it is important that we be aware of this ever increasing possibility among missioners in today's increasingly violent world.

The Nature of Trauma

Trauma has been defined in many ways. Robert Grant characterizes trauma as involving "overwhelming life experiences" which cannot be integrated into one's belief system (see Grant 1995 and 1994). "Events are experienced as traumatic when they overload an individual's capacity to cope with, protect self/others, and make sense of overwhelming experiences" (Grant 1995: 73). Such events erode what Judith Herman calls "the ordinary systems of care that give people a sense of control, connection and meaning" (Herman 1992: 33). The result is thus feeling out of control or powerless, alone or alienated, confused and helpless.

The concept of "trauma" embraces two distinct but necessarily related aspects, that of the "external" event or stimulus, called a traumatic event or "stressor" (Doehring 1993: 1), and that of the "internal" or "intrapsychic" response provoked by the event. Traumatic events or stressors can also be of two kinds: what Herman calls either "disasters" when the force behind the event is that of nature, or "atrocities" when the force is other human beings (Herman 1992: 33). Natural disasters are those

---

POST TRAUMATIC STRESS SYNDROME

- Difficulty falling asleep or staying asleep
- Irritability or outbursts of anger
- Difficulty concentrating
- Hypervigilance
- Exaggerated startle response
- Physiologic reactivity upon exposure to events that symbolize or resemble trauma
- Persistent avoidance of stimuli, thoughts activities, or feelings associated with trauma
- Inability to recall an important aspect of the trauma
- Minimizing the experience
- Disinterest in activities formerly enjoyable
- Detachment/estrangement from others
- Restricted range of affect (e.g., numbness, repressed emotions, etc.)
- Compulsive behavior (e.g., drugs, food, alcohol, attitude)
- No vision of the future (passivity, hopelessness)

Figure 2.2 Post Traumatic Stress Syndrome adapted from the American Psychiatric Association

with which all of us are familiar, such as fire, flood, earthquake, hurricane, tidal waves (tsunamis). People all over the globe on every continent have experienced various kinds of such natural disasters. Neither have missioners working in these areas been immune to these.

The second kind of traumatic stressor is that which is caused, immediately or ultimately, directly or indirectly, by human beings inflicting harm to other human beings. Examples of such events are ecological disasters caused by humans such as toxic waste spills, rain forest destruction, chemical and nuclear toxic poisoning. Human disasters include car accidents and plane crashes, due to human negligence, carelessness or error. What Herman refers to as "atrocities" are the kinds of traumatic stressors, even more devastating on the human psyche, i.e., those which are *purposely* designed and carried out by humans intending to inflict harm on other human beings.This would include war, bombings, shootings, disappearances, murders, massacres, terrorist intimidation, threats, and sexual, domestic or other forms of physical and psychological abuse. Both Grant and Herman conclude that all such traumatic occurrences can lead to feelings of being unable to cope with reality, and *chronic* exposure to trauma , can lead to a sense of losing one's self or identity (Grant 1995: 73). Thus, given what we have already said about a missioner's sense of identity in today's world, and especially during times of transition in his or her life, this added experience of trauma in the mission field is a factor that needs to be taken seriously by missioners and by all who journey with them during such critical times.

One other aspect of trauma, and perhaps the most significant one, is called "psychic traumatization" which is the "*intrapsychic* response to an acute or chronic life-threatening traumatic stressor" (Doehring 1993: 1). Simply put, this is the psychological (and physical in some cases) *effects* of the traumatic events on the human beings involved. This vital dimension of trauma is very complex indeed, and in recent years it has received an increasing amount of attention, given the increasing violence and civil war throughout our world and in the human community. While violence may come from without, trauma is always "subjective."

Traumatic events occur inside the psyche of individuals. The *subjective* experience of a traumatic event varies from person to person and from one event to another. It is also the case that there are levels of objective severity to traumatic events and it is possible to conceptualize stressors as falling along a continuum of stressfulness of different dimensions, such as the threat to life and physical integrity to a more purely psychological focus, for example, the witnessing of an atrocity or the infliction of harm to a loved one (Wilson 1989: 5).

Keeping in mind "Joe's" experience of the guerrilla attack related above, let's take a look at some of the symptoms of trauma.

Symptoms

Symptoms of trauma are many and complex, but they are interrelated and tend to "cluster" into three main groups: physiological "hyper-arousal" (or hyper-vigilance); cognitive "intrusion" (or re-experience), and emotional "constriction" or numbing (see Herman 1992: 33-50).

Hyper-arousal reflects the persistent expectation of ever present danger. Because of a traumatic experience, such as the guerrilla attack, physical or sexual abuse, torture, terrorist threats, seeing others murdered or disappeared, the missioner's system may go into a state of "permanent alert." This hyper-vigilance is one of the most readily detected symptoms of post traumatic stress. "The traumatized person startles easily, reacts irritably to small provocations, and sleeps poorly" (Ibid.: 35). Research shows that traumatized persons suffer both from generalized anxiety and specific fears, reacting strongly to unexpected stimuli, especially specific stimuli associated with the traumatic event. For example a missioner who was tortured or threatened through electronic devices may have a fear or a strong reaction to the presence of such devices. One who has lived with bombings and gunfire may start at the sound of an overhead plane or the drilling of a manhole in the sidewalk.

Intrusion refers to a continual interruption or "intrusion" of the trauma into the life of the traumatized person. "The traumatic moment becomes encoded in an abnormal form of memory, which breaks spontaneously into consciousness, both as flashbacks during waking states and as traumatic nightmares during sleep. Unlike ordinary memories, research shows that traumatic memories (or dreams) return in the form of "vivid sensations and images" (Ibid.: 37-38). The person seems to relive the moment of trauma over and over again. Another characteristic of intrusion is that the person often feels impelled to reenact the moment of terror, in some ways trying to gain control over it or in some way "integrate" it into one's world of meaning. At the same time, the person also makes great effort to avoid reliving the traumatic experience, because of the distressing emotional effect it has on them (Ibid.: 41-42).

Constriction is the term used to refer to a sort of "shut down" of the self-defense system of the traumatized person. It is described in terms such as numbing, surrender, disconnectedness, detachment. Some complications from this state of constriction would be recourse to addictive behavior producing a numbing effect. Other symptoms would be withdrawal, alienation, or depression. A returning or transitioning missioner who has been traumatized by his or her experiences may have little or no support, or, because of his or experience, may feel that there is no one with whom to share. Feeling alone and confused, perhaps dealing with forms of hyper-vigilance and intrusion, unable to pray, separated from his/her network of friends or colleagues, he or she might begin to withdraw, become depressed, maybe begin to drink, alone, attempting to escape the pain, the memory, the fear or pervasive anxiety. As Grant notes, "Many of these

behaviors are not only self-destructive, but can also be life-threatening. .
. . Without treatment, the more radical symptoms go underground within
a few months of the original insult. The costs to health, prayer life and
interpersonal relationships for failing to receive timely treatment are
tremendous" (Grant 1994: 154-155).

When we recognize symptoms of what might be post traumatic
stress in a missioner, it is important to encourage and support him or her to
seek serious professional counseling. This is not always easy to do. It might
seem "foolish," "wasteful," "an exaggeration," weak. There were no
counselors and therapists in the region of Zaire where I was for twelve
years. We were hard pressed to find a spiritual director–that is, one who
actually had some formation as such. Most victims of trauma tend to
minimize it. Remember, missioners are used to "toughing things out." We
can be experts at minimizing and denying very real needs. Oftentimes
others have no idea we have lived through. Grant cites the following case:

One Catholic sister, returning home from a war-torn Latin America
country, was exposed to considerable carnage and the murder of three of her
community members. Over the course of her first six months back in her
country of origin, she was emotionally fragile, had trouble sleeping, and
rarely talked. What no one knew was that she was constantly becoming re-
traumatized by terrifying flashbacks over which she had little control. Her
community, due to the fact that she did not pull herself together in what
they consider to be a reasonable amount of time, thought that she was
mentally unstable and having a breakdown. In actuality she was struggling
with several common post-traumatic reactions. To make matters worse, she
was referred to a psychiatrist who knew very little about post-traumatic
reactions. He concurred with the community's perception of her mental
instability (Grant 1995: 73).

Perhaps Grant seems a little harsh here toward the religious
community. In fact often the reaction of an uninformed group may indeed
seem uncaring and unsupportive. Elsewhere Grant notes, however, that this
is due more to ignorance than to a lack of care. Our intention here is
precisely to help us be more aware and better informed about the strong
possibilities of various kinds of post-traumatic stress symptoms in the life
of missioners, especially those returning or transitioning from turbulent
situations.

One of the characteristics of traumatization is the difficulty in
expressing it or sharing it with others. It has been found that traumatic
memories, unlike ordinary memories, "lack verbal narrative and context"

(Herman 1992: 38). Rather, traumatized people relive their trauma in their thoughts, dreams and sometimes actions. Earlier we recounted the experience of a friend who had witnessed a massacre of youth gathered for a peace rally. He had not been able to share that event with *anyone* since it had happened, over a year prior to his finally telling his FROM group. He let himself cry that night, as he told us what had happened, and we cried with him. Our role was to receive his story, embrace his pain.

Post-Traumatic Stress Disorder (PTSD)

Research continues to reveal both the necessity and complexity of attending to trauma victims and survivors. A particularly common set of symptoms has been detected in post-war victims or survivors of other forms of violence and abuse. This set or "complex" of symptoms has been termed "Post-Traumatic Stress Disorder" (PTSD). Wilson tells us that all traumatically stressful experiences "disrupt the physiological and psychological equilibrium of the person":

> In some persons, especially those who have endured extremely prolonged and physically arduous experiences, there may be relatively permanent changes to the nervous system functioning that result in chronic hyperarousal and a cognitive information-processing style that functions in trauma-associated ways in nearly all situations. This disequilibrium . . . affects all four levels of "organismic functioning": physiological, psychological, social-interpersonal, and cultural (Wilson 1989: 22).

Post-traumatic stress disorder, representing a convergence of accumulate knowledge in the area of traumatic stress response, is considered "a unique phenomenon, (sometimes called a mental disorder), which has features that overlap with other disorders, especially depression, anxiety, and dissociate syndromes" (Ibid.: 23). Another way Wilson defines PTSD is as "a human reaction to abnormally stressful life experiences which disrupt the physical and psychological equilibrium of the person"(Ibid.: 29). Basing his work both on his own experience and the findings of others in the field, Grant describes the three kinds of Post-Traumatic Stress Disorder (PTSD), i.e., simple, complex and secondary or vicarious. We will study these briefly, as well as the three main categories of symptoms: "hyperarousal," "intrusion," and "constriction" (Herman

1992: 35-47).

Simple PTSD

Simple post-traumatic stress disorder could be defined as resulting from "an event that is outside the range of usual experience that would be markedly distressing to almost anyone . . . ." (Grant 1994: 149). Grant explains that the following kinds of symptoms can occur as a result of *exposure to a single event* which is perceived as injurious or life threatening to self or others. It is called "simple" precisely because the trauma stressor is one event or experience, rather than a series of them. Examples of such events are natural disasters (earthquakes, floods) accidents (plane, motor vehicle) or possibly isolated deaths due to unusual circumstances or systemic poverty and injustice (e.g., the deaths of innocent children, victims of malaria or malnutrition). Although singular and isolated, nevertheless, such events as we have seen above, experienced by a missioner even once, can be extremely traumatic and trigger reactions such as described above: sleep disturbances, hypervigilance, fear and avoidance of circumstances similar to the event, withdrawal.

An "Anglo" friend and colleague is pastor of a small rural parish with a largely Latino population. Several years ago a fire broke out in the parish church one night, destroying it almost completely. The entire church community was devastated, including its pastor. At the time he was pursuing part time studies at CTU. He had planned to take a quarter off to go to school full time. The fire changed his plans. He had to drop out of school altogether for the next two years. Temporarily traumatized and immobilized, he and his parishioners joined together in mourning their loss and seeking a temporary gathering place for worship and other activities. For several months they shared worship space with another Christian congregation in the town. Then they moved into a makeshift auditorium. They lived in this "liminal" space physically and psychologically for over two years, as they gradually began to envision their future. Now they have begun to rebuild, not only a place of worship, but a community of strength and courage, renewed and deepened in its faith and commitment to be church for one another and for others.

Complex PTSD

According to Herman and Grant, this second form of stress disorder results from "repeated exposure to events of a traumatic nature, often spanning a period of several years" (Ibid.: 150). I believe it is more and more likely today that missioners returning from their field of ministry will have been traumatized by embedded situations of terror, intimidation, instability, oppression or suppression, exploitation or violence. One may have been a target of continued threats, or aware of the threats of those surrounding him or her. One may have been "warned" about the kind of work he or she does, forbidden to organize groups or gather for any purpose but prayer. Missioners today, like our friend who was awakened at midnight by a guerrilla attack, have often lived on the brink of danger–for themselves and/or the villagers and townspeople with whom they work. Some have had to flee in the middle of the night, leaving home and belongings. Or others have had friends, co-workers and parishioners "disappear," with the effort to try be strong for the bereaved, they have often not been able to adequately mourn the loss to themselves. Often missioners are the confidants of guerrillas and generals, dictators and rebels. Another missioner, home from over twenty years in Latin America, was plagued by panic attacks. He finally began to seek therapy, realizing that although he had left the country, permeated with a terrorist guerrilla presence, the terror and trauma of that presence had not left him. How many missioners today have lived through similar and worse kinds of trauma? Often they are coming from countries whose recent histories have been wrought with civil war and internal genocide: in Central and South America: Guatemala, El Salvador, Colombia and Peru, for example, or in many other parts of Africa, e.g., Rwanda and Burundi, Sudan or Sierra Leone.

Secondary or Vicarious Post Traumatic Stress Reactions

Among that which has begun to be written in recent years about trauma, Robert Grant has attempted to point out the degrees and ways in which traumatization has impacted the life of the church, and in particular members of Catholic religious congregations of men and women. His chapter on trauma in ministry is the only work we have read thus far which makes an explicit connection between trauma and the life of a missioner.

Being a missionary can be very dangerous. In certain locations physical hardship, disease, and frequent exposure to violence are an inherent part of the missionary package. Ministry can be peppered with years of direct experience with and exposure to crime, psychological intimidation, military and terrorist threats, kidnappings, armed coercion, torture, mutilation, rape, and murder. Repeated robberies and home invasions by burglars, soldiers, and terrorists are also not uncommon. Similarly, daily conditions characterized by destitution, oppression, disease, and domestic (as well as street) violence can wear down the most dedicated of missionaries (Ibid.: 72). He adds in another place:

> Experience with any of the above, let alone all of them, involves considerable trauma. Senseless and brutal violence can destroy feelings of safety, beliefs in justice, as well as feelings of personal efficacy and faith in humanity. Beliefs in a just God are also seriously threatened. Doubts about mission, vocation and personal sanity are common effects of continual exposure to trauma and injustice (Grant 1994: 148).

Possibly the experience most common to missioners is this kind of "vicarious" trauma. Grant describes this in terms of those "consistently working with victims of violence, oppression and exploitation . . . ." (Ibid.: 151). He comments that ministers working in cultures permeated by this kind of violence and oppression, those ministering to traumatized populations, often take on or incorporate the trauma of those with whom they work:

> Increased agitation, free-floating anxiety, intrusive thoughts and feelings, emotional numbness, social withdrawal and depression are common reactions, as are reduced abilities to cope, increased interpersonal problems, feelings of powerlessness, guilt (from not being able to do more), helplessness and cynicism (characterized by viewing all human interactions from a predatory perspective). Trauma is toxic and toxicity is contagious (Ibid.: 152).

In addition, Grant comments that ministers such as missioners working with oppressed or traumatized populations, tend to become either "over or under-invested in those with whom they work" (Ibid.). These are common defenses or ways of dealing with the situation that missioners have often learned to develop. How many of us have not dealt with cynicism, withdrawal, or dissociation from situations we find beyond our ability to help. On the other hand there are those who get over-involved, becoming caregivers and often creating unhealthy relationships of codependency. This can be played out in many ways, from exaggerated financial support to the "adoption" of homeless or of children. This over-investment is often appraised by the general population as emotional imbalance or transgression of appropriate boundaries. In the example above from "Kathy" we can see both of these reactions operating: an original under-investment, counteracted later by an over-investment. All of these secondary post traumatic stress reactions are in some ways attempts at coping with our feelings of anger or powerlessness in the face of situations of "violence" to our sense of human dignity.

Another way in which many missioners deal with this vicarious PTSD is in activism. Building, or planting, churches, schools, hospitals and clinics, starting programs, etc., however well intentioned they may be, are often ways of coping with trauma. They are, in some cases, well strategized–if often unconscious–defenses to keep us from dealing with the pain, the alienation, the fear, the guilt. If this happens while missioners are still on "active duty," how much more difficult for someone who has no more work to hide in. A transitioning missioner may have been traumatized, often unbeknownst to self, by any number of circumstances. We often tend to minimize this kind of trauma because the "violence" has not been perpetrated directly or immediately at ourselves. But we can live–vicariously–the tension, the pain, the agony of the situation and those around us.

If missioners are not able to share this distress, or if they neglect the need to do so, plunging themselves quickly into new tasks and positions of responsibility, they may have to pay a high price physically, emotionally and sometimes financially. Sufferers of PTSD are especially vulnerable to times of change and transition, since this heightens their insecurity and need to be "on the alert." Let us recall that trauma is not the only kind of psychological and physiological disequilibrium a transitioning missioner might be experiencing. We have already seen that hypervigilance, intrusive symptoms such as sleep disturbance, inability to focus or concentrate, fits of weeping or emotional constriction such as withdrawal or detachment, may also be symptoms of unresolved grief. Whatever be the source or the cause of the missioners' feelings, the important thing is that they are able to experience them, name them and share them with others who care.

Moving On: Some Concluding Comments

Anyone who has ever experienced the pain of grief could hardly be so insensitive as to ask the question concerning the need for healing. The most obvious reason growing out of the feeling of distress is simply that it hurts. It hurts desperately. Agony cries for relief. Normal life is disrupted. There are sharply unpleasant emotions, physiological distress, an inability to think clearly, a sense of the loss of meaning, the inability to perform one's usual job and engage in useful projects, a lack of enjoyment in activities that formerly produced pleasure. No one wants to live this way. We naturally seek healing" (Switzer 1970: 182).

A pitfall of missioners is to try to "spiritualize" their experience rather than experience it! How many of us have said, or heard said from a missioner filled with pain and anger, "Well, it must be God's will."

> *So what if my heart is breaking? So what if I'm damned angry at that superior. So what if I've been hurt by my pastor, colleague, friend. So what if the people are still going to bed hungry and the babies continue to die? So what if I never got to say "good-bye."*

Often missioners have been too well-trained, as a popular U. S. song put it a few years ago: "Don't cry out loud. Just keep it inside, and learn how to hide your feelings. Walk tall and proud . . . ." This is not just part of a "western"–or some might say–a "masculine" mentality. It's another part of the "missionary myth." "Be tough." "Stay in control." We must attend to those "so whats" if we are to authentically discover God's presence in our experiences.

In some ways this "spiritualizing" is an unconscious attempt to abort, as it were, the transition process. As Bridges puts it, we try to "start a new journey, without unpacking our baggage from the old one" (Bridges 1980: 18). As we have said, every transition–like every good story–has a beginning, a middle, and an end (from → through → to →). Maybe you are one of those people who likes to jump to the end of the novel before you decide if you are going to wade through it. Well, this may work for some in reading novels and short stories. But it won't work in life. We must live *through* the transition, if we are ever to come to its end. We will indeed find God with us in this journey, and in the journey of others along the way, but only if we first allow ourselves to *know and feel* our experience in its depths, from its most anguished suffering to its most profound joys. This process of healing and integration does not happen alone or in a vacuum. The missioner in transition, especially during this liminal "non-space and time," needs a community.

Unfortunately, many communities (be they religious, family, local, etc.) are not well prepared to welcome returning or transitioning missioners. As Grant points out, oftentimes in religious and church organizations "the prevailing sentiment held by leadership is that everything will 'work out' in time or as a result of a vacation or some other type of renewal experience" (Grant 1994: 60). Often, however, more than time is needed to heal hurts, unresolved grief, separation anxiety, fear of the future, or the sometimes devastating effects of trauma. Sending a missioner to a ten-day or week-end workshop, assuming that this will take care of re-entry is often the opposite of what is needed. It could give the missioner the impression of being "sent away" by the community she or he needs for healing and moving on. It might also give both the missioner and the receiving community the impression that the workshop or seminar will "take care of everything."

The community needs to assure its transitioning members that they are consistently supported and affirmed by one another in the quest for the meaning of life and in significant caring for one another. The community also provides the symbols and rituals with the power both to strengthen their communion and, as one aspect of its strengthening function, to dramatize the major events, including the crises, of life. Finally, the community provides the rituals which gather up and express in verbal form these life commitments, the faith, the hope the love of those who share a common life style, i.e., cross-cultural ministers and missioners. In the specific context of death, for example, the funeral is both the symbol and the reality of the mobilization of the community to sustain those persons in distress as it pushes them along in their grief work (Switzer 1970: 213-214).

On the other hand, many lay missioners may have to struggle to find a community to support them. They often are not able to afford the luxury of even a week-end workshop, let alone a 6-month sabbatical. They are forced to get out, find a job—sometimes a house or apartment, and begin rebuilding their "normal" life again. Until recently, most attention has gone rather quickly to the "letting begin" phase of this transition process. Lay missioners, sometimes married with children, often have no choice but to move quickly into a new situation. The future is forced upon them before they have time to deal with the present. Financial security is often one of the factors producing added stress. But sooner or later, they too will find themselves still in the process of letting go and trying to "let be." The transition with each of its phases–"from → through → to → . . ."–will not be denied.

Carolyn Osiek, in an entirely different context, but with words that I find quite applicable to missioners in transition, speaks of this liminal time and space as an "impasse," pointing out that "the way out is the way through":

> Depression, emptiness, and joylessness are symptomatic of the experience of impasse. There is a sense of having been abandoned: by friends . . . who said they understood; by those to whom one looked for leadership and inspiration; by God. All forms of support previously relied upon seem to have been pulled out. It is a death experience, a dark night, to which all the descriptions of such abandonment and desolation in the spiritual classics are applicable . . . . Is there anyway out of this predicament? A way must be found, but it can only be found by remaining in darkness, *with* the sense of impasse. As with all suffering, there is no resolution by dodging or attempting to deny the pain. The way out is the way through . . . . In this transforming process, religious symbols and belief foundations will inevitably change. The old ways that were meaningful before the advent of darkness and impasse are dead and cannot be revived. But eventually they will be replaced by new images and symbols, so that what was once considered loss will begin to appear as gain (Osiek 1986: 23-24).

It is precisely to these transforming "images and symbols" that we now turn in Chapter Three.

Chapter Three:
"In the Desert": Exploring Images

*The image that I had during my time of transition to the
States from Bolivia was that of being suspended by a rope
attached somehow to the sky. I didn't know where to go or
where to land, but was sort of swinging back and forth not
knowing where I was heading. At first I was anxious and
uncomfortable because I was surrounded by people who
all had their ministry in place, and I envied them. I also
felt somewhat out of place in the U.S. culture because of
all the technology: computerized gas fill-ups, computerized
offices . . . and the language that all of this implied. I was
in Bolivia for ten years and hadn't fully realized that ten
years was a long time to be away from the fast-paced
developments of U.S. society. I am sure all of this added to
my sense of self swaying in the wind. I don't think I ever
felt that way before, in such a prolonged state of floating.
("Harry," Spring, 1997).*

In the Introduction I described my first close up encounter with
mountain climbers, watching them as they hung suspended literally
"between a rock and a hard place," as the saying goes. It struck me at the
time that this image is a fitting extended metaphor for the life of a
missioner, particularly when he or she is "in-between" mission assignments.
Often we feel like one of those climbers: having had to let go of one
foothold or handhold, without yet having a secure grip on the one ahead.
Sometimes it's hard even to know in which direction to go. The missioner
quoted above describes his transition in precisely such terms. He felt like
a climber "suspended by a rope attached somehow to the sky . . . swinging
back and forth . . . swaying in the wind." It's an image that seems to capture
well the transitional stage of liminality, the "betwixt and betweenness" of
it–"a prolonged state of floating." Even the very term liminality, as we

noted earlier, is the translation of an image, its Latin root *limen* meaning "threshold." A missioner in transition (for that matter anyone in a transitional phase in his/her life) is indeed "standing on the threshold," having left one place behind, not yet having entered another.

This chapter is about those images through which we express ourselves. These images help us interpret our feelings and make sense out of our experience, both that of the past, as well as that of the present. As in Chapter Two we stressed the necessity of getting in touch with the feelings and emotions that are an integral part of our experiences, now in Chapter Three we want to show how images are key in helping us name those feelings, sometimes expressing what cannot be said in any other way. Again, we take our lead from Patricia O'Connell Killen and John de Beer. They remind us that "we give shape and voice to our feelings in the language of imagery" (35). I will briefly discuss what I mean when I use the word imagery, and how it has been expressed in both spoken language and literature. Then, using actual images of missioners such as the one expressed above, we will discover ways of exploring our images, first of all as images in themselves, and then as they relate to our Christian tradition, particularly through images found in Scripture. As I indicated earlier, in outlining the process developed by Killen and de Beer, I am convinced that exploring our *images* will help us discover "the heart of the matter," in our case, the *heart* of our own transition. This discovery sparks new insight and often, a renewed understanding of our missionary journey, leading us ever deeper into the mysterious Reign of God, the Spirit among and within us.

The Power of Images

To many people "metaphor" is merely a poetic ornament for illustrating an idea or adding rhetorical color to abstract or flat language. It appears to have little to do with ordinary language until one realizes that most ordinary language is composed of "dead metaphors," some obvious, such as "the arm of the chair" and others less obvious, such as "tradition," meaning "to hand over or hand down." Most simply, a metaphor is seeing one thing as something else, pretending "this" is "that" because we do not know how to think or talk about "this," so we use "that" as a way of saying something about it. Thinking metaphorically means spotting a thread of similarity between two dissimilar objects, events, or whatever, one of which is better known than the other, and using the better-known one as a way of speaking about the lesser known (McFague 1982: 15).

A Spontaneous Form of Human Expression

In our language we unconsciously use imagery. We have found this to be true in conversation with others, both in groups or on a one-to-one basis. Most of us naturally tend to speak in images, especially when we are describing an event or an experience. "It was like she just shut the door in my face." "My best friend reads me like a book." "I'm so excited I could burst!" Our conversations, news media and all forms of literature are filled with images and metaphor. What's more, McFague stresses that "metaphorical thinking constitutes the basis of human thought and language" (Ibid.: 15).

From the beginning of this work we have used images to speak of the missioner's transition: journey, mountain climbing, unpacking baggage. Even as we write this we are thinking of some of the expressions we used in Chapters One and Two: crossing cultures, transitioning, "missionary images" such as treasure hunter or migrant worker, liminality, i.e., being "on the threshold," having a burden lifted from our shoulders, and so on. But often we don't even recognize the metaphor in the words we use because those words and expressions have become common and their meaning is widely understood. One missioner, Susan, wrote to me recently, *"Without going into a lot of detail, I share with you that when I returned from El Salvador I was at a very low ebb--physically, emotionally, spiritually."* Perhaps some of us reading her sentence have never seen the ocean, or, if we have, we may never have experienced the tide at its "ebb." Nevertheless, we probably know what Susan is talking about because this metaphor has become a part of our vocabulary.

We point out the spontaneity in our use of imagery and metaphor, what McFague might call, the "indigenous" form of language (Ibid.: 14), in order to emphasize the important role it will play in missioners' integrative process of reflection. As they attempt to recall experiences, vivify memories, grapple with loss, answer unanswered questions, deal with "unfinished business" (another metaphor!), describe often ambivalent feelings of both their past and their present, images will surface. One missioner writes, *"Helpless, insecure and frustrated, I feel like a bloody stump, a broken mask, a blind man . . ."*(Tim, Spring, 1993). Images are powerful tools. They say what often cannot be expressed in any other way.

"Packed with Meaning"

When we begin to "unpack" our narrative–moving from experience, through feelings, to an image (which, in some way, expresses both our experience and feelings,) we are already in the reflective process of making meaning out of our experiences. This "meaning-making" is one of the essentially human acts (see Keagan1982).

Images symbolize our experience. They capture the totality of our felt response to reality in a given situation. That felt response is potent with meaning, but we often are unaware of it. Indeed, the sensations that accompany our felt response in a situation embody that unacknowledged meaning. By symbolizing our experience beyond the level of physical sensation in our bodies, our images move us toward discovering their meaning. They direct our awareness toward the experience in novel ways (Killen and de Beer 1994: 37).

One of the reasons that images are so helpful in a missioner's process of articulating, and especially of interpreting and understanding her or his feelings and experiences, is that they provide an "alternative" form to our conscious cognitive activity. They emerge from our unconscious, products of our dreams and imagination. Images are symbolic, sometimes representing realities that our consciousness is not yet aware of. As we explore our images, we can learn from them about the "inner dynamics" of their transition, which is really where the "heart of the matter" lies. Larry Lewis in his autobiographical work, *The Misfit*, reminds us that missioners always "straddle two cultures," that of the outer world and the inner one, adding, "Their straddling demands that they stretch geographically and interiorly" (Lewis 1997: 16). Lewis quotes Thomas Merton:

> The geographical pilgrimage is the symbolic acting out of an inner journey. The inner journey is the interpolation of the meanings and signs of the outer pilgrimage. One can have one without the other. It is better to have both. History would show the fatality and doom that would attend on the external pilgrimage with no interior spiritual integration, a divisive and disintegrated wandering, without understanding and without the fulfillment of any humble inner quest. In such pilgrimage no blessing is found within, and the outward journey is cursed with alienation. (Merton 1967: 92-93).

Missioners in transition need to be concerned about that "inner journey," that "interior spiritual integration," without which, as Merton intimates, the exterior journey, the outer crossing of continents and cultures, will always be a time of exile in which we are never fully "at home" with self, with others, with God. Let us explore, then, some images of some missioners who are in transition, images which emerge from both their outer and inner journey, bridging the conscious and unconscious worlds, between which perhaps the greatest of all "cross-cultural" journeys takes place.

We will approach these images first of all from a psychological perspective by looking at the kinds of processes Robert Johnson offers in *Inner Work* (1986). His is a very concrete and simple approach to the inner world through both dream work and the work of "active imagination." In a second phase, I will apply some of Johnson's processes by exploring three different missioners' experiences. Finally, we will turn to the Bible, the classic authoritative text of the Christian tradition, seeking in these sacred scriptures experiences and images which may serve as "prototypes" of our own.

"Unpacking" the Images

As I indicated above, Robert Johnson has described in simple, clear language a very complex and deep process of exploring the images that emerge from the unconscious. Basing his work on Jung's theory and analysis of "archetypes," Johnson suggests "a four-step approach" to dream work, and, in the third chapter, a similar approach to the exercise of "active imagination." While it is not *necessary* to use his methods, I would certainly encourage anyone to engage in both of these distinct kinds of "inner work" if he or she is comfortable with it. With the careful use of a guide such as *Inner Work*, and/or with the help of a therapist or counselor when needed, the transitioning missioner would no doubt benefit from these kinds of exercises.

What I am suggesting here, however, is that some of the different methods that Johnson offers might also be helpful in aiding missioners to get in touch with their feelings and their inner dynamics, through the exploration of their images, discovering their richness and their many-layered aspects of meaning. I am not talking specifically about dreams, although there is no reason why some important images might not come in dreams. Similarly, I am not necessarily invoking the full use of "professional" active imagination. At the same time, there is no reason why missioners, often well-experienced in the ways of meditation and contemplative prayer, could not feel comfortable exploring their images through this art.

Although we encourage the *overall* experience of theological reflection to be done in a group, *this* particular exercise of exploring our images must first be done alone. Later the missioner may choose to share some or all of his/her exploration with the group. Another reminder is taht we should decide ahead of time what format we are going to use for recording our images and associations. In this way we won't be distracted later by these kinds of details.

What I primarily want to emphasize is that we *be attentive to our images*. When images come to us, they come from some part of ourselves of which we are usually unaware. In the midst of an unexpected, unwanted or simply jostling experience of leaving a mission and going to a new place, wherever it be, our conscious minds, our thoughts and memories may be too occupied to pay much attention to unconscious dynamics within. But our unconscious has something to teach us. It wants to help us in our transition, and in one way or another, it *will* be heard. One of its most common ways of expressing itself is through images. Johnson makes the point:

> This experience, to be sure is symbolic. The images with which we interact are symbols, and we encounter them on a symbolic plane of existence. But a magical principle is at work: When we experience the images, *we also directly experience the inner parts of ourselves that are clothed in the images.* This is the power of symbolic experience in the human psyche when it is entered into consciously: Its intensity and its effect on us is often as concrete as a physical experience would be. Its power to realign our attitudes, to teach us and change us at deep levels, is much greater than that of external events that we may pass through without noticing (Ibid.: 25).

Invitation: "Opening Our Bags"

Johnson's first step in approaching the "active imagination" is what he terms "invitation" (Ibid.: 165-178). In our case, too, it will be necessary to "invite" some images to come to us from our deepest self. Let us take Kathy's example from Chapter Two. We perceived from her narrative how deeply she felt with the women with whom she was working. We recounted that when we first met Kathy, she *was* "a mess and so angry," but she would not have been able to articulate it at that time. Perhaps she knew she was angry, but *why* was she? At whom? And what was she to do about it. Ordinarily a "helper," for almost a year she kept much to herself, not at all her usual extroverted self. About a year after her arrival at CTU, our first Missioners-in-Transition group was formed. As she gained trust in that group, Kathy began to reveal more and more of her anger and frustration. We recall another night when she briefly mentioned an image that seemed to express how she was feeling, namely, like she was in a "deep pit." We all seemed to resonate with her experience and to understand at some deep level what Kathy was feeling. She had used an image which symbolized something that we all could in some way experience. This moment is a good example of what Johnson is referring to as "invitation" (Ibid.: 165). It is something that we have experienced on many different occasions with different groups, "The more [an image] captures a very particular experience, the more it invites resonance with the experience of others" (Killen and de Beer 1994: 40). It was over a year later when she shared a little more about that image.

> *(In Brazil) powerlessness became very real so that I was no longer able to function, even within myself. The result was a growing depression and a realization that I needed to move away in order to see. Returning to the States and beginning to see, the overriding image that dominated most of my time during these three years is a deep pit. I was in the pit, trapped and powerless. I am caught in the pit, almost paralyzed, and there seems to be no way out . . . (Kathy, Spring, 1997).*

Association: "Examining the Contents"

Johnson calls the second step "association." An association is any word, idea mental picture, feeling or memory that pop into your mind when you look at the image. . . . It is literally *anything* that you spontaneously connect with the image"(Johnson 1986: 52). He suggests that we focus on *each image* appearing in the dream or active imagination, and write out every association that we have with each of them. As you know, a dream often contains persons, objects, situations, colors, sounds, or words. Each of these may be considered a distinct *image* in itself. And so we are invited to *notice* what feelings are connected with each image. What comes to mind when I re-image it? It's always good to record the associations in some way, even briefly, for later reflection. (See Ibid.: 52-58).

Images, as well as the associations we make with them, may be expressed in a variety of ways. Although in Chapter One we did mention the power of writing, it is by no means the only expression of feelings, and certainly not of images. Some people may be more comfortable with art forms, body prayer, guided imagery or dialoguing with the image. In groups I've worked with some have expressed themselves through modeling clay; others brought to the group some precious symbolic object out of their personal missionary journey. In another situation participants expressed themselves in imagery by finding some part of nature that seemed to capture what they were feeling. After staying with that object for awhile, we were invited to share with the group our associations with that symbolic object: an autumn leaf rich in colors, a broken reed, a hard stone, a flower. The imagery was rich and powerful. It is important not to force the process. It happens spontaneously. What is important is to be open to alternative means of expression through symbolic images. It may happen that in one's process, the *image* is often the best way–and sometimes the only way–in which we can express our feeling.

In making associations it is important not to discount what Johnson refers to as "colloquialisms." For example, the image of a kite might remind us of the expression, to be "higher than a kite," or the color "blue" in an image might be associated with the colloquialism "I've got the blues." Maybe for some of us it will be a song that often hovers in our unconscious, just beneath the surface. For example, staying with the color blue: "Blue Moon, you saw me standing alone . . ." or "Am I blue? You'd be too . . ." or again, "Blue, blue, my life is blue . . ." Then there is also "Blue skies shining on me.!"

We can see how the meaning of an image is very personal, depending upon one's experience and associations. In Kathy's image, a colloquialism that she might associate with it is "the pits" roughly meaning about "as bad as it gets." Or perhaps the image might call to mind the word "pitiful." Though originally "pitiful" meant "full of pity," or something fully worthy of pity, it is now commonly used to describe something as quite bad, awful, and sad, in addition to deserving our pity. As you can see, this kind of exercise of making associations is actually a way of probing the image for its hidden meaning, of exploring it in order to discover more about it–and about ourselves. Every image can have many layers of meaning and as in a sort of "archeological dig," each layer can tell us something more about the meaning and message of our transition. At the same time, as Killen and de Beer point out, an image helps us avoid "distanced analysis" of our experience that really "disguises premature interpretations" and judgments of it (Killen and de Beer 1994: 39).

Making associations leads to another step in Johnson's approach, that is, exploring what he calls "inner dynamics"(Johnson 1986: 65-86). He defines *inner dynamics* as "anything that goes on inside you, any energy system that lives and acts from within you." He continues, "It may be an emotional event, such as a surge of anger. It may be an inner conflict, an inner personality acting through you, a feeling, an attitude, a mood"(Ibid.: 65). The images that surface symbolically represent something that is going on inside of us. In a certain sense they have already given a name to some inner dynamic. Let us remind ourselves that the point of this kind of inner work is to "build consciousness," to gain insight into the conflicts an challenges that our life presents, to discover and draw on our own inner resources (Ibid.: 13). Attempting to discover the quality, emotion, movement, inner person or "space" within us that relates to a dominant image is a way of moving toward a greater awareness or consciousness of the "why" of our feelings or behavior. This, in time, leads to insight as to how to interpret and deal with them. We begin to have a sense of where to go from here. And that gives us hope.

Images and Our Experience

We will now "unpack" three different "bags" by reflecting theologically upon some concrete images which missioners have shared, adapting for our purposes Johnson's method of working with dream images. Our reflections will begin at three different starting points: (1) A Lived Personal Narrative, (2) A Cultural Text, and (3) A Text from Tradition. Regardless of the starting point, however, each reflection begins in *experience* and is *theological* in nature, entering at some point during the reflection into explicit dialogue with Tradition (which will be introduced in the next part of this chapter).

Beginning with Experience: "Unpacking Kathy's Images"

Let us spend some time unpacking Kathy's image of being in a deep dark pit. We have already begun with her narration of her experience, and the images that enabled her to put that experience into words: *Powerlessness . . . no longer able to function . . . a growing depression . . . to move away . . . to see . . . trapped . . . almost paralyzed . . . no way out . . .* Another important image is that of *"many 'forces' coming down on me*." Finally, there is the "overriding image" of **THE PIT**, what McFague might call a "model," i.e., "a dominant metaphor or a metaphor with staying power (McFague 1982: 23). *"I am caught in A DEEP PIT . . . ."*

Kathy herself has already made some associations with being "caught in a deep pit." Let us now try to elaborate on those with a few associations of our own. Caught. What do I associate with being caught? Trapped, powerless, disempowered, on a hook, possessed, held, not free, on a trapeze, caught in mid-air, risk, flying, caught in the wind, caught up–with myself, in myself, with someone else, with the others. Now, imagine yourself in a deep pit: dark, down, narrow, endless, bottomless, at the bottom, alone, afraid, unable to move, unable to escape, unable to see the light, "unfree." A deep well, a hole, a crater, a cell, a jail, a tunnel, black, dark, damp, dry, empty.

Kathy speaks of "many forces coming down on me." With what do we associate these "forces"? What might they represent? Weight, heavy, burdensome, holding me down, pinning me down, enemies, powerful, armed forces, weapons, soldiers, war. What inner dynamics might Kathy associate with her images? Questions one might ask are: "What is going on inside of me this image speaks of?" "What traits do I have in common with this image?" For example: Where am I in a deep pit? How? What is the deep pit within me? How am I caught? Who is holding me? What is trapping me?

In her journeying with our group, counseling and spiritual direction, Kathy identified one major dynamic within her represented by her image, i.e., being *depressed*. Actually it was her image that helped her to realize that she *was* depressed. She gradually recognized that she was cutting herself off more and more from others, closing herself in, allowing herself to dig deeper and deeper into that "pit," becoming more and more depressed, alone, angry, frustrated. The deeper she dug her hole, the less able she was to move, becoming less and less free, not knowing which way to turn. It was getting lonely and dark.

Our inner dynamics also have to do with our belief systems, attitudes and values, our "positions" toward life and everything and everyone in it. What might this image be telling me about these? If we think back to Kathy's experience with the woman from her *favella*, we might sense that in some way her own beliefs and values were being smothered or compromised in the way she was living. She was paralyzed, and remained so, without a clue as to how to break loose from the system she was stuck in. Killen and de Beer also suggest other ways of exploring the image by asking deep theological questions in human existential terms: "Consider what existence is like from within the image. Notice what is broken and sorrowing in the image. What possibilities for newness and for healing are present or implied?"(Killen and deBeer 1994: 88). Different questions or approaches to the images will depend on where each missioner is in his or her transition. The important thing is to allow the image to lead us deeper into our experience and ourselves. "By entering the space of the image we open ourselves to new insight, to new learning, to being changed, and potentially to revelation" (Ibid.: 41).

Kathy felt like a fragile animal when trapped: at first hurting, withdrawn, afraid, then becoming more and more angry, aggressively lashing out at anyone near. She was feeling utterly helpless, powerless at the bottom of that pit, as she says, "*unable to function . . . almost paralyzed and there seems to be no way out.*" Again, Kathy acknowledges that she recognized her depression through *attending to the image.* She later shared that she had finally found "*the courage to enter the pit and find myself there, to feel again and to recognize the forces that I felt were keeping me powerless and in the dark.*" At some point in relating some of this transitional experience, Kathy said, "*God was not helpful to me during this time because the only image I had was Jesus, sympathetic but also powerless in the face of all these forces.*"

Beginning with a Cultural Text: Unpacking Silence

Another good source or starting point for theological reflection is culture. A "cultural text" could be a work of art, music, film, literature, or many other sorts of communication media or expression of a culture. Other expressions of cultural texts might be missioners' artifacts, objects of art, clothing, jewelry–or simply objects possessing symbolic value for oneself, e.g., a piece of cloth or a photograph. Yet another way of expressing culture is through one's own creativity, e.g., design, clay modeling or sculpture, painting, dance or photography. Virtually anything that expresses any aspect of a given culture can be considered a "cultural text."

The reflection then proceeds to explore experiences, feelings, images, and tradition (not necessarily in that order). In my experience of beginning with a cultural text, I have used films and novels which in some way represent cross cultural or mission experiences. Thus, the position of the author or narrator, the setting, the characters, the theme might be expressions of different cultures or cultural and/or religious points of view. This can be a particularly good way to help missioners get in touch with their experience and feelings, but in a vicarious way at first. Killen and de

Beer remind us that "the flow of reflections, beginning with cultural texts, is from the *cultural situation* to the *tradition* and our own *experience*" (Ibid.: 101). The images in a novel, short story or film can sometimes express better than we, our own feelings from our past mission experience as well as our oftentimes ambivalence in the midst of transition.

One powerful example of this kind of reflection is Shusako Endo's novel, *Silence* (Endo 1969). I was first introduced to it during my own transition, and have suggested *Silence* in several transition and re-entry groups. Quite a number of missioners have found it a rich source for an even deeper reflection on their own missionary journey and their understanding of mission. It is based on the seventeenth century persecution of Christians in Japan, a time in which there was a brutal effort to exterminate Christianity–and every Christian–from the country. Many Christians, including some missionaries, went underground; most were cruelly tortured and executed. Some apostatized and lived. Endo's plot centers around a Jesuit named Sebastian Rodrigues, who left Portugal for Japan to carry on the underground apostolate, and perhaps especially, to atone for–or hopefully refute–the apostasy of his former teacher and provincial, Christovao Ferreira. David Bosch summarizes the novel in an article on the missioner's vulnerability:

> Eventually Rodrigues, too, was captured and tortured. And much of Endo's novel deals with his ordeal and his refusal to renounce the faith. For many months he refused. All along he prayed fervently, prayed to God for guidance, for a clear direction to go. But there was only silence, as though God did not hear him, or was dead and did not exist. Then, one evening, the interpreter said confidently, "Tonight you will certainly apostatize." To Rodrigues this sounded like the words addressed to Peter: "Tonight, before the cock crows you will deny me thrice" . . . . Then Ferreira explained why he himself had apostatized. It was not because of being suspended in the pit, he said, but because " . . . I was put in here and hear the voices of those *people* for whom God did nothing. God did not do a single thing. I prayed with all my strength; but God did nothing"
>
> It was this silence of God that has given Endo's novel its title–the silence of a God, a Christ, who did not respond to prayers or to torture. Still, in the end the silence was

broken. Christ did speak to Rodrigues–not, however, the beautiful, haloed, and serene Christ of his devotions, but the Christ of the twisted and dented *fumie*, the Christ whose face had been distorted by many feet, the concave, ugly Christ, the trampled-upon and suffering Christ . . . . (Bosch 1994: 74).

Endo's *Silence* is itself a reflection on images, not only the image of the trampled, crucified Christ, but of countless other images which fill the pages of the novel, images of God, faith, suffering, and death: the Christians "hanging in the pit;" Ferreira, the former Jesuit provincial, now "the honorable Sawano," clean-shaven, pig-tailed, and dressed in a black Japanese kimono; the apostate and traitor, Kichijiro, "thin and dirty like the tattered rags he wore" (Endo 1969: 189); the moaning of the peasants of Tomogi, Mokichi and Ichizo, hanging from their stakes at the edge of the dark, pounding sea, and so many more.

As an example of how a cultural text can be the beginning of the process of theological reflection, following are excerpts from two missioners' reflections on Endo's *Silence*:

> *During my mission in Kenya, there were times when I came in contact with tremendous suffering, the suffering of the poor, and the seeming silence of God. I recall the day when I watched helplessly, with fear and dismay, as uniformed men trampled on the vegetables of the poor street vendors in Nairobi. These vendors, who had no other means of livelihood had taken their produce to the streets. This was illegal and they paid for it. Those who were caught were thrown into prison, and all of them-- hundreds of them–lost all of their belongings . . .*
>
> *The novel by Endo paints once again for me a vivid picture of human pain and the reality of evil . . . . When I recall the image of those two men, Mokichi and Ichizo, hanging there on the beach to be overpowered by the stormy waters, I marvel at the human capacity to inflict pain on others . . . . It is this haunting sense of apparent abandonment by God which gives the novel its powerful and eerie atmosphere. I sometimes saw the "silence of God" as something I could not fathom . . . . I wondered, "What does one do?" In Endo's novel, the dilemma is*

evident. "What is the purpose of being a missionary among suffering people?" . . . I am reminded that when the situation is charged with human suffering, there is a greater opportunity to relinquish false power and a false sense of security . . . . We are called to accompany the suffering Christ in his brothers and sisters. While immersed in the adversity and hardships that can be an inescapable part of life, we are challenged to remain hopeful, trusting that God's is the final victory . . . . (Kate, Fall, 1995).

Another missioner, using *Silence* as a starting point for his theological reflection, finds himself connecting three "protagonists": Endo's Rodrigues (*Silence*), Luke's "Rich Fool" (Luke 12:16-21), and himself:

In Luke's passage God zaps the "rich man" right between the eyes: "You fool, this night your life will be demanded of you; and the things you have prepared, to whom will they belong?" (Luke 12:20). And who is the a "fool"? Because he only thought of himself and what he wanted to keep for himself. He had his own expectations. And Shusaku Endo tries to pierce the bubble of his protagonist's expectations just as directly. One moment Rodrigues is filled with feelings of happiness and self-worth; the next moment he's running for his life. . . . I find his reaction very understandable, because I was doing the same thing in my life. I was becoming discouraged with myself, with what I was not accomplishing, with others who were not meeting my expectations, with life in general. . . . Though the life situation was changing all around me, I still wanted to hang on to my own expectations, and to what little sense of peace and security I had left. So does Rodrigues.. So did the "rich fool." . . . But foolish, too, Rodrigues, and foolish me! The signs that our worlds are about to fall apart are all there. Yet we fail to recognize them . . . .

As I write this now, the temptation is just to forget the whole thing. I've been stuck in the same groove for so long that it has become a kind of rut. But it's my rut and I know it well . . . I can hear God calling me "You fool!," trying

*to get through to me . . . . Part of me wants to pretend I'm
deaf, and another part of me knows that I can't. I thought
I had life figured out reasonably well, but I know I was
"fooling" myself. It's time for me to listen I have to listen
and respond if I want to live more fully . . . .* (Terry,
Spring, 1993).

Beginning from Tradition: Unpacking Exodus 40: 34-38

Sometimes a scriptural text itself or a particular aspect of the
tradition generates images and thus begins the theological reflection on
one's experience. My own transition bears this out. Just as Anne's
experience, which will be described in more detail later, speaks of her rediscovery of freedom through her long trek across the desert, I also spent
several years wandering in a sort of "desert experience." In particular,
during my first year back from Zaire, I was wrestling with the obstacles of
my own resistance. It was indeed a liminal time, a space of confusion,
murmuring and tears. It was a period of waiting and wondering where God
was leading me. But while it was a time of "desolation," somehow
throughout it all, I did not doubt that God *was* leading me somewhere,
although I did not know where and I did not know the way. There were
many "consoling" confirmations of God's presence guiding me at that time.
(I would caution, however, that this divine presence is not always a clear
nor *felt* experience during this time. We recall that Kathy seemed to lose all
hope in God during her first two years of transition. She was angry at this
God who seemed as powerless as she felt in her deep pit) .

For me, although it did not negate or take away the painfulness or
confusion, I did *know* in my gut that God was with me in that journey
through the desert. This became explicit for me one day through a particular
passage from Exodus.

Then the cloud covered the meeting tent, and the glory of
the Lord filled the Dwelling. . . . Whenever the cloud rose
from the Dwelling, the Israelites would set out on their
journey. But if the cloud did not lift, they would not go
forward; only when it lifted did they go forward. In the
daytime the cloud of the Lord was seen over the Dwelling;
whereas at night, fire was seen in the cloud by the whole
house of Israel in all the stages of their journey (Ex 40:34-
38).

It was simply part of some reading that had been assigned for a class I was taking at the time. But as I read that excerpt, it was as though I had never heard or read it before. It was not the chronological historicity nor the theology contained in the passage which struck me. Rather it was the *image* it contained, that familiar "cloud by day and fire by night." From that moment this image began to sustain me in all the stages of *my* journey. In fact my own truly *theological* reflection upon my personal experience really *began* when I encountered anew this passage from Exodus.

It seemed clear to me that in the midst of my own "desert wilderness," God was present in the cloud which seemed to hover over me. In this sense it was an ambiguous image for me. It seemed that as long as "the cloud did not lift," I could not go forward. I had to remain in this state of liminality, of discernment, waiting for the time when I could move on in my journey. On the other hand, humbled, I knew that *God was in that cloud*, at times *overshadowing* me as it did the Dwelling. This same "cloud" would later *overshadow* Mary, throwing her life into the mysterious ambiguity of awe and confusion, joy and suffering. There were times when I seemed to be making "progress," and other times I seemed to be moving in circles, or just not moving at all. I learned, in the desert, to be patient and wait for God to show me the way. This passage seemed to make explicit for me what I was experiencing in faith.

There were even times when I seemed to be privileged to be in "the Meeting Tent," in dialogue with God. Samuel Terrien explains that this presence and dialogue took place without the "dramatic frills" and "emotional thrills" of the theophanies of Mt. Sinai. In its "homely character," he describes, it was more like "a chat" (Terrien 1978: 178). As for myself, I was sometimes "complaining," sometimes asking "Your ways, O Lord, make known to me, teach me your paths" (Ps 25:4), but mostly hearing God ask me to be patient and wait: "Be still, and know that I am God"(Ps 46:11).

Finally, after about one year of being in this wilderness, the moment came during a directed retreat when "the cloud lifted" and I knew which route I had to take. It was only then that I too could continue into another stage of my journey. It was this Scriptural image which enabled me to take some distance from my own experience, reflect upon it, while at the same time living through it, and gain wisdom and insight from the lived experience of others before me.

Images in Dialogue With Tradition

I came having crossed over the Red Sea into the
wilderness, the desert of having almost nothing left–no
path, just endless shifting sands . . . . (Anne, Spring 1997)

At this point let us have for awhile an even more explicit dialogue
with that very important aspect of our Christian Tradition, the Bible. "Our
reflection becomes theological when we use questions arising from themes
in our Christian heritage to explore an image that emerges from our
experience" (Killen and de Beer 1994: 42). I am convinced that all of our
theological reflection grows out of our life "Experience," in that broad
sense with which we have defined Experience (with a capital "E").
"Experience" is the "stuff" of which one's life is made, the interaction and
influence of *one's lived narrative* (or personal experiences with a small
"e"), together with one's *culture, religious tradition,* and one's particular
"*horizon*" or *standpoints* in life. Thus it is that our theological reflection on
this vast world of Experience may have different starting points, "taking
off" as it were, from different runways. All of these reflections nevertheless
contain the same basic elements which are part of the process of theological
reflection, (i.e., narration of a situation or event, attending to feelings,
exploring images, discovering the heart of the matter, seeking insight,) and
all of this in the context of a dialogue with Tradition (see Fig. 3.1).

One's Lived Narrative ↔ A People's Lived Narrative
(Personal experiences) ↔ (collective experiences)
One's culture ↔ Cultural Context

Experience → **Image** → **DIALOGUE** → **Image** → **Tradition**

One's Tradition(s) ↔ Traditional Context
One's Horizon ↔ A People's Horizon
(personal stance, beliefs, positions) ↔ (beliefs, positions, convictions)

Figure 3.1. Dialogue: experience, images and tradition

Throughout the process, we are always conscious of permeable
walls along the way, through which flows a continuous dialogue between
our Experience and the body of Christian Tradition. This religious
Tradition, while an element within one's individual life Experience, is also

far greater than that, embodying the Experience of God's people through time and history. Thus it is necessary to invite, consciously and explicitly, our Tradition into our process, seeking its wisdom, even as we bring to the dialogue the wisdom of our own personal Experience.

Although we might draw on any number of sources from our Tradition for this vital aspect of our theological reflection, I will focus our attention in this chapter on the Sacred Scriptures of Christians, i.e., the Bible. It has been my own experience, and I have found it to be that of most of the missioners with whom I have worked, that a Scriptural image will emerge from among others as a significant and dominant metaphor during times of crisis, grief, or other kinds of life changing transitions "from → through → to" We see this in our examples above, i.e., beginning with a cultural text or with a source from Tradition. Another missioner wrote:

> *After a nervous breakdown (some today might call it a severe case of "burn-out,") and needing to come home, I took time off for rest, counseling and healing... As the end of that year was approaching I needed to make a DECISION: Either to stay home or to go back. The decision came one day unexpectedly like a volcanic eruption! After months of hesitation, now suddenly there was no doubt. I wanted to go back! It was a **surprise**. It was **a gift**. What came to my mind was the image of Abraham being willing to sacrifice his only son Isaac (Gen 22: 1-19). It seemed to me that I was called to sacrifice my "Isaac"–to throw reason to the winds and to trust God . . . Abraham named the place "The Lord provides" (Ed, Spring, 1997).*

Scripture as the "Classic Text"

Perhaps biblical images arise spontaneously for most missioners because usually they are persons of prayer, steeped in the tradition of the Scriptures. These are the images that many a missionary kid or an aspiring nun or priest has grown up with. They have often been assimilated and have found a place in the unconscious, if not conscious, memory. Scripture is, as Scripture scholars and theologians alike are quick to point out, "the classic text of the Christian tradition" (McFague 1982: 54), and as such it has intrinsic authority.

The fundamental model was first worked out and decisively

appropriated in the Old Testament. That model was reaffirmed, restated, and reintegrated in Jesus. Christian faith is faith which relates itself to this classic model. The God in whom Christians believe is the God who was known in the Bible; the Jesus in whom they believe is the Jesus of the New Testament (Ibid.: 61).

At the same time in speaking of the Bible as a "classic" text, McFague also demonstrates that it is "the *poetic* classic of Christianity," by which she means to emphasize that "the essence of a great poetic text is that through its particular images it does speak universally, and is open to diverse interpretations. As a "Christian classic," it gives shape to many dimensions of Christian experience and understanding of God. As a "poetic classic," it has, as does any great work of art or literature, an enduring and universal power to move and or transform the hearer or reader (Ibid.: 60-61).

Scripture and Metaphor

Another reason why I suggest the Bible as a primary source of dialogue for missioners with their Tradition is that the Bible is *rich in metaphor*. If, as McFague insists, the Bible has a "reforming and revolutionary power" (Ibid.: 63), much of that power comes from its metaphorical nature. It is not difficult for those who are familiar with the Bible to think readily of dozens of examples of metaphorical language. The parables are classic examples of different types of metaphor: "The kingdom of heaven is like . . ." (Mt 13: 24, 31, 33). "A sower went out to sow . . ." (Mt 13: 3-9). Then there is the Gospel according to John with its rich symbolism and metaphor: "The light shines in the darkness, and the darkness has not overcome it." (John 1:5); "I am the Good Shepherd." (Jn 10:11); "I am the way, and the truth, and the life" (John 14:6). Just this past Sunday, as I participated in the Liturgy of the Word, I could not help but notice the metaphors in each reading:

> Woe to the shepherds who mislead and scatter the flock of
> my pasture, says the Lord. . . . You have scattered my
> sheep and driven them away. . . . I myself will gather the
> remnant of my flock from all the lands. . . . I will raise up
> a righteous shoot to David; as king he shall reign and
> govern wisely. . . . This is the name they give him: "The
> Lord our justice" (Jer 23: 1-6).

> It is he who is our peace...breaking down the barrier of hostility that kept us apart (Eph 2:14).

> Upon disembarking Jesus saw a vast crowd. He pitied them, for they were like sheep without a shepherd (Mk 6:34).

Peter W. Macky's theory is that the biblical writers used much metaphor because it is the form which best enabled them to communicate their "central purposes":

> It is likely that the ultimate purpose the biblical writers had was usually *relational*, to serve as mediators enhancing the relationship between God and their hearers. As a means to that end the writers often used *dynamic* speech, seeking to illuminate hearers' minds (*pedagogical*), to move hearers (*affective*) and so bring them to commit themselves to becoming God's children, servants and friends (*transforming*). And as a further means, one that could draw hearers on a journey of discovery, the writers often used *exploratory* speech, evoking wonder, and a desire to know better, thereby stimulating readers to take the narrow path that leads down into the depths (Macky 1990: 248).

"Metaphors, especially concrete ones," are very often the most effective way to practice these three types of speech-acts, i.e., relational, dynamic and exploratory, "which are the most profound of all the biblical writers' purposes for speaking" (Ibid.: 17). Biblical metaphor goes far beyond the cognitive and informative purposes of speech, or even language's affective purposes, e.g., the arousal of the emotions. The metaphor in Scripture has the power to reach into the human heart and "to illuminate darkness, solving puzzles so the hearer responds, 'Oh, now I see!' . . . to change hearers' attitudes, values and commitments" (Ibid.: 16).

Creative Imagining and Scriptural Metaphors

Probably the most relevant dimension of metaphor for our purposes here is its "exploratory" potential. This "mental exploring" is done by "presenting an experience of some kind and inviting hearers (usually implicitly) to explore imaginatively how their own experience may be illuminated by the one presented" (Ibid.: 16-17). This is the invitation to which I hope missioners will respond: to use our imagination and seek in the Bible the kinds of experiences and images which may illuminate our own experiences, interior movements and images. This can be done through a form of knowing which Macky calls "re-creative [or creative] imagining", i.e., "the process of hearing a word or phrase or description and *re-creating* what probably was being imagined by the speaker" (Ibid.: 11). He gives an example from Matthew: "Come to me, all you who labor and are burdened, and I will give you rest" (Mt 11:28). Here, Matthew was inviting his hearers to re-create an image of their own experience: of bearing a heavy load, of being weary from hard work, and of resting at the end of a long day.

Although I'm not necessarily invoking the exact same relationships between missioners' personal images and those to which they will turn for "illumination" in the Bible, nevertheless I believe that this insight into the metaphorical nature of biblical language sheds some helpful light on the process. I have found it powerful for missioners to enter into some sort of encounter with biblical images, experiences, personages, or themes which somehow speak of their own transitional process. It doesn't matter whether the image be related to a moment in the past, present or imagined future. To necessarily organize or "categorize" our associations in this way would be too analytical for the process at this stage. That kind of organization will eventually fall into place when we later begin to *interpret* our experiences, (feelings, images) in search of "the heart of the matter," that organizing principle or theme for our own personal journey.

All that we want to do at this point is allow free flowing associations between our lives and the lives of our ancestors in faith, i.e., both the personages and the writers of the biblical text. I hope that, in the midst of transitional turmoil, we can simply enter into a "conversation" with the biblical text. This conversation can become a truly *creative* dialogue between the biblical writer (in his or her personal, historical context), the words or text itself (in its context), and the missioner, or any believer for that matter, in her or his personal, historical, liminal situation. With the help of modern biblical criticism, we can enter into a simple process of biblical reflection, more readily accessible to missioners struggling within the mysterious context of a certain "rite of passage," i.e., their own missionary transition.

Dialogue Initiated by Personal Images

As I've noted earlier, we may begin theological reflection from different *starting points or sources*. We have seen how we can reflect upon our journey by beginning with our Personal Narrative or *Experience*, a text from *Tradition* (e.g., Exodus) or from *Culture* (e.g., *Silence*). In any case, whatever the starting point, *we may explore our personal images in dialogue with Scriptural images*. This will vary according to individual ways of thinking and processing experience. However, in my experience with missioners in transition I have found their *narrated life situation* to be the most common and effective starting point for reflection. Thus I want to offer here an example of an in-depth theological reflection that begins with that narrated experience. It unfolds in two movements: first, a free association from the missioner's image to biblical images; second, a focusing in on one particular biblical image which seems to generate the most energy.

The exploration which follows does not represent the *actual* exploration of the missioner herself. I have, however, tried to preserve the *essence and integrity* of her experience and insights, but with a certain anonymity. One's deepest reflections are sacred and should always be reserved for a support group, counselor, spiritual director, soul friend, or for oneself alone. "It has to be clear that only *you* will ever read these pages [that you write]; otherwise it will be very difficult to be honest in what you record" (Johnson 186: 164).

Kathy's Images and Scriptural Associations

Then let us turn again to Kathy's image as related above and begin to "brainstorm," as it were, allowing ourselves to freely explore whatever *Scriptural* associations come to mind when we think of "*being caught in THE PIT, trapped and powerless.*" What Scriptural images come to you? What Scriptural personages have experienced "the pit" in one way or another? Are there any images which come to mind from other images in Kathy's experience: being "trapped and powerless," "almost paralyzed," there seems to be no way out."

There was Joseph, who was thrown into a cistern by his brothers (Gen 37-50). "So when Joseph came up to them, they stripped him of the long tunic he had on; then they took him and threw him into the cistern, which was empty and dry"(Gen 37: 23-24). Or we can recall Jeremiah, who was also thrown into a cistern where he "sank into the mud" (Jer 38:6). We might also think of John the Baptizer in the depths of his prison cell (cf. Mt 11:2-6), or Lazarus buried in a tomb for four days (Jn 11:1-44).

Maybe the image speaks more to you of being paralyzed, calling to mind the paralytic being lowered through the roof by his friends (Mk 2: 1-12). Or does the word "powerless" call to mind the image of the woman who had been afflicted with hemorrhages for twelve years (Mk 5: 25-34)? There's the man who had been sick for thirty-eight years, and had no one to put him into the healing waters (Jn 5: 1-18), or Luke's woman who was "bent over, completely incapable of standing erect" (Lk 13: 10-17).

After we have taken some time with a passage, and allowed such images just to freely come into our consciousness, we then observe which image seems to give us the most energy, the one that seems to capture our feelings and draw our attention. Then we allow ourselves to sit with that image and just let it lead us where it will, but this time try to get inside the experience of the subject/s in the text from the tradition. We can do this first of all by asking ourselves the same kinds of questions that we did with our original image, by making associations, by imagining ourselves in *their* position. Depending upon the missioners and the situations of transition in which they find themselves, this Scriptural image might invite some serious reflection, prayer, and even study, in order to better make connections between our own lives and experiences, and those that come to us from our Tradition.

Of the different Scriptural associations which I make with Kathy's images, it is that of the prophet Jeremiah which seems most powerful. The following reflection on his experience is an example of how missioners might develop an in-depth reflection on a scriptural text to which they feel drawn. Perhaps for some this kind of in-depth study might not be helpful. The purpose of a Scriptural study or reflection in our context of transition is for the sake of deepening our understanding of our own experience, gaining insight and wisdom from the connections made between our lives and our tradition, and deepening our faith and hope by getting in touch with that of our ancestors. It is essential that each person discover his or her way of making that vital faith connection.

Kathy's Image and Jeremiah: A Prophet Who Found Himself "In the Pits"

"This man ought to be put to death . . . ." King Zedekiah answered: "He is in your power," for the king could do nothing with them. And so they took Jeremiah and threw him into the cistern of Prince Malchiah, which was in the quarters of the guard, letting him down with ropes. There

was no water in the cistern, only mud, and Jeremiah sank
into the mud (Jer 38: 5-6).

At first, it is the *image* which is the point of connection here. The
very words, "and Jeremiah sank into the mud," seem to capture for me what
Kathy was feeling during this time–as though she were in the bottom of an
empty cistern, sinking deeper and deeper "into the mud." When we
approach this part of our reflection with an attitude of prayer, wanting to be
attentive to the Spirit's lead, I don't believe it is by chance that one or the
other Scriptural text will seem to stand out for us as significant. The image
is the apparent connection with the missioner's life and transition, but there
are usually other, sometimes more significant, connections when we reflect
upon an image within its context.

Jeremiah's vocation as prophet, especially the second period of his
life after the death of the young and zealous king Josiah, presents one of the
most challenging of the pre-Exilic era. Carroll Stuhlmueller refers to that
period as "that long long trek across the dreary plateau of failures"
(Stuhlmueller 1977: 48). It is said that "misery loves company." If Kathy
experienced misunderstanding, frustration and failure in her vocation and
mission, she can certainly turn to Jeremiah for company and consolation.
Jeremiah's repeated failures and sufferings (Ibid.: 105). Jeremiah's life and
suffering–the suffering particularly affirms the prophet's message as
authentic–revealed to us both in the more biographical prose accounts of the
prophet's ministry as well as in the more poetic "confessions," both
recorded in the book bearing the prophet's name. Believed to be written
down by Jeremiah's faithful disciple and "secretary," Baruch, the book of
Jeremiah reveals a sensitive man. He was "the most personal of prophets .
. . a man of gentleness and peace, forced in spite of himself to preach a
message of condemnation and ruin, a man whose innocence is cruelly
wounded by the incomprehension and aggression he encounters" (Brother
John 1985: 105). Stuhlmueller calls him "the person of prayer *par
excellence*" (Stuhlmueller 1977: 52). Although Jeremiah spent most of his
life searching for "the meaning of his vocation" (Ibid.: 45), he was able "to
be at peace in the midst of darkness and mystery . . . the surest indication
that one is following the intuition of God's will" (Ibid.: 52). This was no
small challenge for Jeremiah, nor is it for any of us, especially when going
through the "darkness and mystery" of a life-changing event, such as a
missionary transition.

Jeremiah began his prophetic ministry in 627 BCE. The same year
marked the death of the Assyrian king, which was followed by civil war and

the ensuing collapse of that great empire. About the same time, the young king Josiah at Jerusalem denounced the Assyrian gods, and would shortly launch his vigorous "Deuteronomic reform" (2Kgs 22:1-23:27). The beginning years of Jeremiah's ministry were not unlike Kathy's in Brazil, indeed not unlike those of many a missioner eager with one's first "missionary fervor."

The first six years of Jeremiah's preaching career (627/6-621) were years of excitement over hopes, ideals and undreamed-of possibilities. Achievement came quickly. This success, thought Jeremiah, must certainly demonstrate the genuineness of God's call and the nature of his vocation (Ibid.: 47-48).

"Then," as Stuhlmueller quickly reminds us, "came a series of reversals" (Ibid.: 48). Although Jeremiah agreed with its goals, he didn't agree with the *way* in which Josiah and his immediate entourage was ruthlessly imposing the reform. It seems that he was more or less a silent and somewhat credulous observer during those years. Shortly after that, however, at the death of Josiah in 609 BCE (2Kgs: 23:29), things indeed turn from bad to worse. In accounts like the one cited above, where he was left to die in a cistern, we are told that he was often accused of inciting the people, arrested, beaten and jailed more than once (37:21; 38:13, 28); he spent a night "in stocks"(20:2) and, suspected of treason, in a dungeon (37:16); he was threatened with death (26:1-9), sometimes fleeing for his life (36:19), and finally exiled to Egypt (43:6) "where we lose his trail" (Brother John 105).

Jeremiah, indeed, is no stranger to incomprehension suffering. It is especially with his "interior crisis" that we can identify and connect Kathy's inner turmoil. We can imagine Kathy, in a different time and place, expressing her solidarity with the people of her neighborhood, as Jeremiah voiced his own solidarity with his compatriots caught in corruption:

> My grief is incurable, my heart with me is faint. Listen! the cry of the daughter of my people, far and wide in the land! Is the Lord no longer in Zion, is her King no longer in her midst? [Why do they provoke me with their idols, with their foreign nonentities?] "The harvest has passed, the summer is at an end, and yet we are not safe!" I am broken by the ruin of the daughter of my people. I am disconsolate: horror has seized me. Is there no balm in Gilead, no physician there? Why grows not new flesh over the wound of the daughter of my people? Oh that my head

were a spring of water, my eyes a fountain of tears, that I might weep day and night over the slain of the daughter of my people! (Jer 8:18-23).

Stuhlmueller, in his exegesis on another verse, this one taken from one of Jeremiah's confessions (12:1-5), gives us insight into the darkness of Jeremiah's own "deep pit." "You, O Lord, know me, you see me, you have found that at heart I am with you" (12:3a). Stuhlmueller writes:

> The Hebrew word implies, "You explore, walking with my footsteps. As I plunge into the darkness of my heart, you God, are there with me." Jeremiah must search into darkness to be where God is to be found. God's answer to Jeremiah, written indeed by Jeremiah after long, silent prayer, says literally in the Hebrew: "If you have run with legs (that is, with other human beings) and have fallen exhausted, how are you going to get along galloping against horses? If in the land of peace, you seek to find your confidence, how are you going to fare in the jungle of the Jordan?" (Jer 12:5) (Ibid.: 49-50).

And he adds, "We can think and ponder and pray long over that verse of Jeremiah. Basically, what it says is: "Jeremiah, things will get worse before they will get better . . . ." (Ibid.: 50). God asks Jeremiah to "hang in there," to hold onto faith in that deep darkness, no matter what. Is this not the ultimate demand in every Christian vocation, certainly in every missioner's? Throughout one's ministry, and perhaps even more so when one's mission is abruptly changed or apparently ended, one's "mission" is not doing what one *thinks* God wants, but doing that which *God has known even before one is formed in the womb* (see Jer 1:5). Stuhlmueller develops this thought in terms of every apostolic vocation:

> A vocation, then, according to Jeremiah, is not doing what one thinks God wants of a person. It is doing that which God has known even before one's conception. A vocation can, in fact it must, begin by responding to apostolic opportunities. Yet, such a response is only the occasion, not the deepest meaning, of a vocation. In the most profound level of the heart, a vocation is a personal union with a God who seeks everyone in peace and love. A

vocation must not degenerate into personal ambition. Rather, it means losing one's self totally in God, there to find one's self again in the union of all persons with God. How is such an interior conviction to be established? In Jeremiah's case, it demanded that his apostolic dreams crumble like paper houses. Somehow he had to sustain repeated failures and difficulties. Only then would he confess deep within his heart: My desire for God must be none other than God's desire for me . . . . (Ibid.: 51).

Jeremiah, because of an interior conversion, was able to sustain and communicate hope, even when he was personally overwhelmed by the misunderstanding and even contempt of those around him, and by personal discouragement and a sense of failure in his life's dream and mission. We will develop further such thoughts of interior "conversion" in the next chapter.

Dialogue Initiated by a Scriptural Theme

Another authentic and valuable way of proceeding in theological reflection is by starting with a *theme*, in this case, a scriptural theme. Here the dialogue with tradition is initiated by tradition itself. Having looked at one missioner's images and scriptural associations from different perspectives, I now offer this final image or recurring biblical theme of "journey" as a model, or dominant metaphor, for the life of a missioner, a life that is always, in one sense, in "transition," always conscious of moving toward the kingdom.

The Biblical Journey

In his book, *The Pilgrim God*, Brother John of Taizé does in a profound and amplified way what I am encouraging missioners to do in their journey, i.e., "search through the Bible for ways the image [of journey] could illuminate our understanding of faith" (Brother John 1985: 3).

The image of the journey as a key to the Bible has one great advantage: its dynamic, open-ended character. In addition to corresponding well to the mentality of our time, it enables us to grasp the progressive quality of God's self-revelation, and the dimension of risk, of adventure, which is so fundamental to the life of faith.   . . .   As for Abraham, the journey and the risk only begin when one says yes to God's call and sets out on the road of the promise (Ibid.: 4).

In the Introduction to his work, Brother John explains that he worked with "pilgrims" in the literal sense, doing Bible studies with young adults who came to spend some time in Taizé in France. He describes pilgrims "in the widest and in fact original sense: pilgrims as people on the road, sojourners, passing strangers moving on to other horizons"(Ibid.: 3). Thus he developed these studies around the theme of "faith as a pilgrimage." His is a theological reflection, moving from the experience of his own praxis, to the study of biblical images and themes expressing the experience of our mothers and fathers in faith, which study, in turn, sheds new and renewed light on the present experience of faith. Brother John organized his work, around the central image or model of "journey" as a way of understanding the biblical message.

This may well be one of the oldest metaphors for human experience, but it is deeply rooted in the Pentateuch itself. Abraham is called to a new land; Jacob must find God far from home. Joseph must go to Egypt, and Israel must cross the desert to find a promised Land. Not only does the journey motif stress the future to which we go, but also emphasizes our way of life as a *walking* with God and under divine guidance (CSB 1990: RG 53).

Certainly every Christian, having said "yes" to God's call, has embarked on a journey of faith. But the missioner, perhaps more than most, embodies in her or his lifestyle "the dimension of risk, of adventure" which we associate with our mother and father in faith, Sarah and Abraham, and with our ancestors who journey out of Egypt in search of a promised land. The image of journey, as suggested above, provides a variety of dynamic metaphors within it offering many possibilities of comparison with the life of a missioner who is continually moving "from → through → to → from → through → to →." Journey implies the call and/or decision to embark, the preparation (the "packing"), the setting out, the difficulties and delights along the route, long days and long nights, exciting adventure and exhausting fatigue, arriving, "unpacking" and "repacking" to set off again.
The missioner's life, like that of our ancestors, is one full of the

unexpected. This should come as no surprise to us–but it always does!–since the God who has called us is full of surprises. The God who called Abraham and Sarah (Gen 12:1-4) is the God who invites us to uproot our lives from wherever they are settled in and move on "to a land that I will show you"(12:1) It is God who takes the initiative with our ancestors, and with us. And God can take it again and again, in ways we may not always recognize (Ex 3:6-8; Is 43:19, Jn 14:9). Sometimes in a missioner's life, we are treated in ways we would least expect, like Jeremiah and Jesus, unwelcome prophets when we try to speak our truth. At other times ready to settle in and fold up our tent, tired of wandering in a land of liminality, ready to "ask for a king" (1Sam 8:4). Brother John reminds us that keeping a "pilgrim heart" (Ibid.: 53) and a sense of ourselves as always on a journey, is a challenge demanding that radical "desert faith," the faith that assures us that the God who has called us, and calls us again and again, will be with us in our journey: "I will show you"(Ex 3:12); "I will be with you." (Jer 1:8); "I will bless you . . . and you will be a blessing"(Gen 12:2-3; Ex 3:10; Is 6:7; Jer 1:10).

As I reflect on my own life as a missioner, it has been a continual journey "from → through → to." Looking back to my past, when I perceived my initial call to mission, I could have never predicted where and how God would direct me, by what routes God would lead me. In every "present" moment, there has been the temptation to compromise, to settle down, to settle for a more "established" lifestyle. Then God would come along and disturb me again, prodding me to continue the journey into the promise of a future even fuller than the present.

The Exodus-Event

To believe that *God is in the journey*, even in those disturbing transitions that uproot and upset us, demands a kind of radical biblical faith, such as we find expressed in the story of the Exodus.

> To find the core of Israel's faith, the events which more than any other gave an identity to the people of the Bible, it is to the books following Genesis we must turn, and especially to the book of Exodus. . . . We are dealing essentially with the story of an exodus, a liberation from bondage followed by a long march across the desert under the leadership of a man named Moses, toward a land of promise "flowing with milk and honey." Once again we

meet a tale of pilgrimage, and this pilgrimage, together
with the traditions of the patriarchs and even more than
these, will provide the central framework for the
expression of the faith of the Hebrew people in the course
of their centuries-long journey through history (Ibid.: 29-
30).

The biblical journey mirrors each of our journeys. The Exodus-
event symbolizes each of our struggles to be free. If we try to understand
how this event became the "central framework" (or model) in the
expression of faith of the Hebrew people, we missioners might ask
ourselves the same question that "second generation" believers asked
themselves about their own history, i.e., "How did we get here?" Their
answer was clearly a theological one: "God brought us here!":

Later on, when your children ask you what these
ordinances . . . mean . . . you shall say to your children,
"We were once slaves of Pharaoh in Egypt, but the Lord
brought us out of Egypt . . . brought us from there to lead
us into the land promised on oath to our ancestors, and to
give it to us" (Dt 6: 20-23).

Many of us who have been on mission in primarily "oral" cultures
are aware that for the orally transmitted culture there is no dichotomy
between myth and history. What "facts" are altered, transformed or simply
forgotten in the telling, depends on their significance–or lack of it–in the
mind of the transmitters and the hearers. In this kind of culture, as was that
of the Hebrew people at this time in their history, the past and the present
merge into one, because there is no "past" apart from its being continually
actualized in the present. Thus, for us today, if we can "pass over" (in John
Dunne's terms–see Dunne 1977: x) into the "oral" mentality, we can better
grasp what was the experience of our ancestors in faith, and the important
messages contained within the images and story of the exodus-event: God
is with us! God is for us! God delivers us! "But the Lord said, 'I have
witnessed the affliction of my people in Egypt'" (Ex 3:6-10).

In the Wilderness

But in order to pass from Egypt to the Promised Land, the Israelites
had to pass through the desert of Sinai and wander "forty years" in what is

generally called a "wilderness" before reaching the land of the promise. Scholars who have studied this wilderness narrative show that many aspects of this part of Israel's pre-Canaan journey provide us with a biblical lens through which we might understand our own missionary transition. I will continue to rely heavily on Brother John of Taizé here, while turning also to an essay by Robert Cohn (1981). Using Victor Turner's categories, Cohn does a comparative study of the wilderness tradition as a liminal time and space for three distinct groups in Israel's history: the actual wilderness generation, those "refugees" fleeing Egypt, the Babylonian exiles, and the community at Qumran.

Both Cohn and Brother John point out characteristics of this liminal wilderness period in Israel's history, at least in the narrated account of it, which can be helpful to missioners in a theological reflection on their own experience of transition. "First of all," says Brother John, "the desert is a *place of transition*, 'a land where . . . no one lives'(Jer 2:6)" (Brother John 1985: 35). Further, Cohn points out:

> When viewed as a whole, the Pentateuchal picture of Israel in the wilderness is analogous to several of the phenomena which Turner describes. Like the initiates in a rite of passage, for instance, the Israelites pass through three distinct phases: (1) separation, the exodus from Egypt in which the crossing of the Red Sea marks the final break . . . . (2) *limen*, the transitional period of wandering for forty years; (3) reincorporation, the crossing of the Jordan river, conquest, and settlement in the new land (Cohn 1981: 12-13).

A Time of Trial

As a characteristic of that liminal transitional period, wilderness or desert indicates, above all, a place without order, chaotic, uncultivated, undomesticated land. Cohn points out that the attention given to this wilderness narrative by the Pentateuchal authors "indicates that the significance of the wilderness for them transcends its geophysical existence" (Ibid.: 13).

> The wilderness is "betwixt and between," neither here nor there, neither Egypt nor Canaan . . . "a moment in and out of time." The past is wholly cut off, and the future but

faintly envisioned. Slavery is over but freedom is not yet.
There God punishes but also protects. The Israelites are in
a quarantine chamber, able neither to return to the "house
of bondage" nor to proceed directly to the "land of milk
and honey." . . . The wilderness forms the setting for a
trek through a time and space apart, ambiguous, liminal
(Ibid.: 15).

It was a place of difficulties, hardships, cruel desert winds and sun.
"By the harsh conditions it entails, the desert offers an *experience of human
fragility*":

Walking under a burning sun "through a land of deserts
and rifts, a land of drought and darkness" (Jer 2:6), "that
thirsty and waterless land, with its venomous snakes and
scorpions" (Deut 8:15) . . . in the language of
Deuteronomy, we learn humility, our fundamental poverty
before God (Deut 8: 2-3) (Brother John 1985: 36).

Wandering in the wilderness is a time of trial. Brother John
explains in some detail the biblical meaning of "trial" or "test." Sometimes
misunderstood when translated into English or other languages, he points
out that the test is not a "temptation" aimed at making us fail, but rather
"the site of an inner combat with essentially two possible outcomes: refusal
to trust or increased confidence in God" (Ibid.: 38).

In the Bible, a trial is fundamentally an event that reveals
what lies hidden in the human heart, and it does so through
the encounter with a resistance. In the face of this
resistance we are obliged to respond, to act. And so what
was merely implicit and unreflective becomes explicit,
visible; our priorities are made evident and thus become
more pronounced. In this respect the trial is a reenactment,
under the sigh of adversity, of our basic vocation, the call
to "leave everything behind" in order to walk with God
towards the land of promise. It offers us the opportunity to
say "yes" to God once again, a yes stripped of all
imaginary consolations. It proves to us, in the midst of
tears and sorrow, that we are still pilgrims on the road of
the Promise (Ibid.: 37).

I would paraphrase Brother John here in saying that the time of transition for missioners, especially a difficult period of "reentry," offers *us* the opportunity to say "yes" again to our missionary vocation, this time, a yes more stripped, perhaps not of *all,* but of many of our illusions about what mission means, and about what it means to be a missioner, a sojourner, an alien in a strange land (see Ex 2:22; 22:21; 23:9; Dt 23:7). That land may be not only the land of mission in the past, but also the very "homeland" on which we plant our feet now. One missioner in transition wrote:

> *I came with the image of having crossed over the Red Sea into the wilderness, the desert of having almost nothing left–no path, shifting sands . . . . That image is still with me* (two years later)–*however the mountains on the horizon are much closer now (Anne, Spring, 1997).*

A Time of Death

This wilderness period of forty years is indeed a time of dying, not unlike the rite of passage, from one stage to another. Cohn develops this idea, pointing out that there are continual references to dying in the wilderness narrations, especially in the murmuring episodes.

> Were there no burial places in Egypt that you had to bring us out here to die in the desert? Why did you do this to us. . . . Far better for us to be the slaves of the Egyptians than to die in the desert" (Ex 14: 11-12). Would that we had died in the land of Egypt, or that here in the desert we were dead! Why is the Lord bringing us into this land only to have us fall by the sword? (Nm 14: 2-3) (Cohn 1981: 16).

Cohn reminds us that historically this "forty years" was a period of death during which one entire generation died out before another could take up life again in the land of Canaan.

> Significantly, perhaps, the trek narrative does not relate a single birth. Especially after the emphasis on the amazing fertility of the enslaved Hebrews in Egypt, the silence is striking. The natural process of generation is halted in *t' s* time and space apart when Israel is ground down, n t ouilt up. Yet as soon as the people cross the Jordan, all those

who had been born in the wilderness are circumcised; the natural life cycle resumes (Josh 5: 5-7) (Ibid.: 16).

For a missioner in transition or reentry, this period also often demands a kind of dying: dying to dreams that will never be realized; to illusions about missionary life; to relationships that will be difficult, if not impossible, to sustain; dying to one's identity as a "missioner," to a certain extent, the dying of one's very self. Anne shares with us a part of her experience of "dying" and the images which helped her begin to understand it. She refers to a moment in her life as her "Red Sea Experience":

*Everything in my life seemed to fall apart at once: my parents died within a short space from one another. My best friend left our religious community. And we were more or less "thrown out" of our ministry–which meant everything to me--by the apparent conspiracy and mutual consent of the local bishop and my congregation's superior. At that time I felt that I had literally lost everything, including my self confidence. At some moment within that period, I drew a picture (which I wasn't accustomed to doing at all). I pictured myself with a big bag, like a knapsack, thrown over my shoulder. The bag had the initials of my religious congregation on it. I had just "crossed the Red Sea," and was standing before the tombstones of my parents. Behind me was the Red Sea. Before me stretched **a desert of endless sand**. No plants. No life. Just sand as far as I could see into the horizon . . . .*

*My life went on like that for a long time, trying to get where there was some life. The image was always very present to me. Then, I don't know when, at some point during the next year or two, I began to see the faintest glimpse of mountains far ahead . . . . Gradually, as I worked my way across the desert, the mountains began to get bigger and closer, until at some point I found myself at the foot of them, smack dab up against a sheer straight cliff of hard solid stone. . . . . The MOUNTAIN loomed straight up before me, like a huge stone wall. It seemed **insurmountable**. I didn't know what to do, or where to turn. I was through the desert now, but I didn't know how*

to face that mountain . . . I knew I couldn't go back, but
there seemed no way to go forward (Anne, Spring, 1997).

A Time of Consolation

Anne says that it took her several months before she could begin to
even think about that mountain and what it might mean in her life. She
remembers dreaming once during that period about a huge, thick, stone wall
and it seemed that there was something ominous on the other side. It is only
in recent months, and after having worked in spiritual direction with her
images, that she is beginning to gain insight into what the mountain, the
insurmountable stone wall, is about. Finally arriving at the point where she
could ask herself what it had to do with her life, with what she had
experienced and what she was carrying around in that bag, that wall is
"beginning to crumble":

> *It's only now, three years later, that the Mountain is*
> *beginning to crumble, little by little, as I'm finding healthy*
> *ways to express all of my anger and grief, anger at the*
> *injustices that were done, my grief at the death of my*
> *parents, and my friend Mary's leaving, and our departure*
> *from St. Jude's. I'm also beginning to have a new image .*
> *. . (I think it may have grown out of my reading Harriett*
> *Lerner's **The Dance of Anger**) . . .and I am beginning to*
> *dance! Oh sometimes I just bumble around . . . .*
> *Sometimes all of my other images are with me in the dance*
> *. . . . But, having crossed the Red Sea, and the desert, I*
> *am finally beginning to understand what freedom is all*
> *about–and that it is within me . . . (Anne, Summer, 1997).*

A Time of Ambiguity

A "wilderness period" of "betwixt and between" is almost always
a difficult time and space, as we also saw in Chapter Two, but for pre-
Canaan Israel, it was also a time of unusual divine intervention and
protection. Brother John calls this *"a place of unparalleled intimacy with*
God":

Almost nowhere else in the Hebrew Scriptures do we see

such a concentration of signs and wonders: The water from the rock, the quails and the manna, the purification of the waters, and so on: the wilderness road is punctuated by attentive gestures of God's loving kindness, as [God] gives [the] people to eat and to drink (Brother John 1985: 42).

Cohn points to George Coats's form-critical study which indicates that the primary wilderness traditions "are those which depict a positive relationship between God and Israel. The negative 'murmuring' traditions are secondary. God's presence among them at this time was almost tangible. One of the differences between the gods of most ancient peoples and the God of Israel was precisely this itinerant character of God, *who journeyed with them every step of the way*" (quoted in Cohn 1981: 1).

The Lord preceded them, in the daytime by means of a column of cloud to show them the way, and at night by means of a column of fire to give them light. Thus they could travel both day and night. Neither the column of cloud by day nor the column of fire by night ever left its place in front of the people (Ex 13: 21-22).

It is this precise aspect of "consolation," intermingled with the "desolation" of trials and death, which makes this period of Israel's transition a time and place of *ambiguity*, which, as we have seen, is characteristic of all transition. This ambiguity was one of the strongest experiences of my own transition. In this way too, as with the trial episodes, the wilderness teaches us an important lesson about "the ambiguity of freedom."

En route from one social role to another, from being held by a land to holding a land, the Israelites occupy a precarious status of landlessness. They are free, but rootless. . . . Only those who learn that freedom means nothing left to lose are ground down sufficiently to experience the other side of freedom, the promised land (Cohn 17).

It seems to me that, in the midst of our missionary transition—or, for that matter, at any other time in our life—we need to be especially attentive to the ways God might privilege us with the Divine Presence. The desert is a privileged place. God may surprise in "fire flaming out of a bush" (Ex 3:2), or in "a cloud by day and a pillar of fire by night," (see Ex 13:21), or, like Elijah on Horeb, in the entrance of our cave of refuge, in "a tiny whispering sound" (1K 19:12). However mysterious or obscure, let us not neglect or ignore the signs of that Presence, but let us be willing to let it guide us in our journey, however long or difficult the route.

Indeed it is important to say that the images of the missioner's transition need not be all dark. When we cross over that threshold, we do find ourselves in a sort of "promised land," not without its own problems and challenges. Some have said it is like being in a new room with new furniture. Things are arranged differently and it takes some getting used to, but there are also new windows and doors, bringing new light and different opportunities. Often before we can truly be at "home" in our own missionary journey, we must pass through a necessary time and space of "chaotic wilderness." It is part of our rite of passage, just as it was for our ancestors in faith. Often we too murmur and grumble, as did they, while crossing this "desert" which, as scholars have shown, ultimately gives us the occasion to make more explicit our trust in the God who is with us in our journey.

Moving On: Some Concluding Comments

As we turn to the next chapter, we will still be reflecting upon images, but with more attention to *interpreting them* and to the interpretation of our experience as a whole, seeking to identify, in our transitional process, what Killen and de Beer have called, "the heart of the matter"(Killen and de Beer 1994: 61-62). While they do not name this "identifying the heart of the matter" as a singular step or phase, they do insist upon its importance in the process of theological reflection. It can be discovered in the energy of our feelings and in the power of our images. For my part, I consider this discovery of one's unique heart of the matter as *the crossroads of the journey of transition*. It is the key for opening the new door that awaits us as we cross the threshold of liminality. In Chapter Four, we will continue to dialogue with tradition, but our conversation will turn to a new theme, that of *conversion*. We will look at what conversion means in the context of theological literature, in missioners' lives, and in Scripture. I believe that openness to this often painful process of conversion is the "heart" of every successful transition. As we transverse the desert, we do begin to find life on the other side. It is in walking new paths–or old ones with renewed vision--that we will eventually "come home" in the journey.

Chapter Four
Conversion: Probing the Heart of the Matter

Helpless, insecure and frustrated, I feel like a bloody
stump, a broken mask, a blind man. "Behold the man!"
Me (Jim, Spring 1993).

We have come now to the crossroads of our reflection. As
missioners in transition, having explored our feelings and images in
dialogue with tradition, it is the moment of identifying and articulating "the
heart of the matter." This, simply put, is what emerges as the underlying
significant issue in our experience. In our process of understanding and
integration, "the heart of the matter" becomes the primary focus of our
reflection. According to the model–and in my experience–missioners will
have already, on some intuitive level, identified their "heart of the matter"
through the articulation of their feelings and the exploration of their images.
It is often through these images that we can usually find at least one, if not
many, important issues or focal points for reflection. In fact, in many cases,
the *image has already articulated it*. The advantage of an image is that in
capturing the significant issue intuitively, it retains the emotional or
affective energy expressed through our feelings. That *energy* is an important
indicator of where to look for the heart of the matter.

Getting To the Heart of the Matter

A clay pot sitting in the sun will always be a clay pot. It
has to go through the white heat of the furnace to become
porcelain. Actually, there's nothing wrong with being a
clay pot. It's just that some of us are called to become
porcelain. And it's not just a question of being fired or not.
Some of us explode in the kiln, some collapse before we
reach the kiln, and some develop cracks that refuse to heal.
Yet probably the saddest response of all is to successfully

*survive the firing and refuse to become porcelain. All of us
have furnaces in our lives. It's up to us to glean the
learning from the firings. (Mildred Witte Stouven)*

A couple of years ago a friend handed me the above verses from her
daily calendar. They struck me at the time, and seem like appropriate lines
with which to begin this chapter's reflection on "conversion." As we enter
into that refining fire to reach whatever the "heart of the matter" is for each
of us, it's important to know that approaching it, exploring it, and reaching
it will inevitably demand a conversion on our part–one for which we are
rarely prepared. Perhaps it is easier to remain "clay pots" when, in truth, we
are being called to become porcelain.

We have already seen the revealing nature of images in missioners'
narratives from the previous chapters. Anne, for example, drew an image
of herself carrying a big duffel bag over her shoulder. Only after months of
processing in group and spiritual direction was she able to begin to ask
herself such questions as: *"What does that bag represent? Why am I
carrying it? What is in it? Why don't I put it down?"* As she made her way
"across the desert" she realized that something was weighing her down,
"hindering me from getting to where there was life." Anne's "heart of the
matter" was symbolized in that heavy bag. Another missioner expressed
herself this way:

> *When I first arrived home I felt like a huge rock,
> immovable. For **four** weeks I sat and did almost **nothing**.
> I didn't want to be involved in anything. I just wanted to
> sit. Sometimes I didn't even think, other times I sat
> questioning why I decided to return home. I was asked
> several times to help out with summer work. I said no. I felt
> too immobilized to do anything and I didn't even feel
> guilty. I felt lost and without energy. I felt disintegrated .
> . . . The scripture story that stayed with me for many
> weeks was the woman at the well. The water jar was an
> essential part of life in Kenya. . . . I had left behind my
> water jar in order to come home, and to leave it behind
> was to leave behind my life there (Sue, Spring, 1997).*

For Sue, that last sentence summarized in a clear image what she
eventually recognized to be her "heart of the matter." She *felt* like she had
left her life behind in Kenya. She had no energy, no motivation, no reason

to go on. It was with this issue that she had to grapple during many months of transition. We all find different ways of exploring our issues. Some with words, others through various art forms, such as dance or drawing. One missioner worked in clay. Another group acted out an issue in a role play. One veteran missioner expresses his heart of the matter in a few words, as authentic "crossing over." It is both his challenge and his conviction, as he puts it, "a reliable entry point every time I enter–or re-enter–a new culture."

> *First off, you have to see what is there TODAY, which is always quite different than it was ten or even five years ago. . . . I have re-entered the USA five times, and each time, in a certain way, it was like entering a new country. . . . You have to cross over to another place and come back to yourself, knowing that you too are a changed person. . . . It can be painful, but less painful than crossing over to what you thought it would be like, as it was ten years ago, and less painful than not crossing over at all (John, Spring, 1997).*

Learning to identify the heart of the matter is not easy. It is perhaps the most challenging skill one must learn when doing theological reflection (Killen and de Beer 1994: 80). As we saw in Chapter One, just remembering and retelling events using *nonjudgmental narration* is, in itself, an art. Then what is most important is trying to locate within our narrative those feelings and images which seem to generate the most *energy* in us at this moment. That energy is an indication that it is *this* space that we are being called to explore more deeply. Somewhere within this space will be found the most significant issue in our experience. Finally we must *articulate* the heart of the matter clearly enough, at least initially for ourselves, so that our reflection be *focused*.

Sometimes one may have to examine several issues in order to discover that which holds the most significance at the time. Using an analogy, if you've had pain in your upper back, or maybe in your leg or arm, you may have discovered that the *cause* of the problem lies somewhere in the lower back or spinal column. Oftentimes our bodies have been absorbing the trauma and adapting themselves to the problem, but eventually their will be signs that something is not right, that something needs healing. In the same way that much of our physical pain often signals displaced symptoms of a problem residing elsewhere in our bodies, so too the feelings generated by an event are like "symptoms" of an unresolved issue which needs attention. Ideally this can be done with others, in the context of a supportive faith community.

Often a returned missioner may not believe him or herself to be in need of any help. You have probably encountered those for whom everything is "just fine"–who don't need any "touchy-feely" group to talk to! Although the personalities and the degrees of need may differ, we all need, sooner or later, to reflect seriously upon our experience in the light of our faith, if we want to continue growing as missioners, and as persons. Those who quickly plunge into new work or a new community, claiming no time or space to process what they have left behind, are either in denial or still in re-entry shock. Eventually symptoms will indicate that they too need "a reliable entry point" if they are to carry on fruitfully in their new situation. The jolt or the ambiguity of a transition are sometimes the "kiln" of conversion through which we are invited to become porcelain.

Conversion: A First Look

> No one sets out deliberately upon a journey of conversion: (we are) always called to it . . . launched upon it, by circumstances outside [our] control" (Searle 1980: 38).

As we have already suggested, exploring the heart of the matter will often lead to a "conversion." In the midst of the many and varied factors which make up transition–like each missioner–unique, there is often a common phenomenon. Something within is often in need of healing. Maybe some part of us has been bruised, or broken and badly in need of "resetting." Perhaps something is festering like a sore, and like salt poured on a wound filled with infection, like a bone that needs to be re-broken before it can be set straight, so too, often the resolving of our issues can be quite painful. Sometimes it may be that we have simply arrived at a new crossroads in our life, and we must leave one path behind and turn to another. But in each case, what is demanded of us is some sort of conversion, a "turning around," which may sometimes require a radical "change of heart" (*metanoia*) if indeed we are ever going to get around to really healing the heart of the matter.

A major guide for our reflection on conversion is an article by Mark Searle entitled, "The Journey of Conversion"(1980). I was introduced to it only a few months after my return from Zaire, but I have yet to find a better paradigm for what we are talking about. Searle focuses on features which seem to be characteristic of all periods of transition in human life, offering those features as fundamental to the "pilgrimage of faith or the journey of conversion":

> "Conversion" consists of the successful negotiation of crisis or change; that conversion is a form of "passage" or "transition" whereby a person may pass through to a new lease on life and enter into a new set of relationships with him[her]self, the world around him[her], and with life itself. The journey of conversion, then, would be a journey through crisis, using the term "crisis" here to refer not only to moments of alarm and anxiety but, in the broader sense of any turning point or moment of change (Ibid.: 36).

In this description we find three elements of the phenomenon of conversion which are especially important for our particular understanding of it: (1) the sense of *journey*, which is itself passage or transition, thus a process rather than a fixed moment; (2) the negotiation of *crisis*, crisis being understood in its broad sense as a moment of opportunity—a turning point or crossroads; and (3) the sense of *new relationships* which will mark the completion of this particular passage as part of the longer journey which is life itself.

Conversion is "a highly confusing and controversial issue today largely because the term 'conversion' refers not to one reality but to an enormously wide range of very different human realities" (Conn 1986: 7). While some authors maintain that conversion is essentially a *religious* phenomenon, I consider it a *human* phenomenon often *set within a religious context*. What's more, any authentic study of conversion ought to be *holistic*, including, at the very least, four components: "cultural, social, personal and religious systems" (Rambo 1993: 7).

Conversion as Process

One of the major discussions about conversion in the literature is whether or not is something which is gradual and ongoing, or whether it is a sudden, one-time event. Almost any serious discussion of conversion in the literature will refer back to William James, who offered one of its earliest definitions in his classic *Varieties of Religious Experience* (1902). He describes conversion as a psychological process, gradual or sudden, of unifying a divided self.

With James' psychological study as a foundation, the topic of conversion *as a process* has since been explored by many authors. David O'Rourke emphasizes that, as much as it is a decisive activity, conversion is also a complex process involving long periods of time and interrelated causes and effects, significant people and relationships, inaction and repression, postponements and sufferings. Ultimately it involves all of these elements *"woven together* into the whole that is the person's life" (O'Rourke, quoted in Eigo 1987: 9).

Lewis Rambo provides a very comprehensive definition:

> Conversion is a process of religious change that takes place in a dynamic force field of people, events, ideologies, institutions, expectations, and orientations . . . (a) Conversion is a process over time, not a single event; (b) conversion is contextual and thereby influences and is influenced by a matrix of relationships, expectations, and situations; and (c) factors in the conversion process are multiple, interactive, and cumulative (Rambo 1993: 5).

While more recent scholars in the field do not discount the fact that there may sometimes be a moment within the process of conversion which stands out as a "moment of grace," there seems to be a consensus that conversion is indeed "an ongoing process, at once personal, communal, and historical (Lonergan, quoted in Conn 1978: 14)." The missioner at the crossroads of transition is, I believe, invited to enter into that process. Mission involves a sort of continual conversion, a journey of "turning" and "re-turning" to one's true self, wherein dwells the One who called us in the beginning, and who never ceases calling us. *To live a life of mission is essentially a spiritual process.* Furthermore, we are being called to "mission," no matter where we find ourselves, but sometimes it takes a radical change of heart to recognize that call. In fact, every missioner who wishes to make a successful transition from one culture to another, from one mission to another, *must* be willing to change—not only on the outside, but more radically, on the inside! And this process of "conversion," of "turning oneself around," examining in the light of faith one's unique journey–this is, in fact, the "heart of the matter."

Stages Within the Process of Conversion

Many authors, including Griffin, O'Rourke, Rambo and Searle, find it helpful to articulate the process of conversion in terms of stages, while acknowledging that the process is necessarily a continuous one, and that the "stages" may interact and overlap. since conversion is a process involving a complexity of factors, the description of "stages" varies from author to author. Searle speaks of the stages as three main parts of a story, or "as a drama in three acts": the beginning, middle and end. He describes the unfolding simply:

> The beginning of a story tells of the way things were and of how the seed of circumstance was sown from which the ensuing events then sprang. The story goes on to tell of how that original state of things came to be altered or put in jeopardy, and it concludes by relating how these events were resolved in a new state of affairs (Searle 1980: 36-37).

Searle himself acknowledges that his paradigm is nothing new. The reader will quickly recognize Van Gennep's description of *separation, liminality and reincorporation,* as well as the theme: "from → through → to" which I referred to in Chapter One. Here I offer Searle's model to missioners as they wade through the sometimes murky waters of their own transitional "rites of passage."

> The Setting Out → The Adventure → The Return
> Separation → Liminality → Reincorporation
> From → Through → To → From → Through → To

Stage One: "The Setting Out"

Essentially, then, this first stage of a conversion process involves both the "setting out," and the "setting." Setting is important for any story. Rambo calls this the "context." Usually one can recognize a particular moment or event, a turning point of sorts, which we often identify with the beginning of a conversion process. This is usually the *onset* of the "crisis," (crisis usually considered an essential element of the conversion process.) But neither the crisis nor the conversion happens in a vacuum. There will have been previous events or circumstances, perhaps unnoticed–or if noticed, unnamed–which announce the arrival of a conversion in much the same way that nature announces the arrival of a storm.

Conversion begins with longing or desire, a heart's ache

> for something . . . . This longing may come in the form of
> a nostalgia when things seemed happier . . . or . . . of world
> weariness, a disenchantment and disappoint with the world
> around us . . . . (Griffin 1982: 36).

For missioners in transition this context for conversion may have begun in the past, the overall situation which we are transitioning *from*. Or our present time of transition *through* may also be the context which invites conversion. It could be the people, community, relationships, an institution, a system, an event or series of events--political, religious or economic, local or national. It could be an environment of overt violence or more subtle oppression. "Context embraces . . . people, events, experiences, and institutions . . . the total environment . . . ."(Rambo 1993: 20).

> Conversion takes place within a dynamic context. This
> context encompasses a vast panorama of conflicting
> confluent, and dialectical factors that both facilitate and
> repress the process of conversion . . . . Context embraces
> an overall matrix in which the force field of people, events,
> experiences, and institutions operate on conversion.
> Context is more than a first stage that is passed through;
> rather, it is the total environment in which conversion
> transpires (Ibid.).

Whatever the circumstances which led to it, missioners in transition find themselves in a new environment, being forced to relate to it, sometimes reluctantly. They are challenged to take a new direction, to think in a new way, and to form new sets of relationships: with others, with self and ultimately, with God. Something has already begun to change, if not externally, then internally, usually both.

How does this onset of conversion present itself? This "context" is not readily detected, much less easily articulated, when one is in the midst of it. Searle maintains that this onset of a conversion crisis is "necessarily perceived in images and expressed in symbolic language" (Searle 1980: 39). I have seen it is most often spoken of in descriptive terms, such as we've seen in the narratives: I'm "at a low ebb," "out of rhythm," "lost," "floating in air, swaying in the wind," "in a deep pit," "in a wilderness," "burned-out," or "having a nervous breakdown." One missioner, Terry, whom we met earlier in Chapter 3, describes the context or onset of his own crisis of conversion:

*I found myself swinging between daydreaming as escape
on the one hand, and redoubled effort on the other. But
almost every time I tried to work harder, it did not last very
long. I was just getting more and more tired and
frustrated. And I kept wondering why. I was becoming
discouraged with myself, with what I was not
accomplishing, with others who were not meeting my
expectations and with life in general. What was happening
to me? . . . My confusion was nearly total: physical,
emotional, mental and spiritual. When I tried to pray, after
a few days of extraordinary effort I would fall right back
into lethargy. And that lethargy in prayer spread into most
areas of my life. My personal energy was running out. I
didn't realize it then, but trouble was well on the way.
(Spring, 1993).*

"Marker Events"

As mentioned above, at this crossroads of our transition, a
conversion will often be associated with some sort of external event or
happening in our lives. This is not usually the crux of the crisis, (although
it may be), but rather what Searle (and Levinson before him) calls a "marker
event" (Searle 1980: 39). This event can be thought of as a trigger or
catalyst which will bring about–or bring to awareness–a series of other
"events" and realizations, more internal then external. It often signals the
onset of a conversion process.

How might a missioner in transition experience this marker event?
It could be in the words of a local church community suggesting that it is
time to move on and surrender the leadership to a local church member.
Perhaps it is the voice of a local superior saying that one is needed
elsewhere. It may be the onset of sickness, the death of a family member or
other loved one. Then too, it may be less evident. Sometimes a seemingly
insignificant happening that turns out to be the "straw that broke the
camel's back." In whatever fashion we may experience or express it, this
marker event will often throw us into a new phase of our transition, into a
crisis which some might experience as the "heart of darkness" or perhaps
others as the "winds of a tornado." Although when one is in this phase, it
seems like it will never end. But it will. It can be survived.

One Marker Event: A Personal Story

Every good story has to have a beginning, but in one's own conversion story "one is always somewhat at a loss to know quite where to begin" (Ibid.: 37). We too are "at a loss" if we try to briefly summarize a complex personal experience of several years duration. We acknowledge the context, a predisposition or internal restlessness which was leading, although we didn't recognize it at that time, into crisis–and to a major change in our life's direction. There was, however, a definite "marker event," which seems in retrospect to have marked the beginning of the crisis, of a period of darkness and disorientation.

This "marker event" occurred in March of 1991. I had been working in the equatorial region of Zaire for eleven years. I had spent the last three years in the village of Iboko, coordinating a program of Literacy, Development and Evangelization, based on Paulo Freire's **Pedagogy of the Oppressed** *(1971). Among other aspects of the program, we had a small collective "store," where participants were able to purchase necessities at retail value, and on a sort of "lay-away" plan. On this particular Monday, I went to the office and found it unlocked. Surprised, I assumed John, who had cleaned up the Saturday before, had been careless about locking it when he left the day before. Thinking nothing more of it, I went in and in the dim light noticed that the inner storeroom door was also ajar. This seemed strange, as I was sure to have locked it, and no one else had a key for that room. Still unsuspecting, I entered and saw papers scattered all over the floor. I confusedly tried to recollect if there had been some storm in the last few days that could have blown loose papers about.*

Then suddenly my heart sank. I recognized the papers on the floor as those that had served as packaging for the pieces of cloth that had been on "lay-away." Frantically I opened the large cardboard carton where I had packed them. Empty. Feeling suddenly sick to my stomach, I slowly began to examine the other boxes and the footlocker where the other items were stored. Everything was gone: the bolt of sheet material for burial, the bicycle parts, the machetes and hoes, the "special orders": all were missing. The only things left undisturbed were the literacy materials: books, pencils, chalk, etc. Another item missing was a spare padlock that I had placed in reserve on a back shelf. Few people, except those I worked with, could have known about that padlock. I checked the doors and windows. Apparently none of the locks had been tampered with. The reading room was in its usual order, and neither room had the appearance of having been "searched." It was as though the thief or thieves had known exactly where to go and what to look for.

*I slowly went outside, wondering how to break the news to those who were eagerly awaiting their purchases. I must have looked shocked and confused, because they quickly seemed to understand what had happened, without my even saying it. When I explained, their immediate reaction was concern for ME. "Who could have done such a thing to you?" they asked indignantly. They were shocked and angry. I, acutely aware that these stolen goods were **theirs**, not mine, was at a loss for what to say. When they gradually began to realize the implications of such a loss, their faces fell. They became strangely silent. But they still continued to try to console me and assure me that the goods would be found—that everything would be all right. I sensed that their trust in me assured them that somehow I would "make good" their investments.*

The news quickly spread in and around Iboko—a small village where everyone knows everyone and nothing is private. All sorts of friends—and even a few traditional enemies—came offering advice as to how to pursue the affair. I, feeling somewhat like "Job," tried to maintain my calm—and my integrity. I resisted the constant refrain that the two young men who regularly helped me, John and Rigo, had "obviously" been behind the theft. I resisted believing that my young friends—or any of my collaborators—could have betrayed me. I was still in a state of shock. They came around the next day to state their innocence. John swore he had locked the door, and that someone must have made a duplicate key. They insisted on going themselves in search of some trace of the robbers.

I didn't see them for quite awhile after that.

I became physically ill for several days after this theft. I did not want to see the office and storeroom for weeks. I tried to tell myself that this was only a theft; it happened all the time and to everyone. And yet this experience had affected me on some deeper psychological level: I felt betrayed, deceived, used, abused, misunderstood. I was deflated, discouraged, de-energized. Everything I was and did seemed to be called into question: my ministry, my relationships, my presence among the people–our corporate presence as missionaries, as part of the local Church, (or were we considered "Church" in as much as we were missionaries?). I questioned our purpose, our strategy, our methodology, and even our reason for being there at all. All the doubts and questions that had occasionally surfaced in my life as a missioner, and in particular during my ministry in Zaire over the past eleven years: these questions suddenly seemed to engulf me. My relationship with others seemed to change. I found it hard to trust as before, to have confidence in those with whom I worked. I found myself more conscious than ever of not wanting to become cynical–an attitude I had often perceived in some veteran missionaries.

Over the next months and year, I gradually began to resume my ordinary routine, to again visit the people in their homes and in the villages, to give myself again to my ministry. But things were never quite the same. I lacked the enthusiasm and conviction that had motivated me before. The same questions continued to plague me: Who had really been involved in this theft? Had the two young men been pawns in the hands of some local gang? Had they sold out their loyalty for money? Was the other collaborator involved, to whom I had confided much responsibility and had designated as "Director" of the program. Certain facts that I later discovered would tend to implicate him also. I never knew the answers to these questions, and probably never will. I kept wondering why this affected me so much? I wondered, "Is this what they call "burn-out"?

This event, which threw me into serious questioning

and doubt about the meaning of what I was doing with my life, eventually led me into total confusion and a "dying" process. The theft at our little storeroom was a shock to my system, to my world of values, to my idealized self-created reality. It wounded my pride, my dignity. I felt a loss of my sense of trust in others, especially the feeling of having been betrayed by those I trusted, and even by those I was trying to help! This produced in me all sorts of physical and emotional responses. I was hurt, offended, angry. I felt resentment and indignation. I was confused. I became physically sick; I sensed myself moving into a generalized mood of discouragement–even depression.

In fact, it was probably this incident more than any other factor, which prompted me, a year later, to ask for a "sabbatical." The theft's powerful devastating effect on me seemed to indicate to me that maybe I needed some space, some distance from Zaire and from my work: a time to study, to be renewed. I left somewhat reluctantly in July, 1992, almost a year and a half later. I did not like the idea of leaving Zaire, which was in a new period of interior turmoil. This meant separation from the country and culture I had come to call "home." But when I left, I thought that I would be returning the following year. I knew the year ahead would be significant, but I did not anticipate the kind of conversion I was to undergo. This seemingly isolated incident was the trigger which set off a whole new process of discernment which would change the direction of my life and ministry.

As Robert C. Solomon points out:

Emotions are the life force of the soul, the source of most of our values. . . . Emotions are said to distort our reality; I argue that they are *responsible* for it. Emotions are said to divide us from our interests and lead us astray; I argue that emotions *create* our interests and our purposes (Solomon 1976: 14-15).

This "marker event" had thrown me off-balance. Through this encounter with "reality," I was forced to understand that my particular "vision" had its own logic, but that the world was not just as I would like it to be, or as I perceived it to be. Everyday is filled with injustices and inequalities in relationships on personal and global levels. "The rich get richer and the poor get poorer." I have been brought to this awareness time and again, by the regard of a "poor" person whose eyes speak to me out of some deep well of dignity and pride: "Who do you think you are, anyway? I don't need your pity. I don't want your 'charity.'" I am reminded of the Apostle's words, "If I give away everything I own, . . . but have not love, I am nothing" (1Cor 13: 3). Kegan maintains that all disequilibrium is a crisis of meaning; all disequilibrium is a crisis of identity, which puts the 'self' at risk (Kegan 1982: 240). I have, more than once, been prodded to this disequilibrium by the challenges of friends who want to help me to grow.

For some mysterious reason, however, this time the experience of the theft jolted me into conflict. I was challenged to relativize what had been until now taken as ultimate. Viewed from the old perspective, in which I had long been invested, I experienced this crisis as a boundary loss, disorientation, and as an experience of not knowing what was happening to me, of felt "meaninglessness" (Ibid.: 231). I felt suddenly stripped of my pretenses and defenses. I experienced a kind of rupture or incongruity in my way of knowing and understanding everything around me. In some way, one might say, my "world" was falling apart, and a new one was not yet clear on the horizon.

Stage Two: "The Adventure"

This struggle is the crisis of conversion: the most difficult time of all. It requires of us a kind of introspection and self-reflection which we have not done before. It is, if not the first, the deepest encounter with the self which we have made, a confrontation with our own weakness and failures and inadequacies . . . both a struggle against belief and a struggle against the self . . . accompanied with a sense of uneasiness, of being cut loose from one's familiar emotional moorings, not knowing when, if ever, one will touch land again (Griffin 1982: 91-92).

Searle refers to the second stage of conversion as "the adventure"(Searle 1980: 39), but many are not accustomed to thinking of crisis as an "adventure." Terry, we have seen, refers to crisis as "trouble," and that is probably the way most of us experience it. Griffin refers to this crisis stage as the "Struggle" (Griffin 1982: 102-147); O'Rourke calls it the "Noisy" stage (Quoted in Eigo 1987: 10); and Rambo refers to it simply as "Crisis" (Rambo 1993: 44-65). Perhaps when we look back upon the time, we can recognize each of these elements (adventure, struggle, noise, "the pits") as part of our own wrestling with the heart of the matter. Like Jacob, we often come away from that struggle limping–but somehow mysteriously blessed (see Gen 33: 23-33).

Crisis represents an *essential element* of conversion. Although not the most important, it's usually the most *characteristic* part of any conversion process, often the most noticeable moment. Conversion consists in "the successful *negotiation*" of a particular crisis (see Searle 1980: italics mine). It's evident that death, suffering, and other painful experiences of loss or trauma can challenge one's interpretation of life, calling everything into question. Some crises challenge one's fundamental orientation in life. But other events which, on the surface, may appear to be relatively insignificant, may also eventually *trigger* a crisis. In fact, *cumulative* events often play a crucial role on the path of conversion.

The Heart of Conversion: Surrender

Crisis *alone* is not enough to explain conversion. At the *heart* of conversion is an essential act of letting go, or "surrender." Why is it, then, that crisis has such an impact in leading to–or at least potentially leading to–conversion? Because crisis–certainly a crisis of transition–leads us to "the heart of the matter" by placing us in the "heart" of our humanness. It brings us smack up against our weakness, our vulnerability, our brokenness as human beings, and we are forced to surrender our masks and pretensions. We are challenged to let go of false expectations, both for ourselves and others. Authentic crisis challenges all of our false conceptions and illusions about mission, ministry, community, others, God, and especially perhaps, ourselves.

> Every time you make a choice you are turning the central part of you, the part that chooses, into something a little different from what it was before. (C.S. Lewis, quoted in Griffin 1982: 30).

In reflecting upon this essential aspect of conversion as an "act of surrender," we look in particular to the work of Walter Conn, who in turn based his developmental study of conscience and conversion primarily on Bernard Lonergan's understanding of conversion as essential to self transcendence. For Lonergan conversion is a human phenomenon occurring on three distinct yet interrelated dimensions: intellectual, moral and religious. Thus conversion simultaneously occurs: *cognitively*, through critical understanding and realistic knowing; *morally*, through responsible choices and decision-making; and spiritually, through free and generous love in service of the other.

Most significant for us in Lonergan is his understanding of human conversion as a *process of self-transcendence.* Conversion, then, is demanded by the human spirit's radical drive for "meaning, truth, value, and love" (see Conn 1986: 24). For Lonergan, conversion, like the drive for self-transcendence, must be an intelligent, responsible and free act of surrender.

> The Gospel demand calling us to intelligent, responsible, loving service of the neighbor requires no more and no less than the fulfillment of this fundamental personal drive for self-transcendence. As the criterion of personal authenticity, self-transcending love is also the norm by which every other personal concern, interest, need, desire or with must be judged—and, if necessary, sacrificed. Fidelity to this law of the human spirit, this radical dynamism for self-transcending love, sums up the demand of the Christian life because it is a response to the divine within us—God's gift of love (Ibid.: 24)

Lonergan's definition of conversion as part of self-transcendence provides us with an important insight. Self-transcendence is the authentic self-realization which occurs when one actively moves *beyond one's own self*. It occurs when persons respond to the radical drive within themselves, the always deepening search for meaning, truth, value and love. Sometimes a conversion is being demanded of us which has little to do with the externals: the "projects" or mission assignments we are given. Paradoxically, self-*realization* is not an end in itself, but occurs as a by-product of authentic self-*transcendence* (see Ibid.: 22-25). And this experience of moving beyond one's own self *is* conversion, it is the turning toward something other. It is as much an act of freedom as it is an act of surrender. The point is that conversion does not consist in "simply surrendering," but rather "*surrendering to someone or something*" (Searle

1980: 42). In some mysterious way one is aware that something new has been born.

Surrender and the Missioner in Transition

> If every crisis, every conversion, is a kind of dying to one's previous life and world; if every crisis provokes what Levinson calls "de-illusionment," "a recognition that long-held assumptions and beliefs about self and world are not true;" then the moment of conversion, the turning point, is that moment of surrender (Ibid.: 41-42).

How might we characterize the kind of conversion that is demanded of a missioner in transition? Missioners may sometimes be those who go quietly along leading good lives, virtuous lives, perhaps never feeling quite radical enough to lead "holy" lives. Christian "holiness" is "transformation in Christ" and this is intimately connected to conversion and freedom. To become holy means being open to conversion, being willing to change, not once, but over and over again. In the words of Thomas Merton,

> We are not converted only once in our lives, but many times; and this endless series of large and small conversions, inner revolutions, leads to our transformation in Christ (Quoted in Ibid.: 48-49).

> But while we may have the generosity to undergo one or two such upheavals, we cannot face the necessity of further and greater rendings of our inner self, without which we cannot finally become free" (Quoted in Ibid.: 55).

Many of us are good, just like that clay pot mentioned at the beginning of this chapter. But some of us are called to become better, to become porcelain. For a missioner who has spent two or twenty years doing good for others, and, in fact, being a good person, sometimes it is a moment of transition or re-entry which provides the fire which leads to genuine holiness. This is the "stuff" of which saints and martyrs are made: a surrender which knows how to "drink the cup," how to say–and live–"Not my will, but thine be done." As we saw earlier, Ed described his own surrendering to the "heart of the matter" as being willing to sacrifice his Isaac: *"to throw reason to the winds and to trust in the God who provides."*

It may be that the missioner has to think of "mission" in new ways, yet nonetheless built on her or his previous understanding and praxis. In this case, as Lonergan says, the new horizon is consonant with the old, a development out of its potentialities. On the other hand, it may be a total "about-face" and new beginning. A missioner may be asked to conceive of his or her life and mission in terms of a *totally new paradigm*, demanding new mental and psychological structures–not to mention the physical and geographical changes that a particular transition may demand.

Someone may have spent fifteen years in "the missions" of another continent, and is now being challenged to be "in mission" to the provincial administration of his/her religious order, or to the street people in the city where she or he grew up. I know an experienced missioner who was very involved in a project in a remote part of Asia. He felt that his contribution there was significant and necessary. He was asked to leave that project in the midst of its development in order to work in formation in the United States with seminarians doing theological studies. When he got to the house of formation, he became part of a formation team where there was a ratio of one "formator" for each seminarian. He found himself asking the question, "Is this mission? Is this what I became a missioner to do? There are lots of people around who can do this . . . and better then me!"

In returning to my own story, I had left "my father's and mother's house" years before I had gone off to Africa, not knowing where or what it would be like. I had thought that these were acts of faith–and in fact, they were. But it had seemed so clear then that God was calling me. This was my vocation! But leaving a country which had become "home" and my religious community of many years, this was truly embarking on a new path, in the dark, having no idea where it was leading me. And trusting that *God* was leading me was perhaps the greatest challenge. How could I really believe that I was still following my vocation, even though it appeared that I had *left* it! In some way, I too felt that I was being asked to sacrifice my "Isaac." This surrendering into the arms of a providential God was the greatest act of faith I had made so far, and it was painful and scary.

Stage Three: "The Return"

The return begins . . . when in a hidden and imperceptible way our perception of the situation begins to alter (Searle 1980: 43).

Once a missioner has surrendered, as it were, to a *new* kind of call to "mission" as represented through this transition, the time of turbulence, resistance, mourning eventually subsides. Rambo notes two reactions to having surrendered. First of all, with the initial "enormous burst of both energy and relief," one feels a sense of liberation–"the energy that was consigned to maintain the conflict is now channeled into the new life . . . . "(Rambo 1993: 135). The second phase involves maintaining or sustaining the surrender, being able to consolidate the new life into a firmer growing commitment" (Ibid: 136). Thus, after the conflict has subsided, and one has "made the turn," there comes the need for owning what has happened, for making it a part of one's new reality.

Now, more than ever, there is a need for a certain withdrawal, for a time of prayerful reflection on what has happened in her or his life. A receiving community or support group needs to be aware of the importance of this time of interiorization for the missioner. This is the *actualization* of the surrender in one's life. One has begun the return home.

> It is not that external circumstances change–simply waiting for things to get better is one of the ways of avoiding conversion–but our vision changes. We see things in a new light. . . . This new vision cannot be defined any more than the moment of its coming can be exactly identified. But the knowledge that one has somehow been reconciled with Ultimate Reality, that one has been in contact for once with all that finally matters, is revealed in a nascent mood of optimism, a feeling of deep integration, of wholeness and renewal (Searle 1980: 43).

A new life has begun to quicken, a quiet joy, deep-seated and intangible, a more deeply rooted peace begin to make themselves felt beneath and beyond the continuing darkness and disorder" (Ibid.: 42). Signs of conversion, like little shoots of green, begin to break through the dark soil: sprigs of hope, peace and joy are barely visible. In the process of surrendering, a missioner senses at last that she/he has taken a significant turn and has started out in a new direction.

> As I walked around the farmland in Door County, I identified with the greening of nature that was happening around me and felt new sap flowing in me, new life, and a healing perspective in relation to some of the painful experiences I had had in El Salvador. . . . I am like a tree whose leaves are beginning to open at the beginning of

Spring. "See, I am doing something new! Now it springs forth, do you not perceive it?" (Is 43:19) (Pam, Fall, 1996).
Biblical Conversion and the Missioner in Transition

"Oh, that today you would hear God's voice: 'Harden not your hearts'" (Ps 95:7-8)

Throughout this process of transition, I have encouraged missioners to continue the dialogue between *their own experience* and their Christian tradition. Now we will reverse the process in a sense, and take a look at some experiences of conversion found in Scripture. Much as we did with images, we will allow our own unique experience of conversion to lead us to the Scriptural experiences or passages which resonate, in some mysterious way or other, with our own. Turning to theologians' commentaries on the subject of conversion in the Scriptures as reference points, we will briefly review the most common biblical understandings of "conversion" as found in the Old and New Testaments. Then I will suggest some possible "conversion stories" as models for deepening missioners' experiences of conversion in the midst of their transition and missionary journey. A main source for our reflection here will be my own and other missioners' allusions to Scriptural texts while in the midst of transition.

Conversion: Some Common Understandings

The Old Testament: Shub

In the Old Testament the Hebrew word *shub* is the most common term for any form of conversion. *Shub* is the twelfth most frequently used verb in the Old Testament, appearing 1059 times (see Eigo 1987: 31-74). There are two basic meanings implied in the word *shub*. One involves physical motion, the act of turning to turn from or turning to something or someone. The other meaning adds to the act of "turning" a dimension of relationship, especially covenant faithfulness or faithlessness, as in turning back toward or away from Yahweh (Ibid.: 31-32). One simple translation of *shub* is simply "returning home"(Conn 1986: 200).

But *Shub* in its different forms can help us understand better the many dimensions and meanings of conversion. A passage from Jeremiah (8: 4-5) illustrates this well:

> When [they] fall, do they not rise again? If one turns away
> (*yashub*), does he not return (*yashub*)? Why then has this
> people turned away (*shob bah*) in perpetual backsliding (*m
> shubah*)? They hold fast to deceit, they refuse to return
> (*lashub*) (Ibid.:31).

In the Old Testament, Jeremiah perhaps best reveals the essence of
conversion. It is not so much a matter of external observances of the law or
ritual that matters to God. rather our values and priorities need reordering,
thus "circumcision of the heart" (Ibid.: 44): "Circumcise yourselves to the
Lord, remove the foreskin of your hearts, O men of Judah and inhabitants
of Jerusalem" (Jer 4:4). Dom Marc-François Lacan summarizes that in the
Old Testament "to be converted is to become faithful," and he adds, "To
succeed in this, a person must rely on God in perfect trust" (Quoted in Conn
1986: 87). This theme of unconditional trust in God will be reinforced in
the New Testament understanding of faith.

The New Testament: Metanoia

In the New Testament, *shub* was usually translated into the root
strepho, meaning "to turn." While *strepho* has a covenantal sense in some
of the writings of Paul, the Gospels, use a new series of words to indicate
conversion, all having *meta-* as their prepositional prefix. This word implies
both repenting and reordering one's life.

> To be converted (*metanoein*) is not only to repent for one's
> sins, but also to bring about an interior transformation
> which blossoms out in a change of conduct, in a new
> orientation of life; a spiritual or moral "about face." . . .
> To be converted is first of all to believe in the Good News
> which Jesus proclaims. And what is this news? The
> presence of the Kingdom of God. This is indeed news
> capable of causing whoever hears it to "turn around," on
> the condition that he[she] believe in the one who proclaims
> it (Lacan, quoted in Ibid.: 100-101).

Conversion, far from being simply a once and for all act of
repentance, is also intimately connected with the "Kingdom" or "Reign" of
God: "Repent, for the kingdom of God is at hand" (Mt 5:17). In the
synoptic gospels, faith implies seeking the reign of God, and accepting

Jesus as the inauguration of its presence. Conversion is a condition for entering this Kingdom, not only for "sinners" but also for the just. It would also seem that a permanent state of conversion is a necessary condition for a living and active faith which witnesses the justice and peace of the God's reign. Crosby confirms Lacan's observation:

> The axis of Matthew's gospel is the proclamation of Christian justice which is the fruit of conversion and the requirement of faith. Now, this justice is nothing other than a permanent conversion; Jesus defines the just [person] in a word . . . the one who "seeks," who has never stopped "seeking the kingdom of God and his justice" (Mt 6:33) (Ibid.: 109).

It is precisely to this sense of "permanent conversion" that I invite the missioner in transition, that is, as one who will never stopped seeking God and God's justice. It is my belief that the "crisis" of transition is, in God's own mysterious way, a personal invitation to greater holiness. Whether with a gentle nudge–or a jolting shove–God is saying: "Seek me with all your heart, you will find me . . . and I will give you rest . . . . (see Jer 29:112-13 and Mt 11:28-29).

Biblical Experiences: Some Helpful Paradigms

> O you of little faith...Do not worry and say, 'What are we to eat?' or 'What are we to drink?' or 'What are we to wear?' . . . Your heavenly Father knows that you need them all. But seek first the kingdom of God and its righteousness, and all these things will be given you besides (Mt 6: 31-33).

Conversion demands that we be always ready for the unexpected, ready to make another turn in the road or an "about face;" willing to sacrifice our "Isaac," to become like little children (see Mk 10: 14-15), to place the establishing of the reign of God–in society and in our hearts–before all else, to never cease striving to "be perfect as your heavenly Father is perfect" (Mt 5:48).

We know, however, how easy it is for the "just" to slip into a comfortable life, maintaining the status quo, becoming accustomed to the norms of society–in whatever society or culture in which we find ourselves.

This is why the call to conversion is not reserved only for the obvious "sinners," but for all of us inconspicuous sinners. Let us now look at a couple of classic examples of the call to conversion, one from the Old Testament and the other from the New.

After God's Heart

David's conversion, recounted in the Second Book of Samuel, is one of the best known conversion stories in the Bible. As a paradigm, it allows us to discern "the essentials of an authentic conversion": God initiates it; conversion is a grace; it is necessary to receive it as a grace and to become a witness to this grace (Ibid.: 76-79).

David is a man with a vocation and a mission: to be faithful to Yahweh by observing the law and the prophets, and by governing God's people with justice. David carries out his mission with fidelity and zeal. He is a good and a humble man. We can witness this from his youth, in his devotion to King Saul and Saul's son Jonathan (see 1Sam 16: 14-23; 17: 32-58; and 24: 1-23). Later, as Lacan puts it, "A wise, valiant, and devout king, he remains humble in success, as indicated by his behavior at the time of the entrance of the Arc into Zion (2Sam 6)," (Ibid.: 76). One of my favorite images is of David dancing "with abandon" before the Arch of the Lord.

Yet, gradually, David becomes complacent and eventually begins to slide down a slippery slope. He allows his lust for life and beauty to lead him into a series of serious transgressions, both of his own conscience and of the Law. When David fell, as was typical of his life pattern, he fell hard. It took a harsh encounter with the truth, through the prophet Nathan, to bring David, literally, to his knees before his God (2Sam 11-12). And again, when David came to awareness and repented of his sin, he likewise did it with his whole heart.

Michael Crosby suggests that the stages in David's conversion "can serve as a model in all personal conversion." He outlines them as they are recounted in Second Samuel:

- The sinner remains in sin and justifies it: (2Sam 11: 1-26).
- The sinner is confronted with a realization of the sinful
      situation: (2Sam 12:1-12).
- The sinner admits/confesses the sin: (2Sam 12-13).
- The sinner, guilt-ridden, repents of the sin and atones for
      it: (2Sam 12: 14-25). (See Crosby 1987: 37).

I take the liberty here of paraphrasing these stages in a slightly different way, as they might correspond to Lonergan's dimensions of conversion, and as they might apply to a missioner in transition. Following is an example of how this conversion might resemble a missioner's "rite of passage" "from → through → to." I use here brief excerpts from one missioner (Spring, 1993) as he describes his experience and makes Scriptural associations with it.

1. *"From"*: The missioner still holds on to "illusions" in his/her situation and yet, is gradually becoming vaguely dissatisfied with it.

> *When I had come to the island, I had known there would*
> *be difficulties, but I thought that I could handle them well*
> *enough. I seemed to be able to adjust to new situations.*
> *. . . The weather would be hot, but I could adjust to that*
> *too. After all I came from a land of very cold winters. .*
> *. I knew that I could learn about new ways, new customs.*
> *. . . Sure I was a "proud" person from time to time, but*
> *usually I felt that I tried to be genuinely "humble" toward*
> *others. . . . How is it that now, island of my missionary*
> *dreams, you have become my nightmare? Why have you*
> *become so impossibly humid, so unbearably hot. . . . I*
> *cannot rest. I am weak, irritable, impatient, tired. . . .*
> *Suddenly the former pastor is gone, and I am pastor of*
> *20,000 people! I cannot even speak to them. After all*
> *those years of study, all I can do is say "Hello" and smile.*
> *. . . I feel so frustrated. With myself, with others, with God.*
> *I know that many of my "images" are false, but I hold on*
> *to them for security . . . .*

"Peter said to him, 'Even though all should have their faith shaken, mine will not be.' Then Jesus said to him, 'Amen, I say to you this very night before the cock crows twice you will deny me three times.' But he vehemently replied, 'Even though I should have to die with you, I will not deny you.' And they all spoke similarly" (Mk 14: 29-31).

2. *"Through"*: Something occurs (marker event, sudden change) which confronts the missioner with the human condition, radically clarifying "stubborn and misleading myths concerning reality, objectivity, and human

knowledge," e.g., self-sufficiency, complacency, false expectations, false sense of security, illusions, or lack of compassion (intellectual conversion, see Lonergan 1972: 238).

> *Suddenly, everything had collapsed. Like some strange quirk of fate, everything had turned upside down. I felt disowned, a failure. The only choice I could make was to leave the mission. I had no choice. . . . Yet leaving was like cutting away half of my heart, half of my life. . . . Just to return to the States was shock enough. . . . Helpless, I sought to find walls of protection to shelter me from further storms. It seemed to be the only way to stay alive. Often though, I found myself almost "buried alive."*

> "Jesus said to them in reply, 'Have you come out as against a robber, with swords and clubs, to seize me? Day after day I was with you teaching in the temple area, yet you did not arrest me; but that scriptures may be fulfilled.' And they all left him and fled" (Mk 14: 48-50).

3. The missioner reluctantly accepts the change and enters into transition, reevaluating the criteria of his/her decisions and choices (moral conversion, see Ibid.: 240).

> *This was my frame of mind when I was asked to write about something from my mission experience, as part of a course for returning missionaries. . . . I chose a "nice" story, innocuous enough, I hoped, to prevent further injury to a heart already adrift in a sea of confusion, doubts and fears, sorrow and a lot of hurt. . . . As we progressed in the course, bit by bit, my walls of protection started to come down. As we delved deeper into the many levels of our "simple" stories, I felt free enough to start asking myself some very important questions. . . . I began to see a gift of hope appear . . . .*

> "Now that very day, two of them were going to a village seven miles from Jerusalem called Emmaus, and they were conversing about all the things that had occurred. And it happened that while they were conversing and debating,

Jesus himself drew near and walked with them, but their eyes were prevented from recognizing him . . . ." (Lk 24: 13-16).

4. *"To"*: The missioner struggles with the new demands of faith, but finally allows him/herself to be "grasped" by that which is greater than self, surrendering "without conditions, qualifications, reservations" to the God who continues to call and challenge (religious conversion , see Ibid.: 240).

> I finally turn toward God . . . and ask for help. Why is it that I turn to God "last"? After all of my other choices fail me. . . . This is "holy ground" . . . the "meeting place of God" where just one condition is mandatory: total honesty between myself and God. At last, I allow no more excuses, no more escapes in this holy place. It is time to search for the Truth. I must wait before God for answers. . . . God must bring light to my darkness. . . . How long must I wait? Does it really matter? . . . I have finally come to realize that my views are no longer sufficient for "life." I must see it in a new way . . . no matter how long it takes. . . . There is no half-way in "overcoming myself" to become like Christ. I either make the choice, or not . . . .

> "And he said to them, 'Oh, how foolish you are! How slow of heart to believe all that the prophets spoke! Was it not necessary that the Messiah should suffer these things and enter into his glory?' Then beginning with Moses and all the prophets, he interpreted to them what referred to him in all the scriptures" (Lk 24: 25-26).

Conversion comes to us in strange packages, under unusual conditions, and when we may least expect it. Neither do we *choose it*. Rather, like crisis, "it is thrust upon us"(Searle 1980: 38), sometimes by circumstances which hardly seem conducive to any preconceived notion of a conversion, much less might they seem congruent with "God's will." (E.g., Recall how Marty spoke to us of his "nervous breakdown," which eventually precipitated an authentic conversion, exploding in his life like a "volcanic eruption.") Ultimately, conversion is the consequence of God's enormous gift of love (see Lonergan 1972: 237-243). Every conversion is a call to "Rend your hearts, not your garments, and return to the Lord, your

God" (Joel 2:13).

"The Road Not Taken"

Let us turn now to the New Testament for another model of a conversion process. Michael Crosby presents the Matthean theme of "seeking-finding-selling-buying" as a paradigm for such a process. We have already seen the intimate connection between "seeking the reign of God" and conversion. We are continually called to be seekers after the gifts and fruits of the Spirit, which puts us in a continual state–or should I say *dance*–of conversion. The Synoptics present to us the case of a "seeker" who does not have the courage–or whatever he is lacking–to bring his call to completion. I am speaking of "the rich man" who approaches Jesus with the question: "Good teacher, what must I do to inherit eternal life?" (Mk 10: 17-31; Lk 18: 18-23; Mt 19: 16-22).

The main character in this Gospel account is obviously a good person, a "just" man. He comes to Jesus seeking how to become *better*, how to live his life more fully. In other terms, he is asking how to "be perfect" as his heavenly Father is perfect (see Mt 5:48). Jesus answers by reminding him of the commandments. Perhaps still kneeling before Jesus, he replies: "Teacher, all these things I have observed from my youth." We know that Jesus, looking at him with love, said to him: "'You are lacking in one thing. Go, sell what you have, and give to the poor and you will have treasure in heaven; then come, follow me.'" At that statement his face fell, and he went away sad, for he had many possessions" (Mk 10: 21-22).

This person had evidently entered into a process of conversion. He had found himself restless, in some way looking for "something more." This good person, propelled, as it were, toward self-transcendence by a pursuit of truth and goodness, is seeking the ground of all goodness: "Good Teacher . . . ." And Jesus' response makes this clearer: "Why do you call me good? No one is good but God alone" (Mk 10:18).

What was it that caused this man to come to Jesus in search of that "ultimate good"? Was there a "marker event" that symbolized something of which he had been only vaguely aware until then? Had he suffered a loss? Had there been some death in his family that had caused him to consider more seriously his own quest for "eternal life"? Or had he been listening to Jesus for some length of time and had long been wanting to talk to him. Was it Jesus' "setting out on a journey" from that district that made the rich man want to seize the opportunity to ask his burning question? We can only speculate. What does seem clear however, is that when it came to the moment of surrender, the man could not let go. Both Matthew and Mark report that when he heard Jesus' proposal: "'Go and sell what you have, and give to the poor . . . ,'" his face fell, and he went away sad, for he had many possessions"(Mk 10: 21-22).

Imagine this person to be a "missioner" who has, in fact, kept the commandments from her/his youth, spent many years in the mission field, and is now being asked to make a change, to be stretched beyond his or her normal goodness, to become "porcelain." Sometimes we missioners pride ourselves–if secretly and even unconsciously–on our lack of possessions. We make visits to the United States, Canada or Europe and are overwhelmed, sometimes genuinely distressed at the enormous quantity of "things" that people have. We are sometimes hostile to the capitalist consumerism that seems to perpetuate the systemic poverty of over two-thirds of the world's population–the people we have been serving. All of this may be an authentic response from a missioner who has spent a number of years away from the "First World."

But is it not also true that we missioners have our own possessions, our "Isaacs." Often we have built our own "kingdoms," losing sight of the greater "Kingdom" which is the source and end of our mission. We have our achievements: churches, schools, programs, hospitals and clinics. We speak about "our" catechists, parishioners, base communities; our workers and farmers, our girls and boys, nurses and midwives, as though *we* made them who they are. And sometimes we really believe we did! (Remember Cathy who was so convinced that *she* would change things! She burned herself out in her over ambitious zeal). Another missioner put it this way:

> *My first five years went by quickly. Then I was elected*
> *superior, a tremendous affirmation by the community*
> *because I was the second youngest in a group of over*
> *twenty. Three years later I was re-elected. I had my ups*
> *and downs during those years, was affirmed fairly often*
> *and reveled in that. Then I accepted a parish that had been*
> *empty for almost a year, and stayed there five years. And*
> *for my last eight years I was director of the catechetical*
> *training center for the diocese, after helping to build it.*
> *(Tim, Spring, 94).*

And there are our interior "Isaacs": our pride, our need for affirmation, security or control, our jealousies and rivalries– .netimes among our churches or parishes or organizations, sometimes even among ourselves as colleagues or companions. We have our hurts and wounds that we often protect and nurse more carefully than the patients in our clinics. Look at my own experience? Had I not exaggerated the importance of *my* literacy program or *my* little store? One of the reasons I was so devastated by the theft in the storeroom was that I took it so *personally*. My pride was wounded. I who was so dedicated, so appreciated, respected, accepted by the population. How could this have happened to *me*?!

Transition is often an opportunity to start over, to begin again the process of "leaving everything" to follow Jesus. One of the greatest demands of the Kingdom is putting *all* of our trust in God:

> "Master, master, we are perishing!" He awakened, rebuked
> the wind and the waves, and they subsided, and there was
> a great calm. Then he asked them, "Where is your faith?"
> (Lk 8: 24-25).

> "Look at the birds in the air; they do not sow or reap, they
> gather nothing into barns, yet your heavenly father feeds
> them. Are you not more important than they?" (Mk 6:26).

> "Do not store up for yourselves treasures on earth, where
> moth and decay destroy, and thieves break in and steal. But
> store up treasures in heaven, where neither moth nor decay
> destroy, nor thieves break in and steal. For where your
> treasure is, there also will your heart be" (Mk 6: 19-21).

Jesus invites us again and again to let go of our possessions, to stop clinging to our settled nests of security, to let go of our fears and doubts, as well as our accomplishments and failures. Allowing our transition to renew us is to enter into a conversion, to get our priorities straight, our relationships in order. We did it once perhaps, but over the months and years, we gradually began to take it all back–everything we thought we had left behind in our early missionary fervor and enthusiasm. Often, little by little, we have been accumulating again. And our hearts have become so heavy that there is no way for God's Spirit to move them anymore! What a striking contrast in the Gospel between the one whose "face fell, and . . . went away sad" (Mk 10:22), and the one who "out of joy goes and sells all . . . and buys that field" (Matt 13:44). And what about the woman who, "left her water jar behind and went into the town and said to the people, 'Come see a man who told me everything I have done. Could he possibly be the Messiah?!'" (Jn 4:28-29).

Moving On: *Some Concluding Remarks*

As we began the process of "setting out" and were thrust headlong into "the adventure" of our transition, we recognized at some moment the invitation to surrender "the heart of the matter" to the One who has called us, and continues to journey with us. The conversion is not yet over. In the past when, full of enthusiasm, we set off for our first mission assignment, the time probably arrived when we felt the urge to "look back" even though we had "put our hand to the plough." So it is with the surrender of conversion. At first, perhaps with renewed courage and energy, we are ready to put our hands to new ploughs. But we find ourselves in new and strangely different fields. It will take time to learn the new terrain and to cull the wisdom of our past in order to help us live our new "mission."

> Order is not at once restored, still less is the old order reestablished: to that there can be no going back. Yet gradually one is led to a new set of relationships, more genuine and more realistic, with one's world. The sense of futile restlessness gives way perhaps to a growing sense of new direction and meaningfulness. One's defeats and failures are not taken away, but forgiven. Physical and material losses are not necessarily made good, but perhaps the sense of loss is transformed into that detachment which is the condition of genuine freedom. The disintegration of so much that one had clung to fades before the hope of a richness and wholeness one had not previously guessed possible (Searle 1980: 42).

There remains now one final invitation: that of integrating new insight into our lives. This is the challenge to be explored in the next and final chapter. In some ways one is still "betwixt and between." But now, having come to the "heart of the matter," and surrendered, we are in a different space. We have taken the risk of letting go: of false hopes and unrealistic expectations, of a false sense of self-reliance and security, and of having to be in control our life and destiny. Having offered our "Isaacs" to the One who has called us from the beginning, we have crossed over the threshold and are one step closer to home.

Chapter Five
Coming Home: Integrating Insight

"At every turning point in our journey, we can hope, reasons of the heart will come to light." (Dunne 1978: xi).

In this chapter, we reflect on "homecoming," drawing inspiration from Henri Nouwen's meditation on *The Return of the Prodigal Son* (1992), reflecting upon John Dunne's insights from his own journey of "passing over" and "coming back," and with Thomas Merton's understanding of the "true self" as our authentic "home" within. My hope is that we will arrive at some new insight for truly being "at home" in the constantly changing context of our missionary–and Christian–journey.

Marginality: From Surviving to Thriving

Now we look for a new place to pitch our tent for awhile, until it be time to move on again. We feel, above all we worry, that we'll be overpowered by the desire to move from the tent into a house and so lose our missionary freedom, our missionary values. We don't want to leave either our tents or the tents of the poor with whom we share a corner of this earth (Ron, Summer 1996).

Cultural Marginality

In Chapter One we considered the challenge of the changing identity of the missioner, and what mission means in our global church today. We have been exploring, in the context of our Christian tradition, the transition of moving "from" our mission experience, wading "through" feelings and images of the past and present, which lead us "to" the heart of the matter. Let us now explore our current and future identity as missioners through the concept of "cultural marginality" (see Bennett 1993: 109-135). According to this concept, individuals find themselves marginalized from their own cultural frames of reference.

> An individual who has internalized two or more cultural frames of reference frequently faces an *internal* culture shock. This intrapersonal response is not due so much to external interaction with a single different culture, but rather to the recognition of conflicts between two cultural voices competing for attention within oneself (Ibid.: 112).

When this situation occurs, the subject could get "stuck" in a state of encapsulated marginality or walk toward a dynamic situation of constructive marginality. I believe that the missioner returning "home" or being sent to another culture, will certainly experience this phenomenon, and face this kind of choice.

Encapsulated Marginality

This is an ambiguous state in which one's choices are muddled by conflicting perspectives and a lack of inner responsibility to think and decide autonomously. (See Ibid.: 116-117.) The "encapsulated marginal" represents that which is the worst or most unsettling about "reverse culture shock." As we pointed out in previous chapters, missioners *will* experience culture shock upon reentry or in a process of changing missions. This is the nature of being "betwixt and between." The problem, however, as Bennett suggests, is when one gets *stuck* there, thus "encapsulated." Missioners who are *stuck* in their transition are not unlike an individuals who get "stuck" in adolescence. They are very self-conscious, preoccupied with their sense of marginality, never "at home" with themselves nor with others, because they don't know where they belong. They squirm, uncomfortable with themselves, and neither are others comfortable with them. Some characteristics of encapsulated marginality are seen in Figure 5.1 below.

Such missioners may have a wealth of wisdom and experience to communicate, but they are trapped in a perceived state of "terminal uniqueness," feeling estranged and alienated from the culture from which they've come, from the culture which they are currently in, and consequently, from themselves (see Ibid.: 115). This state of cultural and self-estrangement could lead a missioner to experience an estrangement from God, thus producing the kind of anxiety and sense of meaninglessness and hopelessness that I have sometimes encountered in returning missioners.

Characteristics of Encapsulated Marginality

Loose boundary control
Difficulty in decision making
Alienation
Self-absorption
No recognized reference group
Multiplistic
Conscious of self
Disintegration in shifting cultures
Troubled by ambiguity
Never "at home"

Figure 5.1 Adapted from Bennett: 113

Constructive Marginality

A constructive marginal is not immune to the throes of culture shock. To the contrary, this missioner also has to deal with what Bennett calls "disintegration"(see 112-119). In terms of a missioner's "conversion" this might be considered the process of "dying" in order to be reborn again. "There must be a finding and a losing, and then a losing and a finding" (Dunne 1978: xi). This is a person who has come–usually through reflection with a peer group of others who are also in transition, to experience his or her marginal status as *constructive* rather than destructive. A missioner begins to evaluate life around him or her in terms of the *context,* thus "intentionally and consciously...creating his or her own [new] identity"(Ibid.: 113). The situation of constructive marginality includes the characteristics shown in Figure 5.2.

Characteristics of Constructive Marginality

Self-differentiation
Well-developed boundary control
Self as choice maker
Dynamic in-betweenness
Authenticity
Marginal reference group
Commitment within relativism
Conscious of choice
Intrigued by complexity
Never not "at home"

Figure 5.2 Adapted from Bennett: 113

As missioners we know that the cultural context has influenced our way of knowing and being, i.e., our values and standpoints on political or religious issues, our way of thinking and of viewing life, our spirituality–our way of praying and being in the world with God and others. If we have been faithful to our vocation as missioners, we will have been continually forging our identity, allowing our "evolving self" to be influenced by, even as we influence, the vitality around us. Just as we have learned from the people and cultures where we have been in the past, we can be confident that we have something new to learn from the people and culture that surround us in the present, which will, in turn, carry us gently into a new future full of hope. "For I know well the plans I have in mind for you, says the Lord, plans for your welfare, not for woe! plans to give you a future full of hope" (Jer 29:11). The *constructive* marginal recognizes that the future is "full of hope," and has come to be at home with him/herself, thus realizing that "one is never *not* at home in the world" (Ibid.: 113, 118).

I've emphasized here certain aspects of what it means to be an "encapsulated marginal" (which Larry Lewis might call a maladjusted misfit!) and a "constructive marginal" (a well-adjusted misfit!). I propose that the process explored throughout this book be considered as a sort of "rite of passage" which would facilitate a transitioning missioner's movement *from* encapsulating marginality *to* constructive marginality. This shift or transition in cultural marginality is expressed in Figure 5.3.

Transition in Cultural Marginality

Disintegration in shifting cultures ➜ Self-differentiation

Loose boundary control ➜ Well-developed boundary control

Difficulty in decision making ➜ Self as choice maker

Alienation ➜ Dynamic in-betweenness

Self-absorption ➜ Authenticity

No recognized reference group ➜ Marginal reference group

Multiplistic ➜ Commitment within relativism

Conscious of self ➜ Conscious of choice

Troubled by ambiguity ➜ Intrigued by complexity

Never "at home" ➜ Never not "at home"

Figure 5.3 Adapted from Bennett 113.

Living in cultural marginality implies both subtle movement and active waiting. Let's now deepen our understanding of this movement toward insight.

Insight: Passing Over and Coming Back

> The movement toward insight is like a journey. We travel from experience through feeling to image to new ideas and awareness that can change and enrich our lives. At our most intuitive moments, we may not be aware of the flow of the movement. Bringing it to awareness allows our reflection to become more conscious and critical...It opens us to being more discerning of God's presence and action in our lives (Killen and de Beer 1994: 45).

Theologian John Dunne has written much about a rather unique process of finding one's true self. Paradoxically, this discovery takes place in the context of "the other": other people, times, places, cultures, religions. While not a "missioner" in the ordinary sense of the term, Dunne has, I believe, given us a model for missionary life in his method of doing theology. "My method is my journey," he tells us (Dunne 1978: 151). And for those who know Dunne's works, his novel-like autobiographical writings reveal that his personal journey *is* his theological method. This method and journey are one of "passing over" and of "coming back," which can be traced through all of the books he has written since he wrote *The City of the Gods* (1965), in which he first made his method explicit.

Dunne articulates his method, as he attempts to live it, in his written "spiritual adventures" (See Dunne 1972: ix), each of which attempts to describe an ultimate search for God through sympathetic understanding of the other. One example of "passing over" occurs on a riverboat, a journey which was to lead Dunne not only up the Amazon River, but also from his standpoint of "personal religion" to "the religion of the poor," (Dunne 1982: vii-x).

> When you are willing to be on a personal journey, you step into your own aloneness, say Yes to it, become one with it. "You find a way a lone a last a loved a long the riverrun." At the same time, you find that the way 'a long the riverrun' is a way for everyone, that you have companions on the journey, that we are on a voyage together. A time like that came for me on the riverboat, a moment of vision, a moment of conversion. I saw in that moment how our voyage on the riverboat was an image of the human journey in time. . . . It was a glimpse of the human essence. Passing over to others reveals how we are sources of life to one another; coming back to yourself reveals how we have the source of life within ourselves (Ibid.: 20).

Passing Over and Coming Back

Each leg of Dunne's spiritual–and usually geographical–journeys, like each book, begins from a different starting point, i.e., his personal standpoint or horizon at that given time and place. He then attempts to "pass over," through a process which he calls "sympathetic understanding," to a different standpoint, i.e., that of another person, culture, place, time, religion. He then, in turn, "comes back" to his own original standpoint–which is, however, no longer the same as it was before.. He describes each "passing over" and "coming back" as a "step of the journey [which] begins as a kindling of the heart and ends as an illumining of the mind" (Dunne 1978: 152). This "illumination of the mind" through the heart's way of knowing is what Dunne (after the mind of his mentor, Bernard Lonergan) calls "insight." "It is when reasons of the heart become known to the mind, I believe, that insight occurs" (Ibid.: xii).

> Passing over to others and coming back to oneself, when it does occur, changes one's relationship with others and with oneself, and when it occurs among a group of people . . . it is an image of change in society. . . . It is the image of a society based on passing over and coming back, on sharing the human essence. It is a changing image, much as time is a changing image of eternity (Dunne 1982: ix).

What missioner has not entered "sympathetically into the feelings of another person?" For most of us, one would hope, if we have discovered anything in our years of cross-cultural ministry, it's that, in attempting to teach others, it is *we* who have learned; in healing others, it is *we* who have been healed; in attempting to convert others, it is *we* who needed conversion; in giving to others, it is *we* who have received much more in return. "Passing over" may be expressed and nuanced in different ways, e.g., acculturation, empathic presence, or compassion.

Regardless of what we choose to call it or however we may understand it, this process is, I think, the essence of ministry. But there is the second half of the process. We come to understanding by "coming back to that of our own lives and times." But, as we know, this "coming back" is often the most difficult leg of the journey. I have observed that it is the "coming back" which provides an equal or possibly greater challenge to the missioner. It is, however, this cyclical process which makes the passing over complete, and which leads to a new understanding which Dunne refers to as "insight."

This is precisely what we missioners are seeking as a result of our transition: a new or re-newed understanding of our life, which will be like "a guide" as we continue on our journey into a new context. Dunne has articulated an intentional way of doing theology based on his experience, i.e., he learns and speaks of God by passing over into the lives of others and then returning to his own. Missioners–perhaps unintentionally–have also been doing this throughout our missionary lives. Perhaps we might say that many of us have been living "practical theology" without realizing it. Possibly the difference lies in the intentionality, which can be developed through theological reflection.

I understand Dunne's theological method as unfolding in six moments which correspond almost directly to Killen and de Beer's movements for theological reflection. Dunne's fifth and six moments are waiting for insight, and, once received, allowing the new or renewed insight to become a guide for life. Dunne entered into this process spontaneously initially, simply because he was *attentive to his feelings*. In reading the epic of *Gilgamesh,* he found his own deep concern and uneasy feelings reflected in the hero. The *image* of Gilgamesh and his journey was able to bring Dunne to recognize the *"heart of the matter,"* which he calls his "real gut problem" (Nilson 1987: 48).

> The story of a man who had been so troubled by death that he had embarked on a quest for unending life could be his own story too. He found himself reading the epic not to find data to support a thesis but to gain insight on an issue engaging his whole existence. Having "found that my real gut problem was death, not political theology," Dunne was now at a crossroads. He could continue his work on political theology and relegate his real issue, death, to the private realm of meditation or evade it altogether. Or he could, like Gilgamesh, set out on his own quest by letting his "gut problem" occupy his mind as well as his heart. He could go on his own journey in search of insight into this problem which he had come to see occupying the hearts and minds of humankind across all ages and cultures (Ibid.: 68).

We know which path Dunne took at his "crossroads," and that, as the poet might say, "has made all the difference." As returning or transitioning missioners, we too are at a crossroads. We have a unique opportunity for renewed growth and discovery. Transition can be a privileged time for re-discovering "the other" with whom and to whom we have been ministering, and the ultimate "Other," without whom our life would not make sense. Most especially we have a time and space in our liminal moment to rediscover with renewed understanding, *ourselves*, as ministers and missioners. Yes, we have become, as Lewis says, "misfits." But it is in this very "misfitness," standing at this transitional crossroads of our missionary journey, that we are–literally–on a "threshold of opportunity."

> Missioners who have worked and lived many years in either host or home culture and return to the *other* find it one of the most wrenching of experiences. Returning to the *other*, the other of host or home cultures, is a paradigm of the missioner returning to The Other, The More Than, which alone can give humanity its distinguishing characteristic as human. . . . This analogy of the homelessness, the misfitness of the foreign missioner and his [her] returning again and again to The Other is what roots the missionary vocation in the fundamental structure of human formation . . . (Lewis, n.d.: 8-9).

Integration

But "straddling" two or more cultures does not *automatically* make of the missioner a "sacrament" of transcendence for others, a "beacon" to the "misfit" in all of us. (This kind of straddling could, in fact, make one nothing more than disjointed!) Threshold living can only be sustained by a *deep rootedness* in the Other, who called and sent us in the first place. And this kind of rootedness grows out of our own solitude, where we discover, accept and own the "truth" about who we are. It is the fruit of prayerful, sometimes painful, reflection on one's experience of being "other."

It is in this experience of "rootedness," in knowing oneself somehow steady, in spite of the continuous, sometimes stormy movement of our lives and everything around us, that we "come home" to ourselves, and are able to hear that "tiny whispering sound" within that says, "Be still, and know that I am God" (Ps 46:11). Home is that "place" within where we meet our "truth," where we know who we are, and *whose* we are. No matter *where* we are, when we are home, we are safe and whole. Paradoxically, it is in understanding, accepting and embracing our marginality and vulnerability, our very restless "homeless" condition as human beings, that we begin to find ourselves strangely "at home" in our journey.

In his autobiographical book, *The Misfit*, Larry Lewis names *his* truth. He calls it "the void" that he tried to avoid for much of his life.

Traveling to China and beyond, like the Prodigal, he tried to run away from himself. He found his "home" by remembering where he had met his truth, in "the rear, right-hand side pew of St. Mary's." There he had embraced his misfitness, yet knew he was safe. He felt "not laughed at," because he knew that "God didn't laugh at people," even at a fat little eight or nine year old kid (Lewis 1997: 61).

> As I look back over the three years in China and see how much came together interiorly for me, I realize it was because circumstances outside of me erupted into disorder and provided the occasion for interior disintegration as well. The exterior disintegration occasioned a felt social misfitness, and the interior disintegration revealed long-held memories of childhood social misfitness. The social misfitness of my Childhood had brought me to God Who doesn't laugh. Everything that happened during my time in Wuhan had served to draw me closer to the truth that had originally brought me to that God. The cultural /geographical dislocations of my foreign missionary vocation, going to and from Wuhan, Hong Kong, and my home in the States all served to bring me back to the gateway to the void (Ibid.: 162).

A new and important dimension of our lives as missioners will be in owning and sharing this "otherness" with others, especially with those *who have also experienced it*–but who are as yet unable or unwilling–to name it or claim it. Thus we will be able to strengthen others who, often unknowingly, remain alienated from themselves and others.

But for this to happen, it is necessary to have not only "passed over" into others' lives and cultures, but also to have in some way successfully come back into our own. This is the process of genuine "integration." This does not mean that we will now "fit in." Nor should we ever really want to. But in finding a "home" within ourselves, in that deepest part of our being, we will find peace in our experience of being "other."

> Peace I leave with you; my peace I give to you. Not as the world gives do I give it to you. Do not let your hearts be troubled or afraid (Jn 14: 27).

This peace of soul will not be mistaken nor go unnoticed, for it is a rare commodity in today's world. It is for this reason that I invite missioners-in-transition to claim as their own, to whatever extent they can, and in whatever way it is helpful, the spirituality and lifestyle of "passing over' and "coming back." To live this way means:

> To enter sympathetically into the feelings of another person, become receptive to the images which give expression to [those] feelings, attain insight into those images, and then come back enriched by the insight to an understanding of one's own life which can guide one into the future (Dunne 1978: 53).

It is difficult to synthesize Dunne's thought without oversimplifying it. And this would be an injustice to the very insight of this innovative theologian. As we have seen in earlier chapters, sometimes we just don't know what to do with the images and feelings that we take with us from our ministry. The baggage that we carry with us when we move weighs us down. Or sometimes, as another friend in transition recently put it, "I feel like a rubber band ready to break." If we don't treat that "rubber band" gingerly, it just might break. If we allow our feelings to fester or form hard scabs to hide infection, we remain wounded without healing, and we will be in too much pain to enter into the joys and sufferings of others on our new path, wherever it be. If we cannot treat our wounds, we will never be able to heal others out of our woundedness. We will no longer be able to pass over into the lives of family, friends or into new cultures and times of ministry "back home" or elsewhere. But we know that healing takes time, and we must wait with patience for insight, and for the voice of God calling us home.

Waiting for Insight: Waiting on God

Dunne's notion of "passing over" "coming back," leads one to new "insight." The ultimate "insight," I believe, is coming to know one's "true self," the self that is God's "beloved," the dwelling place of God's Spirit. For Dunne the experience of "waiting for insight" is also a "waiting on God." As he puts it, "The waiting is the praying, and the coming of God is the answer to the prayer, and [God's] coming takes the form of a kindling of light in the darkness. This kindling of light I shall call 'insight'" (Dunne 1981: 3). And he adds, "In waiting for insight . . . [one] is waiting for [one's] heart to speak" (Ibid.: 5). Dunne considers insight not primarily as an intellectual experience, as does his teacher, Lonergan. Rather it belongs "both to the realm of mind and to that of the heart" (Ibid.: 3), for "it is when reasons of the heart to become known to the mind, I believe, that insight occurs" (Dunne 1978: xii).

> That . . . may be the unifying factor . . . listening . . . waiting for insight. In fact that waiting . . . is the willing of one thing . . . in so far as [it] is waiting for one thing: the one thing is like the x in an algebraic equation. it is an unknown quantity, the unknown path [s]he must walk, and [the] willing it is really a willingness to walk it.   . . . Purity of heart . . . consists in waiting for insight, in waiting for [the] unknown path to be revealed. Yet . . . in the darkness; the path is still unknown. . . . That seeing of the way . . . will be the seeing of God, a seeing of the will of God. . . . If God leads by the heart, then God's leading should come to light, as it seems to be doing, when the heart becomes pure, when the heart begins to will one thing (Dunne 1981: 4-7).

Missioners in transition or re-entry really *must* wait. We are, as we have seen earlier, on the "waiting threshold" of neither there nor here. No matter how busy we make ourselves, no matter how much we try to avoid it or rush it: like birth, transition and conversion will happen in its own time. And so we must wait in the darkness of the womb until the time of birthing is over.

The question, then, is not if, but *how* we are going to wait. Are we simply going to resign ourselves to it? Or are we going to *freely choose* to enter into it through *active, yet contemplative, waiting.* Are we willing to wait for God? Surely we know by now that "God's timing is not our timing." Are we able to allow the time for our new selves to be born out of the transition? The spirituality of Merton maintains that "the whole of the spiritual life finds its fulfillment in bringing our entire life into a transforming, loving communion with the ineffable God," and that this communion is both "the *raison d'être* and fruition of our deepest self" (Finley 1978: 19).

Homecoming: Where the Heart Is

Home is where one starts from. As we grow older
The world becomes stranger, the pattern more complicated
Of dead and living. Not the intense moment
Isolated, with no before and after,
But a lifetime burning in every moment
And not the lifetime of one [...] only
But of old stones that cannot be deciphered.
There is a time for the evening under starlight,
A time for the evening under lamplight
(The evening with the photograph album).
Love is most nearly itself
When here and now cease to matter.
[The] old...ought to be explorers
Here and there does not matter
We must be still and still moving
Into another intensity
For a further union, a deeper communion
Through the dark cold and the empty desolation,
The wave cry, the wind cry, the vast waters
Of the petrel and the porpoise. In my end is my beginning.

(T.S. Eliot, "East Coker" V, 190-209)

Upon Arriving

As missioners we have been on many journeys: planes and boats and trains have taken us across oceans and continents. As missionary "mountain climbers" we have trekked across deserts, reached high peaks, and ventured into deep tropical rain forests. We are "nomads" living on the edge of two or more lands. We are "marginals," and it is difficult to know where we belong, where to call "home." In fact, we wonder if we will ever be "at home" again.

These reflections have led us on another kind of "journey." We have moved *from* our past and present experiences, *through* our feelings and images, and *into* the "heart of the matter," with its demand for surrender in an interior conversion. What I now want to emphasize is that the "waiting" in transition (like being in transit between planes when one returns from one's mission assignment) is *a necessary step toward the integration of our experiences, toward "homecoming."* If we are ever to truly "come home," it will be to embrace God within a transformed and enriched self. In the new context, whatever it be, we must expect to live in a certain cultural marginality, and in fact, welcome the kind of healthy tension that comes with it.

Perhaps we have never been on any journey so challenging, so heart-rending, as this inner journey which calls us to become whole and holy. Before us is the invitation we have been "waiting" for, "the invitation of a lifetime." It's like coming to a new bend in the road. In the midst of a transition—perhaps not of our choosing, perhaps freely chosen—if we attend carefully to our baggage, i.e., those feelings, images we bring with us; and if we carefully heed those signposts along the way, i.e., our insights; we can hear God calling us to a new found freedom and to a more fully integrated life. The voice comes from deep within and invites us to "come home."

For some of us, we were ready to leave our mission assignment. Still, it takes time before we are really ready to begin again in new surroundings. We must recognize that we are again in new and unknown territory (even when it—and we—appear to be the same). Perhaps more than ever, it's necessary to unpack carefully and heed the sign posts along the way.

For others, if we're not ready, it's even harder to "come home." We feel "uprooted," especially if we've planted our heart there. I have often heard missioners say, "I left my heart in . . . Tanzania, Brazil, China, Algeria." Oftentimes this is more than an expression, but it is the person's perceived reality. How does one survive "without a heart"? How do missioners begin a new assignment if they can't "put their heart" into it? Is it better then, as some would believe, not to invest oneself anywhere because it hurts too much to uproot it when the journey calls us on? I think not. Maybe these sound like silly or romantic questions. But in fact, we think they are quite real and relevant for missioners—especially in today's increasingly dynamic and mobile world of global mission.

In one FROM workshop a returning missioner asked the group what they thought about "letter-writing." She explained that she had been a year away from her mission in South America, and still continued to receive many letters. There was genuine angst in her voice as she said, "I don't know what to do. I feel like each letter really needs a response, but then I wonder, Am I still holding on? Should I stop answering their letters? Should I cut it off and let go?" Then she added, almost in tears, "The thing is, well, what I mean is, I feel like half of me is still there!"

Half of her *was* still there. As I've said earlier, "Once a missioner, always a missioner." In a sense, missioners don't really ever "hang up our hat"–much less our heart. We just hang them differently, in different places. Mission is not a question of geographical place and linear time. Rather, mission is the passionate commitment that burns and grows, no matter where we are or what we do. It is born in "kairos" time, and is part of the dynamic and ever-changing "kingdom" which is both "here and now"–and also "not yet." At the same time, while in some sense always sojourners on this earth, missioners also need to be rooted, need a "space" within ourselves that we can, in a very real way, call "home." But arriving at this space is easier said than done.

"There's No Place Like It?"

For many missioners, especially those who have been away for many years, even the word "home" may evoke a "yucky feeling" in the pit of the stomach. Home is fine when you're just on furlough or a holiday visit. But the thought of going home *"for good"*–especially when it is coupled with the false idea of having to "leave the mission behind"–can be frightening, revolting, depressing or even devastating to some. I remember clearly when I would come to the U.S. on my "home visits" from Zaire. I would go from parents to other family members and friends in different parts of the country: vacationing, eating out, swimming, relaxing.

In general all of this was tolerable–most of it even enjoyable–because I knew that *this wasn't "home" for me anymore.* I remember feeling as though I were on a fast train ride during those three or so months in the U.S., with everything and everyone kind of whizzing by me in a surreal way. I knew that this lifestyle was only temporary and in a few months I would be back in "reality," in "my world," the place I had come to call "home." My family and friends couldn't understand this, and it hurt them if I tried to explain. So I kept it pretty much to myself.

At the same time, back in Zaire, I was increasingly aware that this was not really my "home" either. In fact, today it is more important than ever that we missioners recognize from the outset, that we are guests in the countries where we serve–even "strangers," as Anthony Gittins puts it (see Gittins 1989). The irony is that oftentimes the longer we stay somewhere, the more we love the people and want to make this place "home," the more we also realize, as missioners, that we need to "work ourselves out of a job," eventually leaving this adopted "home" where, ultimately, we know we don't belong. I believe it was Maryknoller Bishop James Walsh who said something to the effect that missioners must go where they're needed but not necessarily wanted, and leave when they're wanted but no longer needed. A wise missioner knows it's time to leave when the people begin inviting her/him to stay forever!

This is, then, the missioner's dilemma: "loving and leaving." And indeed we do leave parts of ourselves behind us as we go, living in the lives of those who stay behind. And in some ways we *will* always feel like a stranger, not knowing where to call "home." At the same time, this is the missioner's call, both a challenge and gift: to be a symbol for others in this world, attesting to the fact that here there is no "lasting dwelling place." We are *all* nomads, pitching our tents and then taking them up again, like the One who was willing to "pitch his tent among us" (Jn 1:14). So then none of us, at least as Christian believers, is *really* at home anywhere here on this earth. We are all on a journey, and since all human beings–(and maybe even extra-terrestrials like E.T.)!–need a home, we must find our home in the journey.

The True Dwelling Place

> "Whoever loves me will keep my word, and my Father will love them, and we will come to them and make our dwelling with them" (Jn 14:23).

A friend of mine was born in Cuba, lives in Miami, studied in Chicago, and does missionary work in Haiti and the Dominican Republic. I recently asked her where she felt most at home. She answered, laughing, "On the plane!" So how can we, how do we who have traveled the globe, come to rest "at home" in our missionary journey, no matter where we are? In reality we missioners have begun that long journey home a long time ago, "passing over and coming back"–perhaps many times. If we have been faithful to this voyage, carefully attending to all of our "baggage," listening to the voice within that has been leading us like a trustworthy guide, then we have already crossed the threshold and are at the door of our Mother and Father's house:

> Home is the center of my being where I can hear the voice that says: "You are my Beloved, on you my favor rests."
> . . . Jesus has made it clear to me that the same voice that he heard at the River Jordan and on Mount Tabor can also be heard by me. He has made it clear to me that just as he

has his home with the Father, so do I . . . . Faith is the
radical trust that home has always been there and always
will be there (Nouwen 1992: 35-36).

Perhaps Henri Nouwen makes it sound easy to accept this truth, i.e.,
that each of us, with Jesus, is "the Beloved," but the parable often called
"The Prodigal Son" (Lk 15: 11-32), and Nouwen's semi-autobiographical
meditation on it (inspired by Rembrandt's painting), assures us that this
journey to the center of our being is indeed the most challenging we ever
make. This reflection has been all about that journey of coming home:
telling our story, acknowledging our feelings, seeking the heart of the
matter through our images, while listening to the wisdom of our heart and
our tradition, naming our "Isaacs" and offering them to our God. Dunne
reminds us that this process goes on throughout our lifetime (Dunne 1977:
219). If we, as Christians and as missioners, have been sincerely seeking
understanding, and not certainty, Dunne says, then the quest would verify
the saying "Seek and you shall find, knock and it shall be opened to you"
(Ibid.).

What is it that we shall find when the door of our "home" is opened
to us by our Father and Mother awaiting us there? Dag Hammarskjold said,
"We all have within us a center of stillness surrounded by silence" (quoted
in Dunne 1982: 173). Thomas Moore, among others, would probably call
this *center* the "soul" (Moore 1994). Thomas Merton refers to it as "the true
self," (which we will look at more closely in a moment.) Dunne has spoken
of this "center" in a variety of ways. In *The Church of the Poor Devil*, he
refers to it as the "heart of light," "religious essence," "human essence," and
"source of inexhaustible life" (Dunne 1982: 21). Five years later, in *The
Homing Spirit* (1987), Dunne notes that his authentic "coming back" is not
to his "self," but to the *God dwelling within himself*. "I am! Here is the
home of the spirit, where we can hear and say 'I am,' a kingdom of persons,
a life larger than life" (Dunne 1987: 103).

Missioners who find themselves "alone" in their transition might
take consolation from the image of Jesus in a critical moment of his own
transition. Even his most faithful followers didn't understand what he was
going through. When he needed them most they were overcome by sleep.
"They could not keep their eyes open and the did not know what to answer
him" (Mk 14:40). He too found himself alone--but not totally. "Abba . . . all
things are possible to you. Take this cup away from me, but not what I will,
but what you will" (Mk 14:36). "The prime turning point in a life is the
point where [one] goes over, if and when he [or she] does, from God as the

unknown and uncontrollable, to God as Abba" (Dunne 1977: 222). "Our weakness remains, but it is a handed-over weakness, made strong in its openness and abandonment to God's mercy (Finley 1978: 87).

Trust and Gratitude

The essential attitude of being "at home" in our missionary journey is one of *radical trust*. Dunne refers to it below as "unconditional relation." Merton refers to it more as *faith*. No matter what we call it, this attitude is not really achieved by working hard at it. It will come, however, in prayer, if we sincerely listen to the Spirit dwelling within, if we really *want* to trust in "Abba," to enter into that "stillness surrounded by silence."

> We should not look for a "method" or "system," but cultivate an "attitude," an "outlook": faith, openness, attention, reverence, expectation, supplication, trust, joy. All these finally permeate our being with love in so far as our living faith tells us we are in the presence of God, that we live in Christ, that in the Spirit of God we "see" God our Father without "seeing." We know [God] in "unknowing." Faith is the bond that unites us to [God] in the Spirit who gives us light and love (Merton, 1971: 34).

Faith, as we have seen in previous chapters, requires a continual letting go: letting go of control, letting go of all of our illusions and expectations for our lives. Going over to a trust relationship with God involves a change that is quite radical. It means relinquishing control of our life in the central area, where we care and where we also are able to exercise control (see Dunne 1977: 222). Roger Schroeder, member of the Society of the Divine Word and professor at Chicago's Catholic Theological Union, explains his own "letting go" in this way:

> *Since returning to the States ten years ago, I have come to name, value, and "let go of" my missionary experience of the past, so that I can move on to name, value and embrace my new missionary situation of the present. The "best of days" and the "worst of days" of my earlier cross-cultural missionary life have had a tremendous impact in shaping me into the person I am today. I and those I now teach–and learn from–continue to struggle to be a part of*

God's mission—to cross over to and be transformed by not only the poor and other cultures, races, religions, and Christian denominations, but also those of my own culture and nationality. In many ways, I continue to feel like a "stranger" in "my" own land, but now I do not associate feeling "at home" with a particular place, but rather with being "at home" in the missionary journey itself. (Spring, 2000).

This kind of radical trust means living with uncertainty, with the ambiguity that is characteristic of living on the edge. It means living in the "dynamic in-betweenness" which will always be the lifestyle of missioners, no matter where we find ourselves, and no matter how unclear the future may be. Perhaps it was Hammarskjold who best put this radical trust and gratitude into simple words that have become well known to many of us: "For all that has been—Thanks! To all that shall be—Yes!"

The Identity of a Missioner: At Home with One's Self

What I have been doing in this chapter, and actually throughout these reflections, is to invite you, the reader, and all missioners who are in "reentry" or in a "transition" stage of their journey, to find a home within yourselves. This coming "home" means radically encountering one's true self. Let's take a brief look at what this implies

The False Self

To say I was born in sin is to say I came into the world with a false self. I was born in a mask (Merton 1961: 33).

Merton reminds us that our personality, i.e., the empirical identity which we often call our self, is often mistakenly taken to be our "entire self." In this way, that identity which we cling to and protect as our "self," really becomes a *"false self,"* an obstacle to realizing our *"true self,"* that is our "whole self before God," the self we were created to become (see Finley 1978: 18-19).

There are so many idols surrounding us and voices of "false prophets" building up a negative image of both ourselves and our God, making us afraid to encounter either one, telling us *not* to go home. Merton calls this "the false self," the creation of our egotistical illusions and desires.

For Merton this "I" is not the real "I" but an "illusory person," a "non-existence" which perpetuates a state of alienation from God (and thus our true self), a state of sin.

> Every one of us is shadowed by an illusory person: a false self. . . . My false and private self is the one who wants to exist outside the reach of God's will and God's love–outside of reality and outside of life. And such a self cannot help but be an illusion. . . . A life devoted to the cult of this shadow is what is called a life of sin. . . . All sin starts from the assumption that my false self, the self that exists only in my egocentric desires, is the fundamental reality of life to which everything else in the universe is ordered (Merton 1961: 34).

The "prodigal son" had to deal with the illusion of this false self. It took him a long and difficult time to "come to his senses."

> I shall get up and go to my father and I shall say to him, "Father, I have sinned against heaven and against you. I no longer deserve to be called your son; treat me as you would treat one of your hired workers" (Lk 15: 18-19).

Like him, so many of us–and missioners are probably among the best at it–he imagined that we have to *earn* his father's love. Often we too don't dare to go "home" just as we are, i.e., feeling unworthy, useless, confused, a failure, hurt, tired, angry, rejected, guilty, abused–or abusive–and the list could go on. Finley suggests that Merton's basic dynamic of the spiritual life could be summarized in the experience of the alienated prodigal son journeying back home (Finley 1978: 37-38).

Nouwen reminds us also of the alienation of the "elder son" who, while remaining in his father's house, never really feels "at home" there. Rather than trust, gratitude and joy in his life in the service of his father, he is filled with anger, resentment and envy.

> He became angry, and when he refused to enter the house, his father came out and pleaded with him. He said to his father in reply, "Look, all these years I served you and not once did I disobey your orders; yet you never gave me even a young goat to feast on with my friends. But when

your son returns who swallowed up your property with
prostitutes, for him you slaughter the fattened calf" (Lk 15:
29-30).

But the father gently and lovingly reminds the elder son that his
love, his "home" has always been there for him: "My son, you are here with
me always; everything I have is yours" (31). "What is so clear is that God
is always there. . . . Whether I am the younger or the elder son [or
daughter], God's only desire is to bring me home (Nouwen 1992: 74). We,
who have often been caught up in our projects and projections, still
configure God in our image, rather than ourselves in God's. We
continue–though often unconsciously–to think of God's love as conditional
and about home as a place we are not yet fully sure of. While walking
home, or rediscovering it beneath our feet all along, we keep entertaining
doubts about whether or not we are truly welcome there (Ibid.: 47).

The True Self

There is only one problem on which all my existence, my
peace and my happiness depend: to discover myself in
discovering God. If I find [God] I will find myself and if
I find my true self I will find [God] (Merton 1961: 5).

In an authentic "passing over and coming back" we missioners will
discover that the Other, and the "others" into whose lives we have entered,
are to be found within ourselves, that is, within our "true selves." "By our
love and our need for love we become for one another midwives of the true
self" (Finley 1978: 97). As Merton says:

The inner self is precisely that self which cannot be tricked
or manipulated by anyone, even the devil. [The true self]
is like a very shy wild animal that never appears at all
whenever an alien presence is at hand, and comes out only
when all is peaceful, in silence, when [it] is untroubled and
alone. [It] cannot be lured by anyone or anything, because
[it] responds to no lure except that of the divine freedom
(Merton, quoted in Finley 1978: 91).

And in birthing our "true selves" for one another, we find love, for
"God is Love," and in this home we will find our deep and lasting peace. In

entering into the inner dwelling of our heart and soul, we come into the Presence of the One in whose image we–and our brothers and sisters–are made. "Once a missioner, always a missioner." We missioners are, in a metaphorical sense, an "ark of Yahweh," carrying God within us on our nomadic journey. "Now, if I have found favor with you, do let me know your ways so that, in knowing you, I may continue to find favor with you . . . ." "I myself," the Lord answered, "will go along with you, to give you rest" (Ex 33: 13-14).

It is my hope that, no matter where we are, "en route" or "on mission," we will, at one and the same time, always be "at home."

> To say I am made in the image of God is to say that love is the reason for my existence, for God is love. . . . Love is my true identity. Selflessness is my true self. Love is my true character. Love is my name (Merton 1961: 60).

Moving On: Some Concluding Comments

We are no longer who we were before being sent on mission. Nor are we the same as we were during our time of ministry. To the extent that we have "passed over" into other lives, cultures, thoughts, feelings, sufferings and joys, we have changed and we will never be the same again. To the extent that we have "come back" into our own life, culture, thoughts, feelings, sufferings and joys, we will sense that we have somehow found a "home" here, yet with new and renewed horizons. In *The House of Wisdom*, John Dunne speaks of this new-found sense of being "home" as "being in the hands of God." He writes:

> Now I understand what it is "to be in the hands of God." It is this double relation, this to and fro, on the one side the relation of past and present and future to me, the encompassing peace I have felt again and again, that becomes *inward peace* as it enters my heart and soul, and on the other, my own relation to past and present and future, my response to the peace of God, that becomes *self-realization in God* in my "Yes." . . . As I stand in the present with the past behind me and the future ahead of me, I can feel time's arrow as a longing, and I can see it as the tangent of a great circle of love that comes from God and goes to God. "Unconditional relation" means being

heart and soul in the longing, and my heart's speaking is
calling ever more fully into the great circle of love (Dunne
1982: 112).

As for myself personally, it is only because I believe that I am
finally "at home"–at least to a certain extent–with *myself*, with *others* and
with *God*, that I have been able to put this "journey" into writing. I would
not have been ready to do it five years ago. I recognize, with much
gratitude, that I am still on an amazing journey. I don't really know where
it is leading me, but I do know *Who* is leading me, and that makes all the
difference. I am "in the hands of God." With that confidence, I am "at
home in the journey."

Epilogue

The Sharing

We told our stories–that's all.
We sat and listened to each other, and heard the journeys of each soul.
We sat in silence, entering each one's pain and sharing each one's joy.
We heard love's longing and the lonely reachings-out for love and
      affirmation.
We heard of dreams–shattered–and visions fled.
of hopes and laughter turned stale and dark.
We felt the pain of isolation and the bitterness of death.

But in each brave and lonely story
God's gentle life broke through.
And we heard music in the darkness and smelt flowers in the void.
We felt the budding of creation in the searchings of each soul.
We discerned the beauty of God's hand in each muddy, twisted path.
And God's voice sang in each story.
God's life sprang from each death.

And our sharing became One story of a simple lonely search
For life and hope and Oneness in a world which sobs for love.
And we knew that in our sharing God's voice with mighty breath was
      saying . . .

Love each other and take each other's hand.
For you are one though many and in each of you I live.
So listen to my story and share my pain and death.
Oh, listen to my story and rise and live with me.

                                  (Edwina Gately)

     And so our "mountain climbing" adventure is over. Our journey
of reflection comes to an end. But then again, not really. There are more

mountains to be climbed. As T.S. Eliot might have put it, "In our end is our beginning." A missioner's life is in some ways a continual process of "passing over" to others and a "coming back" to self, and to the spiritual adventure that carries us beyond ourselves, a recovering of heart and soul, "when one is heart-free and heart-whole in the journey with God" (Dunne 1978: 151)–and with others. Coming "home" for missioners, as for *both* sons in Luke's parable (Lk 15: 11-32), is not always easy. Perhaps the task is more complex, because we often confuse our "home" (our identity, our "self"), with a geographical place, a culture, a country, a role, a function, a title, etc. While it may be true that every culture and person we have encountered along the way *has* become a part of us and enriches the *whole* of who we are, it is so easy to create of these people, places or accomplishments, false selves, false images, false expectations, perhaps even false gods. And any one of these "false homes" in some way compartmentalizes and minimizes our true "self," and thus makes us less "whole."

The "*from* → *through* → to →*" of a missioner, the "passing over" and "coming back," and the sharing of insights gained in that crossing, can be a part of the human journey which leads missioners to greater wholeness, integration, and integrity of heart and soul. But this inner journey, as we have seen, is very demanding. It requires no less than *all* of ourselves. But even if it is challenging, it is not really so strenuous a "climb." Rather it demands of us an attitude of prayer and discernment, one of contemplation, openness, exploration, patience, perseverance, and, above all, hope. It is, as Dunne has said, and Lewis as well, an active "waiting."

> The waiting is the praying, and the coming of God is the
> answer to the prayer, and [God's] coming takes the form
> of a kindling of light in the darkness. this kindling of
> light I shall call "insight" (Dunne 1981: 3).

There is movement in the waiting, but not movement toward certainty and decisions. It is rather a movement toward "insight," toward understanding with a kind of "certitude of the heart," which brings with it a certain new clarity, courage and peace. "At every turning point in our journey, we can hope, reasons of the heart will come to light" (Dunne 1978: xii). It is the incorporation or integration of these "reasons of the heart" into our lives which enables missioners to "move on" with authentic freedom and renewed hope, precisely because we have found a place of peace within. We have, in a manner of speaking, come "home" to ourselves, where God and others dwell within us in the journey.

Our missionary venture continues. If we have managed to climb mountains and pass through valleys, to support the firing kiln and the rain, we will have, after all, arrived at a new vision. We will recognize that, in some fashion or another, we *have* come "home." At the same time, we know, more than ever, that we are still on the way. I want to close this reflection with a prayer by one who knew what it meant to "pass over" into others' lives, and to "come back" to himself a "new person in Christ." For Archbishop Oscar Romero, I believe it is safe to say, the waiting *was* a praying, and his prayer was one of hope. So until we reach the "not yet" fullness of the kingdom, our *true* home, let us pray together in hope, "*Thy Kingdom come, Thy will be done . . . .*"

> *It helps, now and then, to step back and take the long view.*
> *The Kingdom is not only beyond our efforts, it is even beyond our vision.*
> *We accomplish in our lifetime only a tiny fraction of the magnificent enterprise that is God's work.*
>
> *Nothing we do is complete, which is another way of saying the Kingdom of God lies beyond us.*
> *No statement says all that should be said.*
> *No prayer fully expresses our faith.*
> *No confession brings perfection, no pastoral visit brings wholeness.*
> *No program accomplishes the Church's mission.*
> *No set of goal and objectives includes everything.*
> *That is what we are about.*
> *We plant seeds that one day will grow.*
> *We water seeds already planted, knowing that they hold future promise.*
> *We lay foundations that will need further development.*
> *We provide yeast that produces effects far beyond our capabilities.*
> *We cannot do everything, and there is sense of liberation in realizing that this enables us to do something, and to do it very well.*

*It may be incomplete, but it is a beginning, a step along
        the way,*
*an opportunity for the Lord's grace to enter and do the
        rest.*
We may never see the end results,
*but that is the difference between the master builder and
        the worker.*
We are workers, not master builders,
ministers, not messiahs.
We are prophets of a future that is not our own. Amen.

(Attributed to Archbishop Oscar Romero)

Appendix I
A Process of Naming and Narration of Experience

Introduction to the Process: The participants are invited to think of their cross/cultural or mission experience as a story, or as a sort of novel. The shaping of one's own "story" is the study of God's presence in one's life, i.e., the reflection on one's life is a way of doing practical and personal theology.

I. *"Prologue" or "Introduction"* (*"The Setting Out"*)

You are invited to write 1-2 pages describing or explaining in some way the situation, steps, significant people, etc. which led to your decision to become a "missioner" or to leave your own cultural context to work in another. In other words, *what or who brought or led you to come to this decision*? What preceded your departure for the new culture or country? Do you recall an *image* or *symbol*, a significant song, book, person, quote, etc. that seemed to capture the context of your "setting out" on this journey in mission?

II. *Divisions* (*"The Adventure"*)

A. Divide your missionary or cross-cultural life into several (3-4) *main* parts or divisions. This may be by theme, chronology, places, events or people. These would be like the "titles" of the main parts of your "novel." For example, *Part 1 - "Osaka: Language School"*; *Part 2 - "1st Assignment"*; *Part 3 - "The Incident with Kim,"* etc. For some of you these main parts may become the *chapters* of your story or novel.

B. For some it may be helpful or necessary to divide the main parts into sub-parts or *chapters*. This may depend on the length of your stay in the host country, or upon the variety of experiences you have had. If this is helpful for you, then divide each of the main parts into two or three chapters.

III. *People*

For each of your chapters or main parts, identify at least *1 or 2 significant persons* who stand out in your memory of that time. Briefly describe the persons, and why they are significant in your experience or memory. (The memory of these persons may be positive or negative, or your feelings toward them may be ambivalent: if for any reason these persons come to mind, then they may be significant to your experience).

IV. *Marker Events* *(Moving toward the "Heart of the Matter")*

For each chapter (or main part) identify one or two particularly *significant moments or experiences*. These "marker events" or moments may have been happy, sad, painful, joyful, hard, easy, a "first", etc.

A. Is there *an image, song, symbol, etc.* which seems to capture these experiences for you? Name or express it in some way. Have you had a dream which might seem to represent these particular experiences? If so, what would you "entitle" that dream? Write out the dream if you care to do so.

B. In reflecting upon these marker events or moments, can you identify any *significant issues, conflicts, concerns, etc.*, which seem to recur or stand out in these moments or happenings? Another way of asking this question is to look for any *common threads* running through these moments in each chapter; does anything seem to stand out or strike you as a *recurring theme* or themes? Try to identify and briefly name these themes.

C. Reflecting upon each of the above named issues or themes, try to indicate which of the following aspects you interpret them to be most focused around. (Some of these issues or themes may seem to be a combination of several or all of these aspects. Try also to indicate which ones seem to be <u>most</u> at play).

1) individual	4) spiritual/religious
2) communal	5) psychological
3) cultural	6) other . . .

V. *One Experience* *(Examining the "Heart of the Matter")*

From the significant people and experiences you have identified thus far, choose *one particular experience* and *describe it in as much clear detail as possible.*

A. Is there *an image, song, symbol, etc.* which seems to capture this experience for you? Name or creatively express it in some way. Have you had a dream which might seem to represent this particular experience or theme? If so, what would you "entitle" that dream? Write out or draw the dream if you care to do so.

B. Identify the *particular theme or themes* that mark this particular experience. Describe this theme in more detail than above, trying to indicate what significant movement it might indicate in your own life. If you have not already done so, indicate which *kind* of an issue or theme it seems to be for you, i.e., individual, communal, cultural, spiritual, etc.

VI. *Scripture*

Identify *a theme or person in Scripture* which seems to express, capture, or in some way connect with your experience. Identify *a particular* passage which expresses this theme or focuses on this person. Please cite this passage, quoting it (or a significant part of it if it is long.) Then briefly describe in what way the text, theme, or person, etc. relates to *your experience.* You may choose to express this passage in some artful way, e.g., role play, mime, oral or dramatic presentation.

VII. *Epilogue or Future Script* *("The Return")*

Having reflected upon your recent or past mission experience, *what insights have you gained* for the present and the future? Explain how you see your past affecting or relating to your present mission or ministry.

What are your dreams for the future? If you could plan your future ministry, what and where would it be? Is there *an image* which seems to capture your "dream"? A *Scripture passage or other theme* from the Tradition which particularly relates to it? In brief, describe (act out, dance, symbolize, sing, etc.) how you might imagine the unfolding of your future, in the light of your past and present.

Appendix II
Suggested Resources in Fiction and Film

A. A SELECTION OF RELEVANT NOVELS and/or SHORT STORIES (in chronological order).

Maugham, W. Somerset.	"Rain." *The Maugham Reader* (1921).
Cather, Willa.	*Death Comes to the Archbishop* (1939).
Godden, Rumer (Margaret).	*Black Narcissus* (1941).
Hulme, Kathryun C.	*The Nun's Story* (1956).
Michener, James A.	*Hawaii* (1959).
Achebe, Chinua.	*Things Fall Apart* (1959).
Matthiessen, Peter.	*At Play in the Fields of the Lord* (1965).
Elliot, Elisabeth.	*No Graven Image* (1966).
Endo, Shusaku.	*Silence* (1969).
Naipal, V.S.	*In A Free State* (1971)
Morrison, Toni	*Sula* (1973)
Craven, Margaret.	*I Heard the Owl Call My Name* (1973).
Morrison, Toni	*Song of Solomon* (1977)
Gordimer, Nadine.	*Burgers Daughter* (1979).
Craven, Margaret.	*Again I Heard the Owl* (1980).
Michener, James A.	*The Covenant* (1980).
Naipal, V.S.	*A Bend in the River* (1980)
Gordimer, Nadine.	*Selected Stories* (1983).
Law-Yone, Wendy.	*The Coffin Tree* (1983).
Doerr, Harriet.	*Stones For Ibarra* (1984).
Allende, Isabel.	*The House of the Spirits* (1985).
Hersey, John.	*The Call* (1985).
Lapierre, Dominique.	*City of Joy* (1985).
Moore, Brian.	*Black Robe* (1985).
Michener, James A.	*Texas* (1985).
Ihimaera, Witi	*Whale Rider* (1986).
Achebe, Chinua.	*Anthills of the Savannah* (1987).

Morrison, Toni	*Beloved* (1988)
Walker, Paul Robert	*Hoop Dreams* (1995)
Pilkington, D./Garimara, N.	*Rabbit-Proof Fence* (1996)
Gourevitch, Philip	*We Wish To Inform You that Tomorrow We Will Be Killed with Our Families* (1998)
Kingsolver, Barbara	*The Poisonwood Bible* (1998)
Ortiz, Dianna	*The Blindfold's Eye* (2002)

B. A SELECTION OF RELEVANT FILMS AVAILABLE ON VIDEO AND DVD

"Rain" (1928, 1932, & 1953).
"Stanley and Livingston" (1939).
"Keys of the Kingdom" (1944).
"Black Narcissus" (1947).
"The Nun's Story" (1959).
"Inn of the Sixth Happiness" (1958).
"Lilies of the Field" (1963).
"Hawaii" (1966).
"El Norte"
"I Heard the Owl Call My Name" (1973).
"The Missionary" (1982).
"City of Joy" (1985)
"Ghandi" (1986)
"The Mission" (1986)
"Stones For Ibarra" (1989)
"Black Robe" (1991).
"At Play in the Fields of the Lord" (1991).
"Hoop Dreams" (1994)
"Traffic" (2000)
"Mighty Times" (2002)
"Rabbit-Proof Fence"   (2003)
"Whale Rider" (2003)
"Maria, Full of Grace" (2005)

Appendix III
Ritual: Theory and Practical Suggestions

Ritual and the Missioner's Transition

A few years ago some close friends and I gathered to celebrate a marker birthday. We broke open the Word: with Scripture. We also shared letters, poems and phone calls from family and other good friends who had been a part of the fifty years we were commemorating. Indeed we broke bread and gave thanks! Into the evening, over shrimp creole and wine, everyone shared a favorite memory or two. The following day, a long plane ride gave me time to reflect on that celebration, on its significance and the fifty years that it commemorated. With a familiar ritual, we had marked a rite of passage: "Happy birthday to you, Happy birthday to you!" There was I, as often in my youth, making a wish before a decorated cake ablaze with lit candles. An "ordinary" ritual, one that takes place every year, in many different forms, everywhere in this world. I was passing over a threshold and into a new stature. I had, as it were, become an "elder," and this passage deserved to be celebrated and remembered. In this culture, as in many, it was marked by friends gathering to share food and drink, song and dance, gifts and stories, laughter and tears. It wasn't just *my* celebration. It was also theirs. The ritual, enacted within a community of friends, enabled me to walk through the threshold with courage and joy. While I've made occasional mention of the need for ritualizing the stages of a missioner's transition, this work would not be complete without speaking intentionally about ritual as an *essential* part of the process. For missioners, transition is an opportunity to grow. But as in every rite of passage, the community needs to ritualize the stages to provide the passenger with a sense of safety and *communitas*.

> The primary purpose of ritual is to enable the individual to undergo the journey of conversion, rendering the experience intelligible and less terrifying, and enabling him [her] to complete the journey, through encounter with

the sacred, to newness of life (Searle 1980: 47).

> [Ritual] enables an individual and his[her] community to
> face the truth of their existence . . . [providing] a safe *locus*
> for encountering the Ultimate and Transcendent.   . . .
> [Ritual] assures that the experience has meaning, and thus
> saves the individual from capitulating to fear of the
> unknown and saves him [her] from being lost in anxiety
> and confusion (Ibid.: 50).

The Role of Ritual in Transition

Many rituals are performed unconsciously, as in routine behavior. Though we might not think of them as such, we carry-out many rituals everyday: brushing our teeth, taking our morning coffee, religiously observing an afternoon "siesta," reading the evening newspaper, praying with the children. All of these, in some fashion or another, are rituals which have evolved and have meaning in our lives.

Other rituals, in the more liturgically correct sense of the term, are *consciously* performed, and the actions, gestures, objects involved are *symbols*, carrying a deeper, sometimes unconscious, meaning beyond themselves. Some rituals and symbols have been consciously modified throughout history, such as Christian sacrament and liturgical celebration, which are intentionally performed to enable us to "identify the meaning of our experience in terms of the gospel of death and resurrection and to commit ourselves to God in faith" (Ibid.: 49). Nevertheless, ritual, if it is real and effective, must be intimately connected with life.

In the case of those in transition, or those accompanying them, rituals provide us with the opportunity to *enact* in some way, through physical action and tangible symbols, what we have been experiencing. At the same time these simple moments of ritual put us in touch with the Sacred: the inner self, the immanent and the transcendent, the "now and not yet" of God's "*basilea*" (kingdom or reign).

"The Readiness is All"

In speaking of ritual and conversion, Searle talks about "four moments of readiness through which a person would have to move if the inner process of conversion and the unfolding ritual process were to mesh together in a single movement of transformation" (Ibid.: 52). In effect, we have been talking about these moments of readiness throughout this process of theological reflection. They are the familiar:

1) coming to terms with what we have actually gone through (*from*);

2) realizing the need to face the truth of our life (*from* → *through*);

3) letting go of illusions and the past, and putting one's trust in God and the future (*from* → *through* → *to*);

4) sharing with others the effects of our new life and vision (*to* → *from* → *through* → *to*).

We need be aware of our "readiness" to actually participate in the ritual. All will not be at "the stage" being celebrated or ritualized at the same moment in their transition. For example, one missioner with whom I was talking recently, said that she is still not "at home" in her own particular journey. She believes that part of the reason is because she was so "violently pulled out" of her mission assignment.I asked what had caused that, e.g., the violence in the country at that time? She replied, "I had been asked by my community to come back to administrative work in my province of origin (where I had previously been in administration for fourteen years). I had written a long detailed letter spelling out all of the very real and valid reasons why I needed to stay where I was for the time being. A few weeks later I received a response telling me to finish up the semester and come home." Then she added, " I realize I didn't do any of the appropriate rituals or ceremonies of departure. In fact I did everything I could to avoid any kind of celebration . . . . My heart wasn't in it."

Secondly, while we can create an atmosphere with all of the appropriate elements, and we can perform all of the proper actions, the totality of ritual is something that happens both within as well as without an individual or group. What I mean to say is that we cannot *make* ritual happen, neither for ourselves or others. Ultimately its power to effect change comes from within the inner self not from the ritual itself. It is important for all of us to be creatively involved in ritual which flows from that "Ark" within ourselves, wherein dwells the "Holy of Holies." If we are the facilitators, as much as possible, we must allow the symbols, words and gestures to come from the missioners themselves. Gene Combs and Jill Freedman remind us of another important point:

197

Although the emphasis in ceremonies is on doing something, preparing for the ceremony, thinking about it, and remembering it afterwards all can contribute significantly to the meaning that ceremonies have (Combs and Freedman 1990: 210).

In addition, as in all that we do, whatever be our ministry, ultimately it is the Spirit who gives life. I recall one particular evening during a mission/ministry integration course, each member of the group was invited to create a representation of some gift that was ours by using modeling clay. (In fact, "clay" in itself was symbolic for the African missioner who suggested and designed this activity). One missioner who was taking the course didn't consider himself the least bit artistic and was not enthusiastic about molding with clay. In addition, he wasn't feeling too good about himself at this moment, nor what "gift" he had to offer.

At the end of the allotted time, each participant presented his or her "sculpture" with a brief explanation about what it meant. We had all sorts of creations: boats and villages and clowns holding daisies. When it was his turn the missioner in question firmly placed on the table in front of him a name plate. You know the type, like the executives have on their desks, in gold and wood. His was carved out of clay. The missioner explained to us that the only gift he had to offer at this moment–for better or for worse–was himself.

One of the most poignant moments I experienced occurred at a FROM workshop a few years ago. We had been using a ritual of placing small candles on a large map of the world laid out before us. In the beginning, we had placed our candles on the spot of the world which represented the place "from" which we had originally been sent on mission. Later in the workshop, we moved the candles to the place to which we had been sent, e.g., Guatemala, Zambia, Panama, Peru, Detroit. Then, as the workshop was coming to a close, we were invited to place our candles on that place with which we identified in the present. i.e., the spot on that map where we knew our candle needed to be at this moment. After a brief time of reflection, with quiet music in the background, each participant got up, one by one, and moved his or her candle to its "proper place." After everyone had finished, most of the candles were clustered around the mid-west area of the United States, but one candle remained all by itself. It was still sitting in Peru. A well intentioned member of the group looked at me and said, "Someone didn't move their candle." An elderly sister spoke up softly but firmly, "No, I didn't forget. That's where it's supposed to be. I must leave it there for awhile."

She had *not* misunderstood the ritual. To the contrary, perhaps she had understood it better than most. The first time that I participated in a similar ritual at my own FROM reentry workshop, I recall that I reluctantly went to the map and moved my name from Zaire to Chicago, where I was living at the time. I went through the motions of the ritual. But I actually wasn't at "home" in Chicago at that time. My heart was still in Zaire. In fact, it was at a later workshop that I was conscious of moving my own candle from Zaire to a spot between Chicago and Milwaukee with a peaceful conviction: "Yes, I am at home here now."

Suggested Strategies, Symbols and Rituals

Combs and Freedman, in their context of psychotherapy, point out the importance of developing appropriate rituals or "ceremonies" for the moment, person or group. They "design ceremonies through strategies based on the purposes for which the ceremonies will be used. . . . Each strategy is based on a therapeutic purpose that lends itself to rituals."(Combs and Freedman 1990: 211).

The following simple suggestions have proved useful to me. It is important that they be used with sensitivity, discretion and creativity, but they can be most meaningful and powerful in different stages of transition. For each symbol or ritual, a few related Scripture texts are offered.

The Map

Locating or situating oneself by placing / transferring of candles, flags, pins, names on the locations from which we've come, where we presently are, and to which we're going, or ultimately, where our symbol needs to be at this time.

Some Scripture suggestions:

Gen 12: 1-4   Go forth from the land of your family . . . to a land I will show you.

Deut 8: 1-5   Remember how for forty years now the Lord has directed all your journeying . . . .

Ruth 1: 15-18   Do not ask me to abandon or forsake you . . . .

The Story-Teller

(using symbols: stick, stone, hat/scarf, cloth, stole, etc.)

The "story-teller" represents a certain kind of authority, word, history, tradition within a given community. We can all be "story-tellers" (or perhaps minstrels!) as we tell (dance, sing, mime) our stories: Stories of: mentors, companions, moments (funny, tragic, difficult, powerful), vulnerability, endings, beginnings.

Some Scripture suggestions:

> 2 Samuel 12: Nathan said to David, "In a certain town there were two men, one rich, the other poor."
>
> Matthew 13: And he spoke to them at length in parables . . . .
>
> Luke 7: 36-49: "Simon, I have something to say to you . . . ."

The Walls of Jericho

Figuratively or literally, "encircle" a person, concern, memory, or the like seven times (or seventy times seven times!), knowing that "the Lord has entrusted to you the city" (Josh 6:16).

Scripture suggestion: Josh 6: 2-5

> "I have delivered Jericho and its king into your power. . . .Circle the city, marching once around it . . . for six days. . . . On the seventh day march around the city seven times, and have the priests blow the horns . . . and all the people shout aloud . . . ."

Natural Elements

Water: (bowl, pond, etc.) symbol of birth, life, death, healing, transformation: rituals of washing, blessing, recalling memories of water.

Some Scripture suggestions:

> John 13:12-17
> 2 Kings 5

Fire: (candle, fireplace) A symbol of warmth, heat, light, purification, death, transformation: rituals of burning, offering, incense, memories of fire.

Some Scripture suggestions:

Exodus 3
Acts 28: 1-6
Mark 4: 21-25

Earth: (soil, sand, grass, rock, clay). A symbol of death (burial), life, growth, desert, green, rituals of the hard and impenetrable, the soft and malleable, transformation; memories of earth.

Some Scripture suggestions:

Josh 5:13-15
Mark 4:1-9, 26-34

Wind: (breath, incense, hand-fan): symbol of spirit, power, movement, change, transformation. Rituals of storm, loss, blessing, recalling memories of wind.

Some Scripture suggestions:

1Kings 19
John 20: 19-29

Food: (corn, cassava, bread, fish). Meals shared, food received/given, lack of food, moments of planting, transformation, memories related to food.

Some Scripture suggestions:

1Kings 17
1Cor 11: 17-34

Natural environment: (animals, insects, trees, leaves, plants, sun, moon, stars). Rituals of transformations: caterpillars/butterflies, snake/skins, bears/hibernation; eggs/birds, fish, reptiles; clouds/vapor/rain/ice/snow.

Some Scripture suggestions:

Jonah 1-4
Matt 6: 25-34

Sounds: Music and dance often accompany rites of passage. Sounds may evoke memories of mission or of "home." Include instrumental music, songs, instruments (bells, chimes, drums, flute, guitar, marimbas, rain stick). Consider other common "noises": (car horns, traffic, sirens, phones and doorbells ringing).

Some Scripture suggestions:

Ex 15: 20-21
1 Samuel 16
Psalm 149

Familiar occasions for rituals in most cultures

Birthdays / anniversaries / baptisms / initiations / engagements / weddings / wakes / funerals / planting / harvesting /home blessings / "exorcisms"/ Send offs to battle, mission, new village, new ministry, marriage, new home, to die (Mission sending, mission receiving, mission accomplished, mission continued).

Homecomings: From any of the above, from the hospital, from prison, from rehab.

Parties, Parades, "Showers," Banquets and Feasts,

Homecomings: Parties, Parades, "Showers," Banquets and Feasts

War vets, "When Johnny comes marching home again!" Sports heroes (Super Bowl/NBA/etc.) Olympic champions; prison parolee or freed: "Tie a yellow ribbon").

*A **Final Note:*** These suggestions are by no means meant to be exhaustive. Hopefully they will stimulate your own ideas and creativity and encourage you to improvise.You are encouraged to improvise and add personal or group touches to any basic ritual.

Works Cited

Aden, Leroy. 1968. "Pastoral Counseling as Christian Perspective." In Peter Homans, eds. *The Dialogue between Theology and Psychology*. Chicago: University of Chicago Press. Pp. 163-182.

Adler, Peter. 1975. "The Transitional Experience: An Alternative View of Culture Shock." *The Journal of Humanistic Psychology*. XV. 4 (Fall): 13-23.

Amaladoss, Michael. 1991. "The Challenges of Mission Today." In Jenkinson and O'Sullivan, eds. 359-397.

Arasteh, Reza. 1965. *Final Integration in the Adult Personality*. Leiden: E.J. Brill.

Arnold, Magda B., John A. Gasson, and Charles A. Curran, eds. 1954. *The Human Person: An Approach to an Integral Theory of Personality*. New York: Ronald.

Arnold, Magda B. 1960. *Emotion and Personality*. New York: Columbia University Press.

_____. 1970. *Feelings and Emotions: The Loyola Symposium*. New York: Academic.

Asante, Molefi K. And William B. Gudykundst, eds. 1989. *Handbook of International and Intercultural Communication*. Newbury Park, CA: Sage.

Austin, Clyde N. 1988. "Reentry Stress: The Pain of Coming Home." in O'Donnell, ed. 513-521.

_____. 1983. *Cross-Cultural Reentry: An Annotated Bibliography*. Abilene, TX: Abilene Christian University.

_____. 1986. *Cross-Cultural Reentry: A Book of Readings*. Abilne, TX: Abilene Christian University.

Bennett, Janet M. 1993. "Cultural Marginality: Identity and Issues in Intercultural Training." In Paige, ed. 109-135.

Bevans, Stephen B. 1992. *Models of Contextual Theology*. Maryknoll, NY: Orbis Books. Revised and Expanded edition 2002.

_____. 1994. "Seeing Mission through Images." In Scherer and Bevans, eds. 158-169.

_____. 1999. "Letting Go and Speaking Out: A Spirituality of Inculturation." In Stephen Bevans, Eleanor Doidge and Robert Schrieter, eds. *The Healing Circle: Essays in Cross-Cultural Mission*. Chicago: CCGM Publications. 133-146.

Bishop, Elizabeth. 1994. "One Art." In Joel Conarroe, ed. *Eight American Poets*.

New York: Vintage. Pp. 62-63.

Bosch, David J. 1979. *A Spirituality of the Road*. Scottdale, PA: Herald Press.

_____. 1991. *Transforming Mission: Paradigm Shifts in Theology of Mission*. Maryknoll, NY: Orbis Books.

_____. 1994. "The Vulnerability of Mission." In Scherer and Bevans, eds. 73-86.

Bourne, Edmund. "Does the Concept of Person Vary Cross-Culturally?" in Shweder, ed. 113-155.

Bozarth-Campbell, Alla. 1983. *Life is Good-bye / Hello: Grieving Well through All Kinds of Loss*. Minneapolis, MN: Campcare.

Bridges, William. 1980. *Transitions: Making Sense of Life's Changes*. Reading, MA: Addison-Wesley.

_____. 1991. *Managing Transitions*. New York: Addison-Wesley.

Brown, Raymond, Joseph Fizmyer and Roland Murphy, eds. 1990. *The New Jerome Biblical Commentary*. Englewood Cliffs, NJ: Prentice Hall.

Brueggemann, Walter E. 1977. *The Land*. Philadelphia: Fortress Press.

Caird, George B. 1980. *The Language and Imagery of the Bible*. Philadelphia: Westminster.

Carroll, L. Patrick and Katherine M. Dyckman. *Chaos or Creation: Spirituality in Mid-Life*. Mahwah, NJ: Paulist Press.

CSB:RG. 1990. Donald Senior et al., eds. *The Catholic Study Bible*. Reading Guides. Oxford: Oxford University Press.

Cohn, Robert. 1981. *The Shape of Sacred Space*. Chico, CA. Scholars Press.

Collins, Michael. 1978. *Spirituality for Mission*. Maryknoll, NY: Orbis Books.

Combs, Gene and Jill Freedman. 1990. *Symbol, Story and Ceremony: Using Metaphor in Individual and Family Therapy*. New York: Norton.

Conn, Joanne Wolski. 1989. *Spirituality and Personal Maturity*. Lanham, MD: University Press of America.

Conn, Walter E., ed. *Conversion: Perspectives on Personal and Social Transformation*. 1978. Staten Island: Alba House.

_____. 1981. *Conscience: Development and Self-Transcendence*. Birmingham, AL: Religious Education.

_____. 1986. *Christian Conversion: A Developmental Interpretation of Autonomy and Surrender*. Mahwah, NJ: 1986.

Crosby, Michael. 1987. "The Human Experience of Conversion." In Eigo, ed. 31-74.

Doehring, Carrie. 1993. *Internal Desecration: Traumatization and Representations of God*. Lanham, MD: University Press of America.

Dooling, Richard. 1994. "Bush Pigs." *The New Yorker*. October 10: 1-5.

Dunne, John. 1965. *The City of the Gods*. New York: Macmillan.

_____. 1977. *A Search for God in Time and Memory*. Notre Dame, IN: University of Notre Dame Press.

_____. 1975. *Time and Myth*. Notre Dame, IN: University of Notre Dame Press.

_____. 1978. *The Way of All the Earth*. Notre Dame, IN: University of Notre Dame Press.

_____. 1978. *Reasons of the Heart*. New York: Macmillan.

_____. 1981. "Insight and Waiting on God." In Matthew L. Lamb, ed. *Creativity and Method: Essays in Honor of Bernard Lonergan, S.J.* Milwaukee: Marquette University Press.

_____. 1982. *The Church of the Poor Devil*. Notre Dame, IN: University of Notre Dame Press.

_____. 1985. *The House of Wisdom*. San Francisco: Harper & Row.

_____. 1991. *The Peace of the Present*. Notre Dame, IN: University of Notre Dame Press.

_____. 1993. *Love's Mind*. Notre Dame, IN: University of Notre Dame Press.

Eigo, Francis A. 1987. *The Human Experience of Conversion: Person and Structures in Transformation*. Villanova, PA: Villanova University Press.

Eliot, Thomas Stearns. 1971. *Four Quartets*. New York and San Diego: Harcourt, Brace, Javanovich.

Endo, Shusaku. 1969. *Silence*. Tokyo: Sophia University Press.

Faucett, Robert and Carol Ann. 1991. *Intimacy and Midlife: Understanding Your Journey with Yourself, Others and God*. New York: Crossroad.

Finley, James. 1978. *Merton's Palace of Nowhere: A Search for God through Awareness of the True Self*. Notre Dame, IN: Ave Maria Press.

Gittins, Anthony J. 1989. *Gifts and Strangers: Meeting the Challenge of Inculturation*. Mahwah, NJ: Paulist Press.

_____. 1987. "Communities of Concern and Close-up Country: A Parable of Survival." *Spirituality Today*. 39. 4. Winter: 329-330.

_____. 1994. "Missionary Mythmaking." In Scherer and Bevans, eds., 143-157.

Grant, Robert. 1994. *Healing the Soul of the Church*. Brulingame, CA: R. Grant.

_____. 1995. "Trauma in Missionary Life." *Missiology: An International Review*. XXIII. 1. January: 71-83.

Griffin, Emilie. 1982. *Turning: Reflection on the Experience of Conversion*. New York: Image Books.

Hall, Edward T. 1977. *Beyond Culture*. New York: Anchor Books.

Herman, Judith L. 1992. *Trauma and Recovery*. New York: Basic Books.

Jenkinson, William and Helene O'Sullivan, eds. 1991. *Trends in Mission: Towards the 3rd Millennium*. Maryknoll, NY: Orbis Books.

John of Taizé, Brother. 1985. *The Pilgrim God: A Biblical Journey*. Washington, D.C.: Pastoral Press.

Johnson, Robert. 1986. *Inner Word*. San Francisco: HarperSanFrancisco.

Kegan, Robert. 1982. *The Evolving Self*. Cambridge, MA: Harvard University Press.

Killen, Patricia O'Connell and John de Beer. 1994. *The Art of Theological Reflection*. New York: Crossroad.

Kim, Young Yun. 1989. "Intercultural Adaption." in Asante and Gudykunst, eds.

275-292.

Kohls, Robert L. 1984. *Survival Kit for Overseas Living*. 2nd Edition. Yarmouth, ME: Intercultural Press.

Kübler-Ross, Elisabeth. 1969. *On Death and Dying*. New York: Macmillan.

Lee, Jung Young. 1995. *Marginality: The Key to Multicultural Theology*. Minneapolis, MN: Fortress Press.

Levinson, Daniel J. 1978. *The Seasons of a Man's Life*. New York: Ballantine.

Lewis, Larry. 1983. "Waiting." *Maryknoll Formation Journal*. 4. 2. Summer: 25-36.

_____. C. 1990. "Mirror of the Misfit: Foreign Mission and the Human Mystery." Unpublished Paper.

_____. 1997. *The Misfit: Haunting the Human–Unveiling the Divine*. Maryknoll, NY: Orbis Books.

Loftis, Margaret F. 1992. "Home (Alone) Again: The Re-Insertion of the Returned Missionary." *CMSM Forum*. Spring: 11-16.

Lacan, Dom Marc-Francois. 1978. "Conversion and Grace in the Old Testament" and "Conversion and Kingdom in the Synoptic Gospels." In Conn, ed. 1978. Pp. 75-96 and 97-118.

Longergan, Bernard J. F. 1972. *Method in Theology*. Minneapolis, MN: Wionston-Seabury.

_____. 1978. "Theology in Its New Context." In Conn, ed. 1978. 3-21.

Macky, Peter W. 1990. *The Centrality of Metaphors to Biblical Thought*. Lewiston, NY: Edwin Mellen.

Mbiti, John S. 1969. *African Religions and Philosophy*. New York: Prager.

McFague, Sallie. 1982. *Metaphorical Theology*. Philadelphia: Fortress Press.

Merton, Thomas. 1961. *New Seeds of Contemplation*. New York: New Directions.

_____. 1961. T. P. McDonnell, ed. *A Thomas Merton Reader*. New York: Harcourt, Brace and World.

_____. 1967. *Mystics and Zen Masters*. New York: Delta.

_____. 1971. *Contemplative Prayer*. Second Edition. Garden City, NJ: Image Books.

_____. 1971. *Contemplation in a World of Action*. New York: Doubleday.

Mitchell, Kenneth R. And Herbert Anderson. 1983. *All Our Losses, All Our Griefs*. Philadelphia: Westminster.

Moore, Thomas. 1994. *Care of the Soul*. New York: HarperPerennial.

Nilson, Jon. 1987. "Doing Theology by Heart: John S. Donne's Theological Method." *Theological Studies*. 48. 1: 65-86.

Nouwen, Henri J. M. 1992. *The Return of the Prodigal Son*. New York: Doubleday.

Oates, Wayne E. 1981. *Your Particular Grief*. Philadelphia: Westminster Press.

O'Donnell, Kelly and Michele L. O'Donnell, eds. 1988. *Helping Missionaries Grow*. Pasadena, CA: William Carey Library. 513-521.

O'Rourke, David K. 1978. "The Experience of Conversion." In Eigo, ed. 1-30.

Osiek, Carolyn. 1986. *Beyond Anger*. Mahwah, NJ: Paulist Press.

Paige, R. Michael, ed. 1993. *Education for the Intercultural Experience.* Yarmouth, ME: Intercultural Press.

Patton, Michael. 1990. *Qualitative Evaluation and Research Methods.* Newbury Park, CA: Sage Publications.

Phan, Peter C. 2003. "The Dragon and the Eagle: Toward a Vietnamese American Theology." In *Christianity with an Asian Face: Asian American Theology in the Making.* Maryknoll, N.Y.: Orbis Books.

Polster, Irving. 1987. *Every Person's Life Is Worth a Novel.* New York: W.W. Norton.

Rambo, Lewis R. 1993. *Understanding Religious Conversion.* New Haven, CT: Yale University Press.

Reilly, Michael. 1980. "Developing a Missionary Spirituality." *Missiology: An International Review.* VIII. 4. October: 441-447.

Rende, Michael L. 1991. *Lonergan on Conversion: The Development of a Notion.* Lanham, MD: University Press of America.

Rupp, Joyce. 1988. *Praying Our Goodbyes.* Notre Dame, IN: Ave Maria Press.

Scherer, James A. and Stephen B. Bevans, eds. 1994. *New Directions in Mission and Evangelization 2: Theological Foundations.* Maryknoll, NY: Orbis Books.

Searle, Mark. 1980. "The Journey of Conversion." *Worship.* 54: 35-55.

Senior, Donald and Carroll Stuhlmueller. 1991. *The Biblical Foundations for Mission.* Maryknoll, NY: Orbis Books.

Sheehy, Gail. 1976. *Passages: Predictable Crises of Adult Life.* New York: Dutton.

Shweder, Richard. 1991. *Thinking Through Cultures: Expeditions in Cultural Psychology.* Cambridge, MA: Harvard University Press.

Solomon, Robert C. 1976. *The Passions.* Garden City, NY: Anchor Books.

Storti, Craig. 1989. *The Art of Crossing Cultures.* Washington, D.C.: Intercultural Press.

_____. 1997. *The Art of Coming Home.* Yarmouth, ME: Intercultural Press.

Stroup, George W. 1981. *The Promise of Narrative Theology.* Atlanta: John Knox Press.

Stuhlmueller, Carroll. 1977. *Thirsting for the Lord.* Staten Island, NY: Alba House.

Sullender, Scott. 1985. *Grief and Growth.* Mahwah, NJ: Paulist Press.

Sullivan, Jack. 1985. "Reentry Revisited." *Maryknoll Formation Journal.* Spring: 30-38.

Sullivan, Paula F. 1991. *The Mystery of My Story: Autobiographical Writing for Personal and Spiritual Development.* Mahwah, NJ: Paulist Press.

Switzer, David K. 1970. *The Dynamics of Grief.* Nashville: Abingdon Press.

Terrian, Samuel. 1978. *The Elusive God.* San Francisco: Harper & Row.

Ting-Toomey, Stella. 1980. "Identity and Interpersonal Bonding." In Triandis and Lambert, eds. 351-373.

Triandis, H. And W. Lambert, eds. 1980. *Handbook of Cross-Cultural Psychology:*

Perspectives. Volume I. Boston: Allyn and Bacon.

Turner, Victor. 1967. "Betwixt and Between: The Liminal Period in Rites of Passage." *The Forest of Symbols.* Ithaca, NY: Cornell University Press, 1967. 93-111.

_____. 1969. *The Ritual Process: Structure and Anti-Structure.* Chicago: Aldin.

_____. "Liminal to Liminoid, in Play, Flow, and Ritual." 1974. *Rice University Studies*: 53-92.

Van Gennep, Arnold. 1960. *The Rites of Passage.* Chicago: University of Chicago Press.

Walsh, James E. 1976. "Description of a Missioner." Maryknoll, NY: Developmen Department.

Westberg, Granger E. 1979. *Good Grief: A Constructive Approach to the Problem of Loss.* Philadelphia: Fortress Press.

Whitehead, Evelyn E. And James D. Whitehead. 1979. *Christian Life Patterns.* New York: Doubleday.

_____. *Method in Ministry: Theological Reflection and Christian Ministry.* Kansas City, MO: Sheed & Ward.

_____. *Seasons of Strength: New Visions of Adult Christian Maturing.* Winona, MN: St. Mary's.

Wilson, John P. 1989. *Trauma, Transformation and Healing: An Interpretive Approach to Theory, Research and Post-Traumatic Therapy.* New York: Brunner / Mazel.

Wiseman, Robert L. And John Koester. 1993. *Intercultural Communication Competence.* Newbury Park, CA: Sage Publications.